INDEX TO
THE AMERICAN SLAVE

THE AMERICAN SLAVE: A COMPOSITE AUTOBIOGRAPHY

INDEX TO
THE AMERICAN SLAVE

Edited by
DONALD M. JACOBS

Assisted by Steven Fershleiser

Contributions in Afro-American and
African Studies,
Number 65

GREENWOOD PRESS
Westport, Connecticut • London, England

Library of Congress Cataloging in Publication Data
Main entry under title:

Index to The American slave.

   (Contributions in Afro-American and African studies,
ISSN 0069-9624 ; no. 65)
   Indexes the main work and its supplements, series
1 and 2.
   1. American slave—Indexes. 2. Slaves—United
States—Biography—Indexes. 3. Slavery—United States—
Indexes. I. Jacobs, Donald M. II. Fershleiser, Steven.
III. Series.
E444.A45 Suppl 3   305.5'6 [B]   81-6662
ISBN 0-313-21374-7 (lib. bdg.)   AACR2

Library of Congress Catalog Card Number: 81-6662
ISBN: 0-313-21374-7
ISSN: 0069-9624

First published in 1981

Greenwood Press
A division of Congressional Information Service, Inc.
88 Post Road West
Westport, Connecticut 06881

Printed in the United States of America

10 9 8 7 6 5 4 3 2 1

TO JONATHAN
AS HE BEGINS
TO EXPERIENCE
THE EXCITEMENT
OF LEARNING

CONTENTS

PREFACE

The search for a clearer understanding of the many facets of the American historical experience continues to build in intensity as innovative tools for evaluating and classifying information open new doors and help the research scholar draw new and hopefully more accurate conclusions. This is nowhere more evident than in the area of American social history where many preconceived notions are undergoing reinterpretation. Teachers and scholars are currently focusing more on the country's historical experience from the bottom up rather than merely from the top, where major political figures have usually occupied not only center stage but the whole stage.

American ethnic history, American immigrant history, and American minority history are significant examples of often overlapping areas where such changes in interpretation are occurring. A sense of racial and ethnic solidarity and individuality has been building as research changes our perceptions from the democratic, egalitarian—often assimilationist—"melting pot" views of the old "progressive" historians. More and more people are not only asking how they became what they are; they also want to know what they were and what their ancestors were.

Most nineteenth-century racial and ethnic minorities had neither the time nor the inclination to keep a personal written record of their experiences in a new, often alien, even hostile world. For the American slave, purposely and purposefully denied education by laws both written and unwritten, a rich shared oral history served for many years as a facsimile for the personal written record of slavery. During slave times Northern whites and Northern blacks, particularly, began to gain a sense of immediacy regarding slavery from the more than one hundred published slave narratives. These narratives were written and ghost written by runaways more than willing to attack the brutal institution whose harshness was so deeply etched in their recent memories.

After the Civil War, ex-slaves had the opportunity to be more outspoken. However, as the nineteenth century wore on and white society began to lose any real sense of concern for the plight of blacks, little effort was made to build a greater understanding of what slavery must have been like from the slave's perspective. It is small wonder that the major works written by whites during the first half of the twentieth century dealing with the issue of slavery were those by the likes of Ulrich Phillips, who referred to the African blacks brought to the Americas as "the world's premium slaves." And while Phillips could not justify the existence of the institution of slavery on economic grounds, he could, nonetheless, give strong support to the Southern effort to maintain slavery for reasons of social control.

Since the turn of the century blacks had been migrating northward by the tens of thousands. By the 1930s a demographic and ideological revolution had taken place. Many in both the North and the South were shifting their political allegiances from the party of Abraham Lincoln to that of Franklin D. Roosevelt who promised so many of America's Depression-ridden and down-trodden a "new deal." If, in the end, the New Deal economically left much to be desired, it did make a massive effort to put the nation's people back to work with direct help from the government. Not only were the industrial unemployed given government-sponsored jobs, but artists, musicians, and people of many and various intellectual talents were also employed by the Works Progress Administration. Among these, fortunately, were the men and women who travelled throughout the South interviewing thousands of by then elderly ex-slaves before this rich source of first-hand information disappeared forever.

However, until George Rawick began to edit and compile these narratives more than thirty years after the interviewing began, much of the material remained scattered, appearing every so often during the 1950s and 1960s in a much abridged single-volume format. Now that Professor Rawick's forty-one volumes have been published (40 volumes contain narrative materials), the thoughts and attitudes of more than 3,500 slaves from twenty-six states have been brought together, providing a vast array of valuable information to research scholars, teachers, genealogists, as well as people who possess little more than a general interest in what slavery must have been like from the perspective of those who had lived it. Professor Rawick has performed an important service, tracing down materials dealing with the slave experience from those who recalled, mostly from the vantage point of the 1930s, what the "peculiar institution" was like as they were growing up.

True, many of those interviewed had experienced slavery as young children and had memories somewhat dimmed from more than seventy years in freedom and influenced by the experience of the Depression. Nonetheless, this does not diminish the value of these narrative materials. The index for the forty volumes of slave narratives that appears on the following pages should make the information that is provided within the more than 20,000 pages of interviews more accessible. In many respects this volume is a testament to the efforts of the many graduate students in the Northeastern University history department who, between 1977 and 1981, spent many long hours poring over the thousands of pages of narrative materials to locate information dealing with more than one hundred different subjects. The subjects are as diverse as "African Survivals," "Diet," "Family (Separations)," "Indian Relatives," "Political Participation, Black," and "Slave Surveillance and Patrols." There will be errors, both of omission and commission. The voluminous amount of data within these pages makes the total avoidance of such errors an impossibility. Hopefully they will not negate the usefulness of this volume.

I would like to thank Northeastern University for the help that was provided during the final stages of preparation of this index for publication. Thanks also to the dozen graduate students who labored long and hard for little more reward than the recognition they are receiving here. They are John Corcoran, Irene Di Pietro, Michael Haire, Robert Ladino, Kerry Mangan, Ben Potter, Stephen Smith, Michelle Strauss, John Thomson, Joanna Walsh, Jacqueline Wilkie, and Alicia Williams.

Much deserved praise also goes to a superb typist, Mary Ellen McGinty, who moved rapidly and accurately through the thousands of names and numbers and did all that could have been asked in helping assure the quality of the final product.

Finally, special thanks to the two individuals who were involved in so many phases of the index, especially during the final weeks when so much last minute checking and rechecking had to be done, Steven Fershleiser and Stephen Shore. Steven Fershleiser, especially, played a key role in the project from its inception to its completion.

Hopefully this work will help demonstrate that indexing, while surely a mechanical and often tedious exercise, is much more than just that. A good index can and usually does help immeasurably in furthering valuable humanistic research in areas of broad intellectual concern and interest. Clearly the central goal of this index, in fact of all research indexes, is to make knowledge and ideas more easily accessible. Volumes such as this can help oversee the building of a few more intellectual bridges so that the various groups who have helped to write many of the fascinating chapters of the American historical experience can come to better understand the ideologies and perspectives of their own and other groups. In the end, can there be any more humanistic goal than that?

Donald M. Jacobs
May 1981

HOW TO
USE THIS INDEX

SLAVE IDENTIFICATION FILE

This index is divided into three sections. The first section is a complete slave identification file. All of the approximately 3,500 ex-slaves interviewed are listed in alphabetical order. Beside the name of each ex-slave is the numbered location of the interview in the proper volume or volumes of the narrative materials, the age of the individual (if given, and often approximate), the job or work the person did (field or house, if given), and the state where he or she was interviewed (together with any other states he or she mentions having resided in as a slave).* Some ex-slaves were interviewed two or more times and the volume location of each interview is noted beside the person's name. The individual names are listed exactly as they appear in the narrative materials compiled by George Rawick, even if a nickname (such as "Bob" or "Jim") is given. Some blacks were interviewed who were never slaves, as were some whites. Their classification is noted in the identification file.

The narratives were published in three groupings, the first nineteen volumes in 1972. In the index these are numbered consecutively, 1 to 19. Therefore, if an ex-slave interview appears in volume 3, part 4 of these nineteen volumes, as Rosa Starke's does on pp. 147-50, the listing appears as follows: STARKE, Rosa (3.4, 147-50), 83 yrs. (SC).

Where there are more than two states listed within a volume as in volume 16 where there are six, the material is divided into six parts. As a result, Kansas becomes 16.1, Kentucky 16.2, Maryland 16.3 in the index. An ex-slave interviewed in Maryland would be listed in the following manner: LEWIS, Perry (16.3, 49-50) (MD).

The second set of narratives were published in twelve volumes in 1977. The materials indexed in these volumes are all preceded by the designation

*All state names are given using U.S. postal service abbreviations.

S1 which stands for Supplement, Series One. A narrative from this section would be listed: HOGUE, William P. (Sl-5.2, 378-79), 76 yrs. (OH via VA). This means that William Hogue's narrative is located in the second part of volume 5 (the Ohio narrative section of that volume) in Supplement, Series One. A similar system has been set up for the last ten volumes of narrative materials (Supplement, Series Two) which were published in 1979. An example from these volumes would be: HAWES, William (S2-1.10, 325-26), 54 yrs., free (NE via KY).

The first volume in Supplement, Series Two consists of narrative materials from sixteen different states, thus the designation S2-1.1, S2-1.2, S2-1.3 . . . S2-1.10 and all the way to S2-1.16. S2-1.10 refers to part 10 of volume 1 in Supplement, Series Two. Thus the following designation: COLE, Thomas (4.1, 225-35) (S2-3.2, 783-836), 92 yrs., fed animals; field work (TX via AL and TN) refers to former slave Thomas Cole whose interview materials are located in two separate places in the Rawick volumes: in volume 4, part 1 of the first nineteen volumes and in volume 3, part 2 of Supplement, Series Two. When interviewed, Thomas Cole was ninety-two years old. He referred to the fact that he fed animals as a young slave and that later he did field work. He also noted that he served as a slave in Alabama and Tennessee before coming to Texas.

NAME INDEX BY STATE

The second section of the index lists the name of each former slave alphabetically by state. For example, the listings for Texas begin with ADAMS, Frank L. and end with ZOLLICOFFER, Tobe. The ex-slaves from each of the other twenty-five states are listed the same way with the individual's name the only information provided.

SUBJECT INDEX

The third section is the subject index. Each subject is listed alphabetically and is followed by a numerically ordered, volume-by-volume listing of each reference to that subject. For example, the first subject noted is ABOLI-TIONISM. This subject heading is followed by the specific references to ABOLITIONISM to be found within the forty volumes of narrative materials. In this particular case the notations appear as follows:

ABOLITIONISM
8.1: p. 183
8.2: p. 122
16.4: p. 90

17.1: pp. 152-53, 208, 265, 337
S1-5.2: p. 412
S1-7.2: p. 333
S1-12.1: pp. 128, 129
S2-8.7: pp. 2982-83

Note that in every case where a reference is given to a volume that provides narrative materials from more than two states, after the volume and part are given, and prior to the page listings, the postal abbreviation for the state is noted. For example, under the subject heading AFRICAN SURVIVALS appears the following notation: S1-2.4(MO): p. 187. In this particular volume, narrative materials are included from six states, the fourth of which is Missouri, thus the designation 2.4(MO). The state postal abbreviations are not provided for volumes featuring narratives from one or two states only since determining the state narrative source is quite simple in such cases.

Please note that this index should not be compared to those found at the end of most single volume monographs. They are much more exhaustive, referring to nearly every major and minor topic that is mentioned. This index is, instead, meant to be a research guide consisting mainly of what are felt to be major topics or subject areas found within the forty volumes or 20,000 pages of narrative materials.

INDEX KEY

The following index key lists alphabetically the twenty-six states from which ex-slaves provided narrative materials. The major share of narratives coming from these states are marked with asterisks. Arkansas and Texas (**) clearly have more entries than any of the other states, although the numbers of entries from Georgia, Mississippi, and South Carolina (*) are also significant.

Each state name is followed by the postal abbreviation for that state. These abbreviations are used throughout the index. Following the name of each state is the location by volume and part of each section of narrative materials for that state. For example, narrative materials for Alabama, the first state listed below, are found in volume 6, part 1 of the first set of published volumes, in volume 1, part 1 of Supplement, Series One, and in volume 1, part 1 of Supplement, Series Two.

Narratives that are not listed by state and which come from the Fisk University collection are volume 18, *Unwritten History of Slavery* and volume 19, *God Struck Me Dead*, both of which are included in the first group of volumes published. States for which there are no narratives but which are referred to in the index are Louisiana (LA), Pennsylvania (PA), and West Virginia (WV).

INDEX TO
THE AMERICAN SLAVE

SLAVE
══════IDENTIFICATION FILE══════

AARONS, Charlie (6.1, 1-5), c. 91 yrs., field (AL via MS)
ABBEY, Tabby (S1 - 6.1, 3-4), 103 yrs., field (MS via VA)
ABBOT, James Monroe (11.8, 1-5), 83 yrs. (MO)
ABBOTT, Silas (8.1, 1-2), 73 yrs., (AR via MS)
ABERCROMBIE, Anthony (6.1, 6-8), c. 100 yrs., field (AL)
ABERNATHY, Betty (11.8, 6-7), 75 yrs., (MO)
ABERNATHY, Lucian (8.1, 3-7), 83 yrs., (AR via MS)
ABRAMS, George F. (S1 - 11.2, 57), (SC)
ABRAMS, M.E. (2.1, 1-4), 82 yrs., (SC)
ABROMSON, Laura (8.1, 8-10), 74 yrs., (AR via MO)
ADAMS, Ezra (2.1, 5-8), 85 yrs., field (SC)
ADAMS, Frank L. (S2 - 2.1, 1-4), 84 yrs., field (TX)
ADAMS, Isaac (7.1, 1-5), 87 yrs., house (OK via LA)
ADAMS, Lewis (S1 - 6.1, 5-8), 106 yrs. (MS via IL, TX, and LA)
ADAMS, Louisa (14.1, 1-7), hard work around house (NC)
ADAMS, Mary (2.1, 9), c. 90 yrs. (SC)
ADAMS, Rachel (12.1, 1-8) (GA)
ADAMS, S.B. (S2 - 2.1, 5-9), 79 yrs., field (TX)
ADAMS, Victoria (2.1, 10-12), 90 yrs., house (SC)
ADAMS, Will (4.1, 1-3) (S2 - 2.1, 10-15), 80 yrs., field (TX)
ADAMS, William (4.1, 4-11) (S2 - 2.1, 16-22), 93 yrs., field (TX)
ADAMSON, Frank (2.1, 13-16), 82 yrs., field (SC)
ADELINE, Aunt (8.1, 11-16), 89 yrs., house (AR via TN)
ADELINE, Aunt (13.4, 212-13), c. 100 yrs. (GA)
ADKINS, Ida (14.1, 8-12), 79 yrs., work around the house (NC)
ADWAY, Rose (8.1, 17-18), 76 yrs. (AR via MS)
AIKEN, Liddie (8.1, 19-21), 62 yrs., free (AR via AL)
ALBRIGHT, George Washington (S1 - 6.1, 8-19), 91 yrs., field (MS)
ALBRIGHT, Priscilla (S1 - 3.1, 1-3), 83 yrs. (GA)
ALDREDGE, Jack (S1 - 6.1, 20-22), c. 80 yrs. (MS)
ALDRICH, Jacob (S2 - 2.1, 23-33), 77 yrs., field (TX via LA)
ALDRIDGE, Mattie (8.1, 22-23), c. 60 yrs., free (AR)
ALEXANDER, Alice (7.1, 6-7) (S1 - 12.1, 1-3), 88 yrs., house (OK via LA)
ALEXANDER, Amsy (8.1, 24-27), 74 yrs. (AR via NC)
ALEXANDER, Diana (8.1, 28-29), 74 yrs. (AR via MS)
ALEXANDER, Fannie (8.1, 30-31), 62 yrs., free (AR via TN)
ALEXANDER, Gus (S2 - 2.1, 34-37), field (TX)

ALEXANDER, J.C. (S2 - 2.1, 38-43), 87 yrs., shepherd (TX via KY)
ALEXANDER, Lucretia (8.1, 32-39), 89 yrs., house (AR)
ALFORD, Barney (S1 - 6.1, 23-49), c. 84 yrs., field (MS)
ALLEN, Dinah (S1 - 6.1, 50-51), 90 yrs. (MS via AL)
ALLEN, Ed (8.1, 40) (AR)
ALLEN, Hannah (11.8, 8-17) (S1 - 2.4, 138-46), 107 yrs., house
    (MO via AR)
ALLEN, Jeff (S1 - 1.1, 1-2), 74 yrs. (AL)
ALLEN, Jim (7.2, 1-10) (S1 - 6.1, 52-65), 87 yrs., field (MS via AL)
ALLEN, Joseph (S1 - 5.1, 1-4), 86 yrs., field (IN via KY)
ALLEN, Martha (14.1, 13-15), c. 78 yrs., hard work around the house (NC)
ALLEN, Parson (11.8, 18-19), 78 yrs. (MO)
ALLEN, Ruth (S1 - 2.3, 101-04), over 85 yrs. (MN via MO)
ALLEN, Sarah (4.1, 12-13) (S2 - 2.1, 44-47), 80 yrs., house
    (TX via VA)
ALLEN, Rev. W.B. (12.1, 12-16) (S1 - 3.1, 4-22), 87 yrs., field
    (GA via AL)
ALLEN, Washington (12.1, 9-11), 83 yrs. (GA via SC and AL)
ALLISON, Lucindy (8.1, 41-43), 61 yrs., free (AR)
AMELIA (13.4, 220) (GA)
AMERSON, Richard (S1 - 1.1, 3-9), 60 yrs., free (AL)
AMES, Josephine (8.1, 44-45) (AR)
AMMONDS, Molly (6.1, 9-11) (S1 - 1.1, 10-12), 85 yrs., house (AL)
ANDERSON, Andy J. (4.1, 14-16) (S2-2.1, 48-56), 94 yrs., shepherd (TX)
ANDERSON, Charity (6.1, 12-14) (S1 - 1.1, 13-16), 101 yrs., house (AL)
ANDERSON, Charles (8.1, 46-48), c. 77 yrs. (AR via KY)
ANDERSON, Charles Gabriel (11.8, 20-23), c. 119 yrs., field
    (MO via AL)
ANDERSON, Charles H. (16.4, 1-5), 92 yrs. (OH via VA)
ANDERSON, Cindy (S1 - 6.1, 66-67), 87 yrs. (MS)
ANDERSON, Frank (S2 - 2.1, 57-59), 80 yrs., field (TX via TN)
ANDERSON, George Washington (4.1, 17-20), 82 yrs., carriage driver
    (TX via SC)
ANDERSON, John (16.2, 45-46) (KY via PA)
ANDERSON, Joseph (14.1, 16-18) (NC)
ANDERSON, Josephine (17.1, 2-9), house (FL)
ANDERSON, Mary (14.1, 19-26), 86 yrs. (NC)
ANDERSON, Nancy (8.1, 49-52), 66 yrs., free (AR via MS)
ANDERSON, R.B.(8.1, 53-54), 76 yrs. (AR)
ANDERSON, Sam (S1 - 12.1, 4-10), 98 yrs., field (OK via MS)
ANDERSON, Sarah (8.1, 55-56), c. 78 yrs. (AR via GA)
ANDERSON, Selie (8.1, 57-59), 78 yrs. (AR via AL)
ANDERSON, "Uncle Willis" (4.1, 21-24), 93 yrs. (TX)
ANDERSON, W.A. (8.1, 60-61), 78 yrs. (AR)
ANDREWS, Cornelia (14.1, 27-31), 87 yrs., house (NC)
ANDREWS, Frances (2.1, 17-18), 83 yrs., house (SC)
ANDREWS, Samuel Simeon (17.1, 10-21), 86 yrs. (FL via GA, SC, TX and AL)
ANN, Aunt (S1 - 6.1, 68-72) (MS via SC)
ANNGADY, Mary (14.1, 32-43), 80 yrs., house (NC)
ANONYMOUS (S2 - 1.3, 254), c. 74 yrs. (AR)
ANONYMOUS (S2 - 1.3, 253) (AR via MS)
ANONYMOUS (S1 - 4.2, 401-09), 81 yrs. (GA)
ANONYMOUS (S2 - 1.9, 301) (MD)
ANONYMOUS (S1 - 6.1, 2) (MS)
ANONYMOUS (S1 - 6.1, 1) (MS via SC)
ANTHONY, Henry (8.1, 62-63), 81 yrs. (AR via NC)

ANTWINE, Nancy (S2 - 2.1, 60-62), 84 yrs. (TX)
ARBERY, Katie (8.1, 64-67), 80 yrs. (AR)
ARCHER, Jim (S1 - 6.1, 73-75), c. 79 yrs. (MS)
ARMSTRONG, Campbell (8.1, 68-74), 86 yrs., field (AR via GA)
ARMSTRONG, Cora (8.1, 75) (AR)
ARMSTRONG, Manuel (S2 - 2.1, 63-65), 80 yrs., field (TX)
ARMSTRONG, Mary (4.1, 25-30) (S2 - 2.1, 66-74), 91 yrs., house
   (TX via MO)
ARMSTRONG, Nora (S2 - 2.1, 75-76), 75 yrs., house (TX)
ARMSTRONG, Wash (S2 - 2.1, 77-79), field (TX)
ARNETT, R.C. (S1 - 2.4, 270-71), 89 yrs. (MO)
ARNOLD, George W.(6.2, 1-7), 76 yrs., field (IN via TN)
ARNWINE, Sterling (Stearlin) (4.1, 31-33) (S2 - 2.1, 80-86), c. 85 yrs.,
   house (TX)
ARRINGTON, Jane (14.1, 45-49), 84 yrs., field (NC)
ARTHUR, "Pete" (2.1, 19), 85 yrs. (SC)
ASH, Thomas (6.2, 8-10), c. 81 yrs., field (IN via KY)
   See Crane, Mary (IN via KY)
ASHLEY, Levi (S1 - 6.1, 76-87), c. 81 yrs. (MS via LA)
ASHLEY, Sarah (4.1, 34-36) (S2 - 2.1, 87-91), 93 yrs., field
   (TX via MS and GA)
ASKEW, Gus (6.1, 15-16) (S1 - 1.1, 17), 84 yrs., field (AL)
ATES, Caroline (S1 - 3.1, 23-31), 90 yrs., house (GA via AL)
ATKINS, Lizzie (S2 - 2.1, 92-103), 87 yrs., house (TX)
ATKINSON, Jack (12.1, 17-18), house (GA)
AUGUSTUS, Sarah Louise (14.1, 56-57), 80 yrs., tended animals (NC)
AUSTIN, Bill (17.1, 22-25), c. 100 yrs., field and store work
   (FL via GA)
AUSTIN, Charity (14.1, 58-62), 85 yrs. (NC)
AUSTIN, George (S2 - 2.1, 104-117), 75 yrs., free (TX)
AUSTIN, Hannah (12.1, 19-21), 70-75 yrs., town slave (GA)
AUSTIN, Hattie (S2 - 2.1, 118-20), 75 yrs., house (TX via GA)
AUSTIN, Lou (S2 - 2.1, 121-32), 87 yrs., field (TX)
AUSTIN, Smith (S2 - 2.1, 133-37), 90 yrs., field (TX)
AVERY, Celestia (12.1, 22-31), 75 yrs. (GA)

BABINO, Agatha (4.1, 37-38) (S2 -2.1, 138-42), 87 yrs., field
   (TX via LA)
BACCHUS, Josephine (2.1, 20-25), uuper 70's (SC)
BACCUS, Lillie (8.1, 76-77), 74 yrs. (AR via MS)
BACKSTROM, Susan (S1 - 6.1, 88-89) (MS via MD and AL)
BADGETT, Joseph Samuel (8.1, 78-83), 72 yrs. (AR)
BAILEY, Jeff (8.1, 84-90), 77 yrs. (AR)
BAKER, Anna (7.2, 11-17) (S1 - 6.1, 90-101), 80 yrs. (MS via AL)
BAKER, Blount (14.1, 63-65) (NC)
BAKER, Father (S1 - 1.1, 30-34), field (AL)
BAKER, Georgia (12.1, 37-57), 87 yrs., yard work (GA)
BAKER, Henry (S2 - 2.1, 143-49), 80 yrs., field (TX via VA)
BAKER, James (8.1, 91-96), 81 yrs. (AR)
BAKER, Jane (11.8, 24), 103 yrs. (MO)
BAKER, Julia (S1 - 1.1, 28-29), 81 yrs. (AL via VA)
BAKER, Lizzie (14.1, 66-69), 73 yrs. (NC)
BAKER, Slim (S1 - 2.2, 25-27), 67 yrs., free (CO)
BAKER, Tom (6.1, 17-19), c. 86 yrs., field (AL)

BAKER, Viney (14.1, 70-72), 78 yrs. (NC via VA)
BAKER, William (S1 - 2.2, 28-32), c. 65 yrs. (CO)
BALE, Mrs. Elizabeth Brooks (S2 - 10.9, 4327-29), 92 yrs., white (TX)
BALLARD, General Lee (S1 - 1.1, 35-37), 76 yrs., house (AL via LA)
BALLARD, William (2.1, 26-28), 88 yrs., field (SC)
BALTIMORE, Uncle William (8.1, 97-103) (S2 - 1.3, 19-24), 103 yrs.,
   blacksmith and carpenter (AR)
BAMBURG, Red (S1 - 6.1, 102) (MS)
BANKS, Ephom (S1 - 6.1, 103-04), c. 70 yrs. (MS)
BANKS, Frances (S1 - 12.1, 11-12), 82 yrs., field (OK)
BANKS, Mose (8.1, 101-03), 69 yrs., free (AR)
BANKS, Phoebe (7.1, 8-11), 78 yrs., house (OK via AR)
BANKS, Sina (S1 - 12.1, 13-27), 86 yrs., field (OK via MO)
BANNER, Henry (8.1, 104-06), 89 yrs. (AR via VA)
BARBER, Charley (2.1, 29-33), 81 yrs. (SC)
BARBER, Ed (2.1, 34-37), 77 yrs. (SC)
BARBER, James (S2 - 2.1, 150-52), 79 yrs. (TX)
BARBER, Millie (2.1, 38-41), 82 yrs., house (SC)
BARBER, Mollie (S1 - 12.1, 28-35), 79 yrs., house (OK via AR)
BARBER, Rosa (6.2, 11-12), 76 yrs. (IN via NC)
BARBOUR, Charlie (14.1, 73-77), 86 yrs. (NC)
BARBOUR, Mary (14.1, 78-81), 81 yrs. (NC)
BARCLAY, Delia (S2 - 2.1, 153-58), field (TX)
BARCLAY, Jim (S2 - 2.1, 159-63), 82 yrs., field (TX)
BARCLAY, Mrs. John (Sarah Sanders) (4.1, 39-41), 84 yrs. (TX via MS)
BARDEN, Mrs. Melissa (Lowe) (16.4, 6), 80-90 yrs. (OH via GA)
BARKER, John (4.1, 42-44) (S2 - 2.1, 164-73), 84 yrs., field
   (TX via OH and MO)
BARNER, L.B. (S1 - 12.1, 36-38), 81 yrs., field (OK via TX)
BARNES, Berle (S1 - 11.1, 1-4), 83 yrs. (NC)
   See Barnes, Mariah (NC)
BARNES, Henry (6.1, 20-24) (S1 - 1, 38-43), 79 yrs., field (AL)
BARNES, Joe (4.1, 45-46) (S1 - 2.1, 174-77), 80 yrs., field (TX)
BARNES, Lucy (S2 - 2.1, 178-80), 84 yrs., cared for children (TX)
BARNES, Mariah (S1 - 11.1, 1-14), 83 yrs., cook (NC)
   See Barnes, Berle (NC)
BARNES, Mary (S2 - 1.9, 297-300), 93 yrs., house (MD)
BARNETT, Amelia (S2 - 2.1, 181-86), 94 yrs., field (TX via AL)
BARNETT, Darcus (S2 - 2.1, 187-92), 82 yrs., cared for children (TX)
BARNETT, John W.H. (8.1, 107-08), 81 yrs. (AR via LA)
BARNETT, Josephine (8.1, 109-111), upper 70's (AR via TN)
BARNETT, Lewis (S1 - 5.1, 5-6), over 85 yrs. (IN via KY)
BARNETT, Lizzie (8.1, 112-114), c. 100 yrs. (AR via TN)
BARNETT, Spencer (8.1, 115-18), 81 yrs. (AR via AL)
BARR, Emma (8.1, 119-20), 65 yrs., free (AR via MS)
BARR, Robert (8.1, 122-25), 73 yrs. (AR via MS)
BARRENS, Jake (S2 - 2.1, 193-95), 81 yrs. (TX)
BARRETT, Armstead (4.1, 47-48) (S2 - 2.1, 196-98), 90 yrs. (TX)
BARRETT, Harriet (4.1, 49-50) (S2 - 2.1, 199-204), 86 yrs., cook (TX)
BARTON, Robert (S1 - 5.1, 7-8), 88 yrs. (IN via KY)
BASARD, Elvira (S2 - 2.1, 205-06), cared for children (TX)
BASS, Matilda (8.1, 126), 80 yrs. (AR via MS)
BATES, Anderson (2.1, 42-45), 87 yrs. (SC)
BATES, Frank (17.1, 366), carried water to slaves (FL via AL)
BATES, John (4.1, 51-53) (S2 - 2.1, 212-19), 84 yrs., field
   (TX via AR)

BATES, Millie (2.1, 46-47) (SC)
BATSON, Frances (16.6, 1-2), over 90 yrs. (TN)
BATTIEST, Jane (S1 - 12.1, 39-46), 105 yrs., field (OK)
BATTLE, Alice (S1 - 3.1, 39-44) (12.1, 58-60), c. 87 yrs., house (GA)
BATTLE, Anthony (S1 - 5.1, 161-64), 78 yrs. (IN via NC)
BATTLE, Jasper (12.1, 61-71), c. 80 yrs., field (GA)
BAUGH, Alice (14.1, 82-86), 64 yrs., free (NC)
BAUMONT, Kate Dudley (S1 - 5.2, 277-80), over 80 yrs. (OH via KY)
BEAL, Emmett (8.1, 127-28), 78 yrs. (AR via TN)
BEAN, Abe (S2 - 2.1, 220-23), 84 yrs., field (TX)
BEAN, Joe (S1 - 12.1, 46-51), 89 yrs., field (OK via AR)
BEAN, Nancy Rogers (7.1, 12-13), 82 yrs., house (OK)
BEARD, Dina (8.1, 129-30), 76 yrs. (AR)
BEAS, Welcome (S1 - 11.2, 58), 104 yrs. (SC)
BEATTY, George (S1 - 5.1, 9-10), 75 yrs. (IN via KY)
BEAUCHAMP, Nathan (6.1, 25-26), c. 70's (AL)
BECCA, Aunt (S1 - 6.1, 105) (MS)
BECK, Anne (8.1, 131), 50 yrs. free (AR via MS)
BECKETT, Harrison (4.1, 54-58) (S2 - 2.1, 224-36), c. 80 yrs., field
   (TX)
BECKETT, Ransom (S1 - 11.2, 59-60), 88 yrs. (SC)
BECKWITH, J.H. (8.1, 132-34), 68 yrs., free (AR via NC)
BECKWITH, John (14.1, 87-90), 83 yrs. (NC)
BECTOM, John C. (14.1, 91-98), 75 yrs. (NC)
BEDFORD, Henry (S1 - 5.2, 281-83), 80 yrs. (OH via TN)
BEE, Prince (7.1, 14-16), 85 yrs., field (OK)
BEEL, Enoch (8.1, 135-36), 79 yrs. (AR via TN)
BEES, Welcome (2.1, 48-50), 104 yrs. (SC)
BEES, Will (S1 - 11.2, 61-62), 75-80 yrs. (SC)
BELCHER, John (S1 - 6.1, 106-16), c. 90 yrs. (MS via GA)
BELL, Alex (S1 - 6.1, 117) (MS)
   See Bell, Mary (MS)
BELL, Anne (2.1, 51-54), 83 yrs., house (SC)
BELL, Bettie M. (S1 - 1.1, 44-54), 87 yrs., house (AL via GA)
BELL, Charlie (S1 - 6.1, 118-27), 81 yrs. (MS via AR)
BELL, Eliza (S1 - 12.1, 52-58), 87 yrs., field (OK via MS)
BELL, Frank (4.1, 59-61) (S2 - 2.1, 237-43), 86 yrs., saloon work
   (TX via LA)
BELL, Laura (14.1, 99-102), 73 yrs. (NC)
BELL, Mary (S1 - 6.1, 117) (MS)
   See Bell, Alex (MS)
BELL, Mary A. (11.8, 25-31), 85 yrs., nurse (MO)
BELL, Oliver (6.1, 27-32) (S1 - 1.1, 55-60), planted trees (AL)
BELL, Virginia (4.1, 62-65) (S2 - 2.1, 244-48), 88 yrs., house
   (TX via LA)
BELLE, Sophie (8.1, 137-40), 77 yrs. (AR via GA)
BELLUS, Cyrus (8.1, 141-45), 73 yrs. (AR via MS)
BENDY, Edgar (4.1, 66-67), over 90 yrs., cared for children (TX)
BENDY, Minerva (4.1, 68-69) (S2 - 2.1, 249-53), c. 84 yrs., house
   (TX via AL)
BENFORD, Bob (8.1, 146-48), 77 yrs. (AR via AL)
BENJAMIN, Sarah (4.1, 70-71) (S2 - 2.1, 254-60), 82 yrs., house
   (TX via LA)
BENNEFIELD, Willis (13.4, 235-44), 101 yrs., field (GA)
BENNETT, Carrie Bradley Logan (8.1, 149-52), c. 79 yrs. (AR via MS)
BENSON, George (8.1, 153-54), 80 yrs. (AR)

BENTON, Harriet (S1 - 45-52), 83 yrs. (GA)
BENTON, Kato (8.1, 155-56), 78 yrs., house (AR via SC)
BENTON, Sara (S1 - 1.1, 61-63), 89 yrs., house (AL)
BERLINER, Sara L. Johnson (S2 - 10.9, 4330-41), 97 yrs., white (TX)
BERRY, Fannie (16.5, 1-6) (VA)
BERRY, Frank (17.1, 27-31) (S2 - 1.5, 263-66), 78 yrs. (FL)
BERTRAND, James (8.1, 157-59), 68 yrs., free (AR)
BESS, Jack (4.1, 72-74), 83 yrs., cared for animals (TX)
BEST, Nathan (S1 - 6.1, 128-40), 92 yrs., field (MS via NC)
BETHEL, William (S1 - 12.1, 59-63), c. 92 yrs., field (OK via NC)
BETHUNE, Thomas (S1 - 3.1, 53-61), 88 yrs. (GA)
BETTERS, Aunt Kate (S2 - 2.1, 261-64), 87 yrs., house (TX via MS)
BETTS, Ellen (4.1, 75-83) (S2 - 2.1, 265-80), 84 yrs., cared for
    children (TX via LA)
BEVERLY, Charlotte (4.1, 84-86) (S2 - 2.1, 281-88), c. 90 yrs.,
    house (TX)
BEVIS, Caroline (2.1, 55-56), 96 yrs. (SC)
BIBLES, Della Mun (S2 - 2.1, 289-95), cook (TX)
BIBLES, Johnny (S2 - 2.1, 296-98), free (TX)
BIDDIE, Mary Minus (17.1, 32-38), 105 yrs., boarding house chores (FL)
BIGGS, Alice (8.1, 160-161), 70 yrs., free (AR via MS)
BILLINGS, Mandy (8.1, 162-63), 84 yrs. (AR via LA)
BILLINGSBY, Kate (16.2, 60), 110 yrs., house (KY)
BILLUPS, Ellen (S1 - 6.1, 141), house (nurse) (MS via GA)
BINNS, Arie (12.1, 72-79), c. 88 yrs., house and field (GA via AR)
BIRCH, Jane (8.1, 164-65), 74 yrs. (AR via SC)
BIRDSONG, Nelson (6.1, 33-34), c. 80 yrs. (AL)
BISHOP, Ank (6.1, 35-38), 89 yrs. (AL)
BISHOP, Nancy (S1 - 6.1, 142), house (MS)
BLACK, Beatrice (8.1, 166-67), 48 yrs., free (AR)
BLACK, Francis (4.1, 87-88) (S2 - 2.1, 299-302), 87 yrs., house
    (TX via MS)
BLACK, Henry W. (S2 - 1.10, 303-08), 56 yrs., free (NE via IL)
BLACK, Maggie (2.1, 57-61), 79 yrs. (SC)
BLACK, William (11.8, 32-35) (S1 - 2.4, 147-49), c. 85 yrs., light
    field work and house (hired out) (MO via VA)
BLACK, William Edward (S1 - 6.1, 143-46), 91 yrs., house (MS via NC)
BLACKWELL, Boston (8.1, 168-74), 98 yrs. (AR via GA)
BLACKWELL, Charlie (S1 - 6.1, 147-48), 104 yrs. (MS via SC)
BLACKWELL, Willie (S2 - 2.1, 303-23), 103 yrs., field (TX via NC)
BLAKE, Henry (8.1, 175-79), c. 80 yrs. (AR)
BLAKELEY, Adeline (8.1, 180-93), 87 yrs. (AR via TN)
BLAKELEY, Mittie (6.2, 13-14), 79 yrs., house (IN via MO)
BLAKELY, Sally (S1 - 3.1, 62-67), 80 yrs., house (GA)
BLALOCK, Emma (14.1, 103-09), 88 yrs. (NC)
BLANCHARD, Olivier (4.1, 90-92) (S2 - 2.1, 324-29), 95 yrs., field
    (TX via LA)
BLAND, Henry (12.1, 80-85), 86 yrs., field (GA)
BLAND, Patsy Jane (S1 - 5.1, 11-15), 107 yrs., house (IN via KY)
BLANKS, Julia (4.1, 93-105), 75 yrs. (TX)
BLEDSOE, Susan (16.4, 7-9), 92 yrs., field and house (OH via TN)
BLEWETT, Dig (S1 - 6.1, 149-50) (MS)
BLEWETT, Harold (S1 - 6.1, 151) (MS)
BLEWITT, Peter (S1 - 6.1, 152-54), 87 yrs., house (MS via TX)
BLOCKER, Irena (S1 - 12.1, 64-68), 68 yrs., free (OK via TX)
BLOUNT, Uncle David (14.1, 110-16), field (NC)

BLUFORD, Gordon (2.1, 62-64), 92 yrs., house (SC)
BOBBIT, Clay (14.1, 117-19), 100 yrs. (NC)
BOBBITT, Henry (14.1, 120-24), 87 yrs., field (NC)
BOBO, Vera Roy (8.1, 194), 68 yrs., free (AR via GA)
BODY, Rias (12.1, 86-90) (S1 - 3.1, 68-75), c. 89 yrs., field (GA)
BOECHUS, Liddie (8.1, 195-96), 73 yrs. (AR via MS)
BOGAN, Herndon (14.1, 125-29), c. 76 yrs. (NC via SC)
BOGGAN, Manda (S1 - 6.1, 155-59), 90 yrs., field (MS)
BOGGS, Daisy L. (S1 - 2.4, 137), white (MO)
BODIE, Dan (16.2, 1-4), 79 yrs. (KY)
BOHANNON, Henry (S1 - 1.1, 64-66), over 80 yrs., house (AL via GA)
BOHANON, Georganna (S1 - 6.1, 160-61), 104 yrs., house (MS via VA)
BOHMER, Lewis (7.1, 17-19), 87 yrs., house (OK via TX)
BOLDEN, Lizzie (S1 - 5.1, 1-6) (IN via KY)
BOLDEN, Mary M. (S1 - 2.4, 150-51), 76 yrs. (MO)
BOLDIN, Quentin (S2 - 2.1, 330-35), 86 yrs., field (TX)
BOLDRIDGE, Joe (S1 - 6.1, 162-65), house (MS)
BOLES, Elvira (4.1, 106-08) (S2 - 2.1, 336-39), 94 yrs., house and
    field; brick yard worker (TX via MS)
BOLLINGER, George (11.8, 31-43), 84 yrs., field (MO)
BOLTON, James (12.1, 91-104) (S1 - 3.1, 76-90), 85 yrs., yard and light
    work (GA)
BOND, Maggie (8.1, 197-200), 80's (AR via NC)
BOND, Porter (S1 - 6.1, 166-69) (MS)
BOND, Scott (S2 - 1.3,25-50), 84 yrs. (AR via MS)
BONDS, Caroline (8.1, 201), 70 yrs., free (AR via NC)
BONES, Tom (S1 - 6.1, 170-74), 95 yrs. (MS via VA)
BONNER, Elax (S1 - 6.1, 175-77), 86 yrs. (MS)
BONNER, Lewis (S1 - 12.1, 69-72), 87 yrs., field (OK via TX)
BONNER, Sidney (6.1, 39-41), c. 117 yrs. (AL)
BOONE, Andrew (14.1, 130-37), 90 yrs. (NC)
BOONE, Carl (5.2, 15-18) (S1 - 5.1, 1719), 87 yrs., free (IN via KY)
BOONE, Rev. Frank T. (8.1, 202-09), 80 yrs. (AR via VA)
BOONE, J.F. (8.1, 210-13), 66 yrs., free (AR)
BOONE, Jonas (8.1, 214-15), 86 yrs. (AR via MS)
BOOTH, Ella (S1 - 6.1, 178-79), 80 yrs. (MS)
BOOTH, Etta (S1 - 1.1, 67-68), 94 yrs., house (AL)
BORLAND, Walter (S1 - 5.1, 252-53), 70 yrs., free (IN)
BORMER, Betty (4.1, 109-11) (S2 - 2.1, 340-45), 80 yrs., cared for
    children (TX)
BOST, Mrs. Phoebe (16.4, 10), c. 90 yrs. (OH via LA)
BOST, W.L. (14.1, 138-46), 88 yrs. (NC)
BOSTWICK, Alec (12.1, 106-112), 76 yrs. (GA)
BOUDREAUX, Felice (4.2, 225-27) (S2 - 6.5, 2035-42), 78 yrs (TX via LA)
    See Johnson, Pauline (TX)
BOUDRY, Nancy (12.1, 113-17), c. 100 yrs., field (GA)
BOULWARE, Samuel (2.1, 65-69), 82 yrs. (SC)
BOVY, Joe (S1 - 6.1, 180-82), 89 yrs. (MS)
BOWDRY, John (8.1, 216-17), 73 yrs. (AR via MS)
BOWE, Mary Wallace (14.1, 147-51), 81 yrs. (NC)
BOWEN, Charley (S2 - 2.1, 346-50), 93 yrs., field (TX via AL)
BOWEN, Jennie (6.1, 42-43) (S1 - 1.1, 69-71), 90 yrs., house
    (AL via VA)
BOWMAN, Amanda (S1 - 6.1, 183), c. 90 yrs., house and field (MS)
BOWMAN, Julia (6.2, 19-20), 78 yrs., house (IN via KY)
BOYCE, Angie (6.2, 21), 76 yrs. (IN via KY)

BOYD, Annie B. (16.2, 57-59), 86 yrs., nurse (KY)
BOYD, Rev. Eli (17.1, 39-40), 73 yrs. (FL via SC and GA)
BOYD, Harrison (4.1, 112-13) (S2 - 2.1, 351-54), 87 yrs., house (TX)
BOYD, Isabella (4.1, 114-16) (S2 - 2.1, 355-61), house (TX via VA)
BOYD, Jack (8.1, 218-19), 72 yrs., free (AR via VA)
BOYD, James (4.1, 117-20) (S2 - 2.1, 362-70), c. 100 yrs., field
    (TX via OK)
BOYD, John (2.1, 70-73) (SC)
BOYD, Mal (8.1, 220-22), 65 yrs., free (AR)
BOYD, Nellie (S1 - 11.2, 63-65), house and field (SC)
BOYKINS, Jerry (4.1, 121-23) (S2 - 2.1, 371-74), 92 yrs., house
    (TX via GA)
BOYNTON, Rivana (Riviana) (17.1, 41-46, 367-71), 87 yrs., field and
    house (FL via SC)
BOYSAW, Edna (6.2, 22-24), c. 87 yrs., field (IN via VA)
BRACEY, Callie (6.2, 25-26), field (IN)
BRACEY, Maria (S1 - 11.2, 66-67) (SC)
BRACKINS, Monroe (4.1, 124-29) (S2 - 2.1, 375-90), 84 yrs., cow
    puncher (TX via MS)
BRADDOX, George (8.1, 223-28), 80 yrs. (AR)
BRADFIELD, Nannie (6.1, 44-45), 85 yrs., house (AL)
BRADFORD, Elodga (S1 - 6.1, 184-86), 92 yrs. (MS)
BRADFORD, Sam (S1 - 6.1, 187-88) (MS)
BRADLEY, Alice (12.1, 118-22) (GA)
BRADLEY, Edmund (S1 - 6.1, 189-95), 95 yrs. (MS)
BRADLEY, Edward (8.1, 229-32), 70 yrs., free (AR via TN)
BRADLEY, Jane (2.1, 74), 80 yrs., house (SC)
BRADLEY, Martha (6.1, 46-47), c. 100 yrs., field (AL)
BRADLEY, Rachel (8.1, 233-36) (S1 - 2.1, 1-3) (S2 - 1.3, 51-55),
    c. 108 yrs., nursemaid and weaver (AR via LA)
BRADLEY, Reuben (S1 - 6.1, 196) (MS)
BRADSHAW, Gus (4.1, 130-32) (S2 - 2.1, 391-96), c. 93 yrs., field
    (TX via AL)
BRADSHAW, Tillman (S1 - 3.1, 91-93), over 85 yrs., yard work (GA)
BRADY, Wes (4.1, 133-36) (S2 - 2.1, 397-404), 88 yrs., house;
    sheep herder (TX via AL)
BRAGG, Tolbert (S1 - 5.1, 20-21), 101 yrs. (IN via TN)
BRANCH, Jacob (4.1, 137-42) (S2 - 2.1, 405-19), c. 86 yrs., field;
    cared for animals (TX via LA)
BRANCH, William (4.1, 143-46), 87 yrs. (TX via VA)
BRANDON, David (S1 - 6.1, 197) (MS)
BRANNON, Elizabeth (8.1, 237-40), 40's, free (AR)
BRANON, Ernest (S1 - 6.1, 198-99), 88 yrs., field (MS via GA)
BRANTLEY, Mack (8.1, 241-45), 80 yrs. (AR via AL)
BRASS, Ellen (8.1, 246-48), 82 yrs. (AR via AL)
BRATCHER, Minerva (S2 - 2.1, 420-21), 86 yrs. (TX)
BRATTON, Alice (8.1, 249-50), 56 yrs., free (AR via TN)
BREWER, Dora (S1 - 6.1, 200-03), house (MS)
BREWER, Wiley (S1 - 6.1, 204-06), claims 130 yrs., field and house (MS)
BRICE, Amanda Eilers (S2 - 2.1, 422-27), 87 yrs. (TX)
BRICE, Andy (2.1, 75-79), 81 yrs., field (SC)
BRIDGES, Annie (11.8, 44-51), 81 yrs., house (MO)
BRIDGES, Francis (7.1, 20-23), 73 yrs., field (OK via TX)
BRIDGES, Harry (S1 - 6.1, 207-15), 79 yrs. (MS)
BRIGGS, George (2.1, 80-97) (S1 - 11.2, 68-75), 88 yrs., fed animals
    (SC)

BRILES, Frank (8.1, 251-52), 83 yrs. (AR)
BRIM, Clara (4.1, 147-48) (S2 - 2.1, 428-33), 100 yrs., field
  (TX via LA)
BRISCOE, Della (12.1, 125-32), over 90 yrs., light field work (GA)
BRISTON, Josephine (2.1, 98-103), 73 yrs. (SC)
BRITTEN, Della (3.3, 256-59), c. 74 yrs. (SC)
BRITTIAN, James (S1 - 6.1, 216-21), 85 yrs., house (MS)
BROACH, Sam (S1 - 6.1, 222-30), 89 yrs. (MS via SC and AL)
BROADDUS, Henry (S2 - 2.1, 441-44), 77 yrs., herded ducks (TX via AL)
BROADUS, Ned (S2 - 2.1, 434-37), field (TX via AL)
BROOKS, G.W. (S1 - 2.4, 152), 83 yrs. (MO)
BROOKS, George (12.1, 133-34), 112 yrs., field and house (GA via AL)
BROOKS, James (S1 - 6.1, 231-34), 92 yrs., house (MS)
BROOKS, Lucy (16.3, 1-3), c. 90 yrs., house (MD)
BROOKS, Mary Ann (8.1, 253-54), 90 yrs., house (AR)
BROOKS, Matilda (17.1, 47-51), 79 yrs., field (FL via SC)
BROOKS, Sylvester (4.1, 149-50) (S2 - 2.1, 448-53), c. 88 yrs., field
  (TX via AL)
BROOKS, Waters (8.1, 255-66), 75 yrs. (AR)
BROOME, Anne (2.1, 104-06), 87 yrs. (SC)
BROUSSARD, Donaville (4.1, 151-53) (S2 - 2.1, 454-59), c. 88 yrs.,
  house (TX)
BROWN, Adeline (2.1, 127-30), 96 yrs. (SC)
  See Brown, John (SC)
BROWN, Allen (6.1, 48) (S1 - 1.1, 72), 99 yrs., stable boy (AL via VA)
BROWN, Ben (16.4, 11-14), c. 100 yrs., field and chores (OH via VA)
BROWN, Betty (13.4, 266-68), non-slave (GA)
BROWN, Betty (11.8, 52-55), weaver (MO via AR)
BROWN, Calline (S1 - 6.1, 235-38), 105 yrs., field (MS)
BROWN, Casey Jones (8.1, 267-71), 91 yrs. (AR)
BROWN, Charley M. (S1 - 12.1, 73-77), 63 yrs., free (OK)
BROWN, Easter (12.1, 135-40), 78 yrs., house (GA)
BROWN, Ebenezer (S1 - 6.1, 239-54), 85 yrs., field and house (MS)
BROWN, Elcie (8.1, 272-74) (AR)
BROWN, F.H. (8.1, 275-80), 75 yrs. (AR via MS)
BROWN, Fannie (4.1, 154-55) (S2 - 2.1, 460-63), cook and weaver
  (TX via VA)
BROWN, Fred (4.1, 156-59) (S2 - 2.1, 464-70), 84 yrs., field
  (TX via LA)
BROWN, George (8.1, 281-83), 84 yrs., house (AR via AL)
BROWN, Gus (6.1, 49-50), c. 90 yrs., house (AL)
BROWN, Hager (2.1, 107-14) (S1 - 11.2, 76-86), 77 yrs., midwife (SC)
BROWN, Hattie Jane (S2 - 3.2, 471-73), c. 115 yrs. (TX via MS)
BROWN, Henry (2.1, 118-26), 79 yrs. (SC)
BROWN, J.N (8.1, 284-85), 79 yrs. (AR via MS)
BROWN, James (4.1, 160-62) (S2 - 3.2, 474-80), 84 yrs., carriage
  driver (TX)
BROWN, John (7.1, 24-26), 87 yrs., field (OK via AL)
BROWN, John (2.1, 127-30), 86 yrs. (SC)
  See Brown, Adeline (SC)
BROWN, Josie (4.1, 163-65) (S2 - 3.2, 481-84), c. 79 yrs., house (TX)
BROWN, Julia ("Aunt Sally") (12.1, 141-53), 87 yrs., house (GA)
BROWN, Lewis (8.1, 286-97) (S2 - 1.3, 56-57), c. 83 yrs. (AR)
BROWN, Lizzie Fant (S1 - 6.1, 255-67), 76 yrs. (MS)
BROWN, Louisa (2.1, 115-17) (SC)
BROWN, Lucretia (S1 - 6.1, 267), house (MS via AL)

BROWN, Lucy (14.1, 152-54), c. 75 yrs. (NC)
BROWN, Mag (8.1, 298), 83 yrs. (AR via NC)
BROWN, Manus (S1 - 6.1, 268-72), 79 yrs. (MS)
BROWN, Mary (8.1, 299-300), 78 yrs. (AR via VA)
BROWN, Mary Frances (2.1, 131-36) (S1 - 11.2, 87-90), 88 yrs., house
    (SC)
BROWN, Mattie (8.1, 301-02), 75 yrs. (AR via AL)
BROWN, Molly (8.1, 303-10), over 90 yrs. (AR)
BROWN, Peter (8.1, 311-14), 86 yrs., house (AR via MS)
BROWN, Rina (S1 - 6.1, 273-83), 84 yrs. (MS)
BROWN, Rose (S1 - 6.1, 284-86), 84 yrs., store work (MS via AL)
BROWN, Rosella (S2 - 3.2, 485-88), over 100 yrs. (TX)
BROWN, Rube (S1 - 6.1, 287-89), upper 80's (MS via GA)
BROWN, Sally (S1 - 3.1, 94-110), 85 yrs., field (GA)
BROWN, Sara Mom (2.1, 137-44), 85 yrs. (SC)
BROWN, Steve (11.8, 56-57), cared for livestock (MO via KY)
BROWN, Steve (S2 - 3.2, 489-96), 78 yrs. (TX via AL)
BROWN, Thomas (S1 - 6.1, 290-93), 75 yrs. (MS via TN)
BROWN, William (8.1, 317-23), 78 yrs. (AR)
BROWN, William (8.1, 315-16), 67 yrs., free (AR via VA)
BROWN, Zek (4.1, 166-68) (S2 - 3.2, 497-502), 80 yrs., house
    (TX via TN)
BROWNING, G.W. (S1 - 3.1, 111-17), 85 yrs., field (GA)
BROYLES, Maggie (8.1, 324-28), c. 80 yrs. (AR via TN)
BRUIN, Madison (4.1, 169-73) (S2 - 3.2, 503-11), 82 yrs., field;
    groomed horses (TX via KY)
BRUNER, Peter (16.2, 88-90), 91 yrs. (KY)
BRUNER, Richard (11.8, 58-60) (S1 - 2.4, 153-55), 97 yrs., carried
    water (MO via KY)
BRUNSON, Vinnie (S2 - 3.2, 512-18), 76 yrs. (TX)
BRYAN, Margaret (S1 - 11.2, 91-92), 80 yrs. (SC)
BRYANT, Ida (8.1, 329), 61 yrs., free (AR via LA)
BRYANT, Margaret (2.1, 145-48) (SC)
BRYANT, Mary J. Williams (S1 - 6.1, 294), 78 yrs.(MS)
BRYANT, Robert (S1 - 6.1, 295-96) (MS)
BRYANT, Robert (11.8, 62-69), 75 yrs. (MO)
BRYANT, Tommie (S1 - 1.1, 73), 68 yrs. (AL)
BUCK, Nelson (S1 - 6.1, 297-99), 88 yrs. (MS)
BUCKLEY, Della (S1 - 6.1, 300-02) (MS)
BUCKNER, Dr. George Washington (6.2, 27-35) (S1 - 5.1, 22-26), 85 yrs.,
    house (IN via KY)
BUFFORD, Alex (11.8, 70-72), field (MO)
BUFFORD, Henry (S1 - 2.2, 33-34), over 80 yrs. (CO via GA)
BULLEN, Claiborne (S1 - 6.1, 303-04) (MS)
BUNCH, Julia (12.1, 154-59), 85 yrs., children's nurse (SC)
BUNTIN, Belle (8.1, 330-33), 80's, house (AR via MS)
BUNTON, Martha Spence (4.1, 174-75) (S2 - 3.2, 519-26), 81 yrs.,
    carried food to field slaves (TX via TN)
BUNTS, Queen Elizabeth (S1 - 3.1, 118-30), 73 yrs., yard work and
    house (GA via NC)
BURDEN, Augustus (S1 - 3.1, 131-34), 95 yrs., house (GA)
BURDICK, Amos (S1 - 11.2, 93-94), 70 yrs. (SC)
BURGESS, Jeff (8.1, 334-35), 74 yrs. (AR via TX)
BURKE, Sarah Woods (16.4, 15-17) (OH via WV)
BURKES, Norman (8.1, 336-37), 73 yrs. (AR)
BURKES, Will Sr. (8.1, 338-39), 75 yrs. (AR via TN)

BURLESON, James (S2 - 3.2, 527-30), 86 yrs., helped gin cotton (TX)
BURNES, Mahala (S1 - 1.1, 74-76), c. 98 yrs., house (AL via LA)
BURNETT, Midge (14.1, 155-58), 80 yrs., field (NC via GA)
BURNS, George Taylor (6.2, 36-39) (S1 - 5.1, 27-42), 104 yrs., field
   (IN via MO)
BURNS, Robert (S1 - 12.1, 78-81), 81 yrs. (OK via TN)
BURRELL, Phoebe Jane (S2 - 3.2, 531-33), 87 yrs., house (TX via GA)
BURRELL, Savilla (2.1, 149-51), 83 yrs. (SC)
BURRELL, Wesley (S2 - 3.2, 534-38), 86 yrs., sheep herder (TX)
BURRIS, Adeline (8.1, 340-41), 91 yrs. (AR via TN)
BURTON, C.B. (S1 - 11.2, 95) (2.1, 152), 79 yrs. (SC)
BURTON, Daniel (S1 - 12.1, 82-86), 87 yrs. (OK via TX)
BURTON, James (S1 - 6.1, 305-07), c. 80-86 yrs., house (MS via VA)
BUSBY, Vinnie (S1 - 6.1, 308-12), 83 yrs. (MS)
BUSH, Richard (S1 - 6.1, 313), 90 yrs. (MS)
BUSH, Sam (S2 - 3.2, 539-44), 77 yrs., errands and chores (TX)
BUTLER, Belle (6.2, 40-42), field (IN)
BUTLER, Ed (S1 - 12.1, 87-89), 81 yrs., field (OK)
BUTLER, Ellen (4.1, 176-78) (S2 - 3.2, 545-50), c. 78 yrs., carried
   water to field slaves (TX via LA)
BUTLER, Gabe (S1 - 6.1, 314-28), 83 yrs. (MS)
BUTLER, George Ann (2.1, 153-54), 75 yrs. (SC)
BUTLER, Sarah (2.1, 155-60), 79 yrs. (SC)
BUTLER, Jennie (8.1, 342-45), c. 105 yrs. (AR via VA)
BUTLER, Jennie (S1 - 6.1, 329-30), 88 yrs. (MS via KY)
BUTLER, Marshal (12.1, 160-67), 88 yrs., field (GA)
BUTLER, Solbert (2.1, 161-65), 82 yrs. (SC)
BUTLINGTON, Charles (S1 - 2.4, 156-57), 90 yrs. (MO)
BUTTLER, Henry H. (4.1, 179-80) (S2 - 3.2, 551-59), 87 yrs., heavy
   outdoor work (Tx via VA and AR)
BYNES, Titus (17.1, 52-54, 220-21), 90 yrs., house (FL via SC)
BYNUM, Sallie (S1 - 6.1, 331), 81 yrs. (MS)
BYRD, David L. (S2 - 3.2, 560-72), field (TX)
BYRD, E.L. (8.1, 346), 76 yrs. (AR via SC)
BYRD, Emmett Augusta (8.1, 347-51), 83 yrs. (AR via MO)
BYRD, Mrs. (S1 -3.1, 134-41), 83 yrs., field (GA)
BYRD, Sarah (12.1, 168-71), 95 yrs., field (GA via VA)
BYRD, William (4.1, 182-84) (S2 - 3.2, 573-83), c. 97 yrs., field
   slave and driver for master (TX)

CAIN, Granny (2.1, 166-68), 90 yrs. (SC)
CAIN, Louis (4.1, 185-87) (S2 - 3.2, 584-99), 88 yrs., heavy outdoor
   work (TX via NC)
CALDWELL, James (S1 - 11.2, 96), 71 yrs. (SC)
CALDWELL, Laura (2.1, 169), 77 yrs. (SC)
CALDWELL, Solomon (2.1, 170-71), 73 yrs. (SC)
CALHOUN, Jeff (4.1, 188-90) (S2 - 3.2, 600-10), 98 yrs., driver for
   master; field (TX via AL)
CALLOWAY, Mariah (12.1, 172-76), c. 85 yrs., played with owner's
   children (GA)
CALLOWAY, Walter (6.1, 51-54), 89 yrs., field (AL via VA)
CAMERON, John (7.1, 18-21) (S1 - 7.2, 332-35), 95 yrs., gardener (MS)
CAMERON, Nelson (2.1, 172-75), 81 yrs. (SC)
CAMPBELL, Easter Sudie (16.2, 90-94), 72 yrs. (KY)

CAMPBELL, Ellen (13.4, 221-25), 91 yrs., field (GA)
CAMPBELL, Jack (S1 - 12.1, 90-95), over 75 yrs. (OK via AL)
CAMPBELL, James (16.4, 18-21), 86 yrs., barn work (OH via WV)
CAMPBELL, Patience (17.1, 58-61), field (FL)
CAMPBELL, Simpson (Simp) (4.1, 191-92) (S2 - 3.2, 612-17), 78 yrs. (TX)
CAMPBELL, Thomas (2.1, 176-79), 82 yrs., house (SC)
CANCER, Polly Turner (S1 - 7.2, 336-52), c. 100 yrs., limited field
    work due to health (MS)
CANNADY, Fanny (14.1, 159-64), 79 yrs. (NC)
CANNON, Sylvia (2.1, 180-96), 85 yrs. (SC)
CAPE, James (4.1, 193-96) (S2 - 3.2, 618-25), c. 117 yrs., tended and
    trained horses (TX)
CANNON, Frank (8.2, 1-2), 77 yrs. (AR via MS)
CARDER, Sallie (7.1, 27-29) (S1 - 12.1, 96-98), 83 yrs., house
    (OK via TN)
CAROLINA, Albert (2.1, 197-98) (S1 - 11.2, 97), 81 yrs. (SC)
CARPENTER, Mary (S1 - 3.1, 142-49), 86 yrs., house (GA)
CARRIE (13.4, 219) (GA)
CARRUTHERS, "Uncle" Richard (4.1, 197-201) (S2 - 3.2, 626-38),
    c. 100 yrs., slave driver (TX via TN)
CARTER, Aron (S1 - 7.2, 353-60), 80 yrs. (MS)
CARTER, Cato (4.1, 201-11) (S2 - 3.2, 639-52), c. 101 yrs., house
    and tended cows (TX via AL)
CARTER, George (S1 - 3.1, 150-66), over 90 yrs., field (GA via VA)
CARTER, Joseph William (6.2, 43-49) c. 101 yrs., field (IN via TN)
CARTER, Martha (S1 - 7.2, 361), c. 75 yrs. (MS)
CARTER, Nick (S1 - 7.2, 362-63), c. 110 yrs., dug trenches (Civil War)
    (MS via AL)
CARTHAN, Allen (S2 - 3.2, 653-65), c. 74 yrs. (TX)
CARUTHERS, Belle (S1 - 7.2, 364-68), 90 yrs., house (MS via NC)
CARVER, George Washington (S1 - 1.1, 77-78), 79 yrs. (d.1943), (AL)
CASEY, Esther King (6.1, 55-57), 81 yrs., house (AL via GA)
CASEY, Harriet (11.8, 73-75), 75 yrs. (MO)
CASEY, Joe (11.8, 76-78), 90 yrs. (MO)
CASEY, Julia (16.6, 3-4), 82 yrs. (TN)
CASSIBRY, Georgiana (S1 - 1.1, 79-85), 81 yrs., house (AL)
CASTLE, Susan (12.1, 177-83), 78 yrs. (GA)
CATO, George (S1 - 11.2, 98-100), 50 yrs., free (SC)
CAULEY,Zenie (8.2, 3-4), 78 yrs. (AR)
CAULTON, George (S1 - 3.1, 167-76), 92 yrs., house (GA via VA)
CAUTHERN, Jack (4.1, 212-213) (S2 - 3.2, 666-68), 84 yrs., house and
    field (TX)
CAVE, Ellen (6.2, 50-51), 86 yrs., house and field (IN via KY)
CAWTHON, Cicely (S1 - 3.1, 177-95), 78 yrs. (GA)
CHAMBERS, Abraham (S1 - 1.1, 86-88), 83 yrs., field (AL)
CHAMBERS, Ben (S2 - 3.2, 669-76), 87 yrs., hunted animals; carriage
    driver (TX via AL)
CHAMBERS, Liney (8.2, 5-7) (AR via TN)
CHAMBERS, Lula (11.8, 79-83), house (MO via AR and KY)
CHAMBERS, Lucy (S2 - 3.2, 677-80), c. 86 yrs. (TX)
CHAMBERS, Sally Banks (4.1, 214-16) (S2 - 3.2, 681-85) (TX via LA)
CHANEY, Ned (S1 - 7.2, 369-78) (MS via AL)
CHAPMAN, Amy (6.1, 58-61), 94 yrs., field (AL)
CHAPMAN, Emma (6.1, 62-65), 85 yrs., house (AL via SC)
CHAPMAN, Hannah (S1 - 7.2, 379-85), c. 85 yrs., house (MS)
CHAPMAN, Mr. (18.1, 74-79), tobacco factory (TN)

CHAPMAN, Mrs. (18.1, 73-74), nursed children (TN)
CHAPMAN, W. (S1 - 2.2, 35-36), 66 yrs. (CO via MN)
CHAPPEL, Cecelia (16.6, 5-8), 102 yrs., house (TN)
CHAPPEL, Clara (Clara Williams) (S2 - 3.2, 686-91), 94 yrs., house (TX)
CHARLESTON, Willie Buck Jr. (8.7, 8-9), 74 yrs. (AR)
CHASE, Lewis (8.2, 10-12), c. 90 yrs. (AR)
CHAVIOUS, Hillery (S1 - 5.1, 43-44), 94 yrs., free (IN via VA)
CHEATAM, Harriet (6.2, 52-54), 92 yrs., house and field (IN via TN)
CHEATAM, Henry (6.1, 66-71), (S1 - 1.1, 89-94), 86 yrs., water boy
  (AL via MS)
CHEATHAM, Robert J. (S1 - 5.1, 45-61), over 90 yrs. (IN via VA and KY)
CHESLEY, Harriet (S2 - 3.2, 692-94), c. 85 yrs. (TX)
CHESSIER, Betty Foreman (7.1, 30-32) (S1 - 12.1, 99-102), 94 yrs.,
  house (OK via NC)
CHILDERS, Henry (S2 - 3.2, 695-704), 94 yrs., house (TX)
CHILDRESS, Frank (S1 - 7.2, 386-90), 85 yrs., personal servant (MS)
CHILDRESS, James (6.2, 55-56), 77 yrs. (IN via TN)
CHILDRESS, Wiley (16.6, 9-10), 83 yrs. (TN)
CHILDS, Mary (S1 - 3.1, 196-202), over 90 yrs., field (GA via VA and NC)
CHILES, George Washington (S1 - 7.2, 391-99), 97 yrs., house
  (MS via AL)
CHILES, Henrietta Outlaw (S1 - 7.2, 391-99), over 90 yrs., house
  (MS via NC)
CHISOLM, Silvia (2.1, 199-200), 88 yrs. (SC)
CHISOLM, Tom (2.1, 201-03) (S1 - 11.2, 101-104), 62 yrs., free (SC)
CHOICE, Jeptha (Doc) (4.1, 217-219) (S2 - 3.2, 705-17), 101 yrs.,
  light field work (TX)
CHRISTOPHER, Anthony (Uncle Tom) (S2 - 3.2, 718-24), c. 87 yrs. (TX)
CLAIBORNE, James (S1 - 7.2, 400-01), 77 yrs. (MS)
CLAIBOURN, Ellen (12.1, 184-88), 85 yrs., house (GA)
CLARIDY, George W. (S1 - 12.1, 103-07), 84 yrs., house (OK via AR)
CLARK, Amos (4.1, 220-22) (S2 - 3.2, 725-32), 99 yrs. (1941), heavy
  work and house (TX)
CLARK, Anna (S1 - 2.2, 37-39), 90 yrs., concubine (CO via GA)
CLARK, Cherry (S1 - 7.2, 402), c. 81 yrs., house (MS)
CLARK, Fleming (16.4, 22-25), c. 74 yrs., field (OH via VA)
CLARK, Gus (7.2, 22-25) (S1 - 7.2, 403-07), 85 yrs., field (MS via VA)
CLARK, Laura (6.1, 72-75), 86 yrs., field and house (AL via NC)
CLARK, Mother Anne (S2 - 3.2, 733-36), 112 yrs., field (TX via MS, LA
  and TN)
CLARK, Rena (S1 - 7.2, 418-21), c. 87 yrs., house (MS)
CLAY, Berry (12.1, 189-94), 89 yrs. (GA)
CLAY, Henry (S1 - 12.1, 108-18), c. 100 yrs., field (OK via NC)
CLAY, Katherine (8.2, 13-14), 69 yrs., free (AR via MS)
CLAY, Sarah (S2 - 1.3, 58), house (AR via MS)
CLAYTON, Florida (17.1, 62-64), 82 yrs. (FL)
CLAYTON, Hattie (6.1, 76-77) (S1 - 1.1, 95-98), c. 89 yrs., field
  (AL via GA)
CLELAND, Maria (2.1, 204), 80 yrs. (SC)
CLEMMENTS, Maria Sutton (8.2, 15-27), upper 80's (AR via GA)
CLEMONS, Fannie (8.2, 28-29), 78 yrs. (AR via LA)
CLEMONS, Wadley (6.1, 78-80), 92 yrs., field (AL)
CLIFTON, Matilda (S1 - 7.2, 412-15), c. 115 yrs., house (MS via NC)
CLIFTON, Peter (2.1, 205-09), 89 yrs. (SC)
CLINTON, Joe (8.2, 30-35), 86 yrs. (AR via MS)
CLUSSEY, Aunt (S1 - 1.1, 18-21), 90 yrs., field (AL)

COATES, "Father" Charles (17.1, 65-73), 108 yrs., yard work and
    carriage driver (FL via VA and GA)
COATES, Irene (17.1, 74-79), 77 yrs., baby nurse (FL via GA)
COBB, Frances (S1 - 7.2, 416-22), 84 yrs., house (MS)
CODY, Pierce (12.1, 195-200), field (GA)
COFER, Betty (14.1, 165-75), 81 yrs., house (NC)
COFER, Willis (12.1, 201-11), 78 yrs. (GA)
COFFEE, Anna M. (S1 - 5.2, 284-89), 86 yrs., field (OH via NC and VA)
COGGIN, John (14.1, 176-78), 85 yrs., field (NC)
COKER, Abraham (S2 - 3.2, 737-45), 93 yrs., field (TX via GA)
COKER, Emma (S1 - 3.1, 203-10), over 90 yrs., field (GA)
COKER, Neil (17.1, 80-85), 79 yrs. (FL via VA)
COLBERT, Mary (12.1, 212-25), 84 yrs. (GA)
COLBERT, Polly (7.1, 33-38), 83 yrs., house (OK)
COLBERT, Sarah (6.2, 57-60), 82 yrs., field (IN via KY)
COLBERT, William (6.1, 81-82), 93 yrs., field (AL)
COLE, Alice (S2 - 3.2, 746-64), 86 yrs., house (TX via LA)
COLE, Harrison (S2 - 3.2, 765-74), c. 70 yrs. (TX)
COLE, Hattie (S2 - 3.2, 775-82), 83 yrs., house (TX)
COLE, Jefferson (S1 - 12.1, 119-27), 98 yrs., field (OK via AR)
COLE, John (12.1, 226-29), 86 yrs., house and horse trainer (GA)
COLE, Julia (12.1, 231-36), 78 yrs. (GA)
COLE, Thomas (4.1, 225-35) (S2 - 3.2, 783-836), 92 yrs., fed animals;
    field work (TX via AL and TN)
COLEMAN, Betty (8.2, 36-37) (S2 - 1.3, 59), 80 yrs. (AR)
COLEMAN, Betty (Robertson) (S2 - 3.2, 837-42), c. 85 yrs., house
    (TX via AR)
COLEMAN, Eli (4.1, 236-39) (S2 - 3.2, 843-55), 91 yrs., field
    (TX via KY)
COLEMAN, Ellen Williams (2.1, 216-17), 78 yrs. (SC)
    See Coleman, Rev. Tuff (SC)
COLEMAN, Evvie (2.1, 210-15), 82 yrs., house (SC)
    See Coleman, Henry (SC)
COLEMAN, F.C. (S1 - 3.1, 211-14), 104 yrs., field (GA)
COLEMAN, George (S1 - 7.2, 423-26), 107 yrs., house (MS via VA)
COLEMAN, Henry (2.1, 210-15), 82 yrs., house (SC)
    See Coleman, Evvie (SC)
COLEMAN, Lula (S1 - 7.2, 427-34), 86 yrs., field (MS)
COLEMAN, Luvenia (S1 - 7.2, 435-37), c. 85 yrs., house (MS)
COLEMAN, Preely (4.1, 240-41) (S2 - 3.2, 856-62), 85 yrs., field
    (TX via SC)
COLEMAN, Rev. Tuff (2.1, 216-17), 80 yrs. (SC)
    See Coleman, Ellen Williams (SC)
COLEMAN, William (S2 - 3.2, 863-79), c. 85 yrs., field (TX via TN)
COLES, Charles (16.3, 4-5), 86 yrs. (MD)
COLEY, Annie (S1 - 7.2, 438-46), 80 yrs., field (MS via SC)
COLLIER, Holt (S1 - 7.2, 447-78), 88 yrs. (d. 1936), house and
    personal servant (MS)
COLLIER, Louisa (2.1, 218-23), 78 yrs. (SC)
COLLINS, Bill (S2 - 3.2, 880-82), field (TX via LA)
COLLINS, Elvira (S1 - 7.2, 479), c. 74 yrs. (MS)
COLLINS, Harriet (4.1, 242-45) (S2 - 3.2, 883-96), 67 yrs., free (TX)
COLLINS, John (2.1, 224-26), 85 yrs. (SC)
COLLINS, Mary (S1 - 7.2, 480-82), 113 yrs., house (MS)
COLLINS, Tildy (6.1, 83-86), 84 yrs. (AL)
COLQUITT, Kizzie (12.1, 122-24) (S1 - 3.1, 215-17), c. 76 yrs. (GA)

COLQUITT, Martha (12.1, 237-50), 85 yrs. (GA)
COLQUITT, Sara (6.1, 87-89) (S1 - 1.1, 99-101), c. 100 yrs., field
   (AL via VA)
COLUMBUS, Andrew ("Smoky") (4.1, 246-48) (S2 - 3.2, 897-901), c. 79 yrs.
   light field work (TX)
COMBINED INTERVIEW (13.4, 269-81), "Conjuration" (GA)
COMBINED INTERVIEW (13.4, 282-89), "Folk Remedies" and "Superstition"
   (GA)
COMBINED INTERVIEW (13.4, 290-307), "Mistreatment of Slaves" (GA)
COMBINED INTERVIEW (13.4, 308-64), "Slave Conditions" (GA)
COMBS, J.B. (S1 - 7.2, 483-85), 82 yrs., house; teacher (MS via GA)
COMPTON, Jake (S2 - 3.2, 902-07), 82 yrs., light field work (TX)
COMPTON, Josephine Tippit (S2 - 3.2, 908-13), c. 75 yrs. (TX)
CONERLY, Ike (S1 - 7.2, 486), teamster (MS)
CONEY, Joe (S1 - 7.2, 487-91), c. 80 yrs., house (MS)
CONNALLY, Steve (4.1, 249-51) (S2 - 3.2, 914-18), c. 90 yrs., house
   (TX via GA)
CONRAD, George Jr. (7.1, 39-44), 77 yrs., field (OK via KY)
CONWAY, George (S2 - 1.10, 309-10), 92 yrs., jockey (NE via MO)
COOK, Jerry (S1 - 7.2, 492-500), 84 yrs. (MS via AL)
COOPER, Charlie (S2 - 3.2, 919-27), 90 yrs., field (TX via LA)
COOPER, Frank (6.2, 61-63), 115 yrs., field (IN via KY)
COOPER, Lucius (S2 - 3.2, 928-32), 90 yrs. (TX via SC)
COPE, Ermaline (11.8, 84), 89 yrs. (MO via KS and TN)
CORMIER, Valmar (4.1, 252-53) (S2 - 3.2, 933-36), c. 90 yrs., field
   (TX via LA)
   See Moses, Mary (TX)
CORN, Peter (11.8, 85-95), 83 yrs., cared for livestock (MO via TN)
CORNEAL, Mrs. Phannie (S2 - 1.10, 311-13), 74 yrs. (NE via MO)
CORNELIUS, James (7.2, 26-33) (S1 - 7.2, 509), c. 91 yrs., house
   (MS via LA)
CORNISH, Laura (4.1, 254-56) (S2 -3.2, 937-43), c. 84 yrs., light field
   work (TX)
CORRY, Bouregard (2.1, 227-28), 75 yrs. (SC)
COSBY, Mandy McCullough (6.1, 90-91), 95 yrs., field (AL)
COSTINE, Hannah (S1 - 7.2, 510), 79 yrs., spinning shop (MS via LA)
COTTEN, Betsey (S1 - 7.2, 511), 110 yrs. (MS via VA)
COTTON, Jane (S2 - 3.2, 944-49), 90 yrs., field (TX)
COTTON, Lucy (8.2, 38), 72 yrs., free (AR)
COTTON, T.W. (8.2, 39-41), 80 yrs. (AR via VA)
COTTONHAM, John (S2 - 1.3, 60-61), 70 yrs., free (AR)
COVERSON, Mandy (14.1, 179-81), 78 yrs., house (NC)
COX, Albert (S1 - 7.2, 512-16), c. 86 yrs., field (MS)
COX, Alex (S1 - 7.2, 517), 90 yrs. (d. 1937), foreman (MS)
COX, Elijah (S2 - 3.2, 950-53), free (TX)
COX, (Rev.) John R. (16.2, 32-34), 85 yrs. (KY)
COX, Julia (S1 - 7.2, 518-21), c. 87 yrs., house (MS)
COX, Martha (S1 - 11.2, 105-06), c. 70 yrs. (SC)
COX, Tony (S1 - 7.2, 522-24), 87 yrs., field (MS)
COXE, Josephine (S1 - 7.2, 525-28), 84 yrs., field and house (MS)
COZART, Willie (14.1, 182-86), 92 yrs., field (NC)
CRADDOCK, Ed (11.8, 96-97) (S1 - 2.4, 158-59), 85 yrs. (MO)
CRAFT, Jessie (S1 - 7.2, 529-31), foreman (MS)
CRAFT, Sue (S2 - 4.3, 955-61), 78 yrs. (TX via TN)
CRAGIN, Ellen (8.2, 42-49), over 80 yrs. (AR via MS)
CRAIG, Caleb (2.1, 229-33), 86 yrs. (SC)

CRAIG, Letitia (S1 - 7.2, 532-33), c. 95 yrs., house (MS)
CRANDLE, Bill (S1 - 1.1, 102-04), over 85 yrs., field (AL)
CRANE, Mary (6.2, 8-10), 82 yrs., field (IN via KY)
   See Ash, Thomas (IN via KY)
CRANE, Sally (8.2, 50-56), over 90 yrs., field (AR)
CRASSON, Hannah (14.1, 187-93), 84 yrs., work around house (NC)
CRAWFORD, Isaac (8.2, 57-58), 75 yrs. (AR via MS)
CRAWFORD, John (4.1, 257-59) (S2 - 4.3, 997-1001), 81 yrs., livestock
   boy (TX)
CRAWFORD, John (S2 - 4.3, 962-96), c. 100 yrs. (TX via MS)
CRAWFORD, Rena (S1 - 7.2, 534-35), 75 yrs., personal servant (MS)
CRAWLEY, Charles (16.5, 7-10), field (VA)
CRENSHAW, Julia (14.1, 194-95) (NC)
CROCKETT, Emma (6.1, 92-94), c. 80 yrs. (AL)
CROSBY, Mary (8.2, 59-60), 76 yrs. (AR via GA)
CROSS, Cheney (6.1, 95-102), c. 90 yrs., house (AL)
CROSS, William (S1 - 2.1, 22-23), 90 yrs. (AR)
CROWDER, Zeb (14.1, 196-202), 80 yrs., field (NC)
CROWLEY, Ellen (8.2, 61) (AR via MS)
CRUM, Ed (S1 - 7.2, 536-40), 84 yrs., field (MS)
CRUMP, Adeline (14.1, 203-06), 73 yrs. (NC)
CRUMP, Bill (14.1, 207-11), 82 yrs., field (NC)
CRUMP, Charlie (14.1, 212-215), 82 yrs., carried water (NC)
CRUMP, Richard (8.2, 62-66), 82 yrs. (AR via MS)
CRUZE, Rachel (S1 - 5.2, 290-323), 81 yrs., house (OH via TN)
CULP, Zenia (8.2, 67-69), over 80 yrs. (AR)
CUMEY, Green (4.1, 260-62) (S2 - 4.3, 1002-05), 86 yrs., field (TX)
CUMINS, Albert (8.2, 70-71), 86 yrs. (AR)
CUMMINGS, Josephine (S1 - 1.1, 105), 94 yrs., nursemaid (AL)
CUMMINS, Tempie (4.1, 263-65) (S2 - 4.3, 1006-12), c. 76 yrs., house
   (TX)
CUNNINGHAM, Adeline (4.1, 266-68), 85 yrs. (TX)
CUNNINGHAM, Dinah (2.1, 234-37), 84 yrs. (SC)
CUNNINGAHM, Martha (7.1, 45-47), 81 yrs., white (OK via TN)
CURLETT, Betty (8.2, 72-81), 66 yrs., free (AR)
CURRY, J.H. (8.2, 82-87), 76 yrs. (AR via TN)
CURRY, Katie (S2 - 4.3, 1013-19), c. 104 yrs. (TX via LA)
CURTIS, Mattie (14.1, 216-22), 98 yrs., house and field; tobacco
   factory (NC)
CURTIS, William (7.1, 48-52), 93 yrs., field (OK via GA)
CUSTIS, Lititia (S1 - 1.1, 106-08), 108 yrs., house (AL via VA)
CYRUS, Shadrach (S1 - 7.2, 541-48), 87 yrs., field (MS)

DAILY, Will (4.1, 269-72), 79 yrs., chores and brought food to field
   (TX via MO)
DALTON, Charles Lee (14.1, 223-28), 93 yrs., farm work (NC)
DANDRIDGE, Lyttleton (8.2, 88-90), 80 yrs. (AR via LA)
DANFORTH, Nelson (S1 - 2.4, 160-63), 85 yrs. (MO via TX and MO)
DANIEL, Matilda Pugh (6.1, 103-04) (S1 - 1.1, 109-10), 96 yrs., house
   (AL)
DANIELS, Ella (8.2, 91-94), c. 74 yrs. (AR via NC)
DANIELS, Henry (S1 - 7.2, 549-52), 87 yrs., field (MS via GA)
DANIELS, John (14.1, 229-31) (NC via SC)
DANIELS, Julia Frances (4.1, 273-74) (S2 - 4.3, 1020-27), 89 yrs.,

water girl (TX via GA)
DANIELS, Lucy (2.1, 238-39), 78 yrs. (SC)
DANIELS, Parilee (S2 - 4.3, 1028-46), 91 yrs., chores (TX)
DANT, Henry (11.8, 98-99), 105 yrs., field (MO)
DANTZLER, Juda (S1 - 7.2, 553-57)), house and mail carrier (MS)
DARBY, _____ (S1 - 9.4, 1844) (MS)
DARLING, Katie (4.1, 278-80) (S2 - 4.3, 1047-51), 88 yrs., house
    (nursemaid) (TX)
DARROW, Mary Allen (8.2, 95-96), 74 yrs. (AR)
DAUGHERTY, Ethel (S1 - 5.1, 62-64), free (IN via KY)
DAUGHERTY, Lizzie (S1 - 5.1, 65-66), free (IN)
DAVE, Uncle (S2 - 10.9, 4374-77), mechanic; managed a farm (TX)
    see Julia, Aunt (TX); Woorling, James G. (TX)
DAVENPORT, Carey (4.1, 281-84) (S2 - 4.3, 1052-58), c. 83 yrs.,
    tended sheep (TX)
DAVENPORT, Charlie (7.2, 34-43) (S1 - 7.2, 558-72), 100 yrs., field
    (MS)
DAVENPORT, John N. (2.1, 240-43), 89 yrs., house (SC)
DAVENPORT, Moses (2.1, 244), 89 yrs. (SC)
DAVES, Harriet Ann (14.1, 232-36), 81 yrs. (NC via VA and MO)
DAVIDSON, Alice Moore (S2 - 4.3, 1059-62), 78 yrs. (TX)
DAVIDSON, Hannah (16.4, 26-32), 85 yrs. (OH via KY)
DAVIS, A.K. (S1 - 7.2, 574) (MS)
DAVIS, Alice (8.2, 97-98), 81 yrs. (AR via MS)
DAVIS, Annie (S1 - 1.1, 111-16), 78 yrs., house (AL)
DAVIS, Campbell (4.1, 285-88) (S2 - 4.3, 1063-68), 85 yrs. (TX)
DAVIS, Carrie (6.1, 105-08) (S1 - 1.1, 117-20), c. 83 yrs., house
    (AL via GA)
DAVIS, Charlie (8.2, 99), 76 yrs. (AR)
DAVIS, Charlie (2.1, 245-49), 88 yrs., field (SC)
DAVIS, Charlie (2.1, 250-53), 79 yrs. (SC)
DAVIS, Clara (6.1, 109-10) (S1 - 1.1, 121-25), 72 yrs. or 92 yrs. (AL)
DAVIS, D. (8.2, 100-08), 85 yrs. (AR via MS)
DAVIS, Heddie (2.1, 254-59), 72 yrs. (SC)
DAVIS, Henry (2.1, 260-62), 80 yrs. (SC)
DAVIS, James (8.2, 109-15), 96 yrs., field (AR via NC)
DAVIS, Jeff (8.2, 116), 85 yrs. (AR)
DAVIS, Jeff (8.2, 117-21), 78 yrs. (AR via AL)
DAVIS, Jerry (14.1, 237-40), 74 yrs., watched animals (NC)
DAVIS, Jesse (2.1, 263-66), 85 yrs., house (SC)
DAVIS, Joe (S1 - 7.2, 575) (MS)
DAVIS, Jordan (8.2, 122-23), 86 yrs., house (AR via MS)
DAVIS, Lizzie (2.1, 288-98) (S1 - 11.2, 107-14), 70's (SC)
DAVIS, Louis (S1 - 7.2, 576-89), c. 79 yrs. (MS via AR)
DAVIS, Louisa (2.1, 299-303), 106 yrs., house (SC)
DAVIS, Lucinda (7.1, 53-64), 89 yrs., field (OK)
DAVIS, Lucy (11.8, 100-01) (MO via KY)
DAVIS, Margaret (S1 - 2.4, 164-65), over 85 yrs., nursemaid (MO)
DAVIS, Mary (S2 - 4.3, 1069-74), 73 yrs. (TX)
DAVIS, Mary Jane Drucilla (8.2, 124-25), 73 yrs. (AR via GA)
DAVIS, Minerva (8.2, 126-29), 56 yrs., free (AR via TN)
DAVIS, Minnie (12.1, 251-64), 78 yrs., yard work (GA)
DAVIS, Mose (12.1, 265-71), master's son's playmate (GA)
DAVIS, Nelson (S2 - 4.3, 1075-78), c. 100 yrs., carriage driver
    (TX via GA)
DAVIS, Ollie (S1 - 7.2, 590), c. 78 yrs. (MS)

DAVIS, Rosetta (8.2, 130), 55 yrs., free (AR)
DAVIS, Tob (S2 - 4.3, 1079-86), 87 yrs. (TX)
DAVIS, Virginia (Jennie) (8.2, 131-33), c. 46 yrs., free (AR via NC)
DAVIS, Wallace (2.1, 304-07), 88 yrs. (SC)
DAVIS, William (4.1, 289-94) (S2 - 4.3, 1087-95), 92 yrs., house
    (TX via TN)
DAVIS, William Henry (2.1, 308-12), 72 yrs. (SC)
DAVIS, Winnie (8.2, 134) (S1 - 2.1, 4), 100 yrs., cook (AR)
DAVIS, Young Winston (17.1, 86-92), 81 yrs. (FL via GA)
DAVISON, Eli (4.1, 295-97) (S2 - 4.3, 1096-1108), 93 yrs., field
    (TX via WV)
DAVISON, Elige (4.1, 298-301) (S2 - 4.3, 1109-18), cared for animals
    (TX via VA)
DAWKINS, Elias (2.1, 313-18), 84 yrs. (SC)
DAWKINS, Frank (S1 - 7.2, 591) (MS via VA)
DAWKINS, Jake (S1 - 7.2, 592-99), 92 yrs., field (MS)
DAWSON, Anthony (7.1, 65-72A), 105 yrs., field (OK via NC)
DAWSON, Mollie (S2 - 4.3, 1119-59), 85 yrs. (TX)
DAY, Annie (S2 - 4.3, 1160-62) (TX)
DAY, James Hickey (S2 - 4.3, 1163-67), 82 yrs. (TX via TN)
DAY, John (4.1, 302-04), 81 yrs. (TX via TN)
DAY, Leroy (8.2, 135-36), 80 yrs. (AR via GA)
DEANE, James V. (16.3, 6-9), 87 yrs., field (MD)
DEBNAM, W. Solomon (14.1, 241-46), 78 yrs. (NC)
DEBRO, Sarah (14.1, 247-53), 90 yrs., house (NC)
DELL, Hammett (8.2, 137-46), 90 yrs. (AR via TN)
DEMPSEY, Mary B. (16.4, 33-34) (S1 - 5.2, 324-25), 87 yrs. (OH via KY)
DENNIS, Edie (12.2, 20-22), 110 yrs. (in 1901) (GA)
DENSON, Nelson Taylor (4.1, 305-06) (S2 - 4.3, 1168-92), c. 89 yrs.
    (TX via AR)
DERRICOTTE, Ike (12.1, 272-84), 78 yrs. (GA)
DESSO, Jake (S2 - 4.3, 1193-1200), 73 yrs. (TX)
DICKENS, Charles W. (14.1, 254-58), 76 yrs. (NC)
DICKENS, Margaret E. (14.1, 259-62), 76 yrs. (NC)
DICKERSON, Nelson (S1 - 7.2, 600-09), field (MS)
DICKEY, James (8.2, 147-48), 68 yrs., free (AR)
DIGGS, Benjamin (8.2, 149-50), 79 yrs. (AR via NC)
DILL, Will (2.1, 319-23), 75 yrs. (SC)
DILLARD, Benny (12.1, 285-99), 80 yrs. (GA)
DILLARD, George (6.1, 111-12), 85 yrs., field (AL via MS)
DILLARD, Lizzie (S1 - 7.2, 610-11) (MS)
DILLIARD, Ella (6.1, 113-16), upper 70's, house (AL)
DILLON, Kate (8.2, 151-52), 82 yrs. (AR via MS)
DILLWORTH, Mattie (S1 - 7.2, 612-17), 112 yrs., house and field
    (MS via KY)
DIRT, Rufus (6.1, 117-18), c. 92 yrs., slave driver (AL)
DISCUS, Malinda (S1 - 2.4, 166-70), 78 yrs. (MO)
DISCUS, Mark (S1 - 2.4, 171-77), 88 yrs., field (MO)
DIVINE, Mary (11.8, 102-06), 85 yrs., nursemaid (MO via TN)
DIVINITY, Howard (S1 - 7.2, 618-19), c. 105-110 yrs. (d. 1930),
    personal servant (MS)
DIXON, Alice (8.2, 153-56), over 80 yrs. (AR)
DIXON, Bud (S2 - 4.3, 1201-06), 92 yrs., field (TX via LA)
DIXON, Emily (S1 - 7.2, 620-24), c. 108 yrs., field (MS)
DIXON, Luke (8.2, 157-60), 81 yrs. (AR via VA)
DIXON, Martha Ann (8.2, 161-63), 81 yrs. (AR via NC)

DIXON, Sally (S1 - 7.2, 625-30), field (MS via GA)
DIXON, Thomas (2.1, 324-25), 75 yrs. (SC)
DOCKERY, Railroad (8.2, 164-65), 81 yrs. (AR)
DODGE, Clara (S1 - 7.2, 631), house (MS)
DOGAN, M.W., Dr. (S1 - 7.2, 632-34), 74 yrs., free (MS)
DODSON, Mary (S2 - 4.3, 1207-13), 89 yrs., nursemaid (TX)
DOMINO, Amy (S2 - 4.3, 1214-17), nursemaid (TX via AL)
DOMINO, Ed (S2 - 4.3, 1218-20), 79 yrs. (TX)
DONALD, George (S1 - 7.2, 635), 79 yrs. (MS)
DONALD, Lucy (S1 - 7.2, 636-41), c. 80 yrs. (MS)
DONALSON, Callie (8.2, 166-68), 72 yrs. (AR via TN)
DONATTO, Mary (S2 - 4.3, 1221-24), 82 yrs. (TX via LA)
DORRAH, Isabella (2.1, 326-28), 75 yrs. (SC)
DORSEY, Amelia (S1 - 3.1, 232-35), 85 yrs., cared for slave children
    (GA via NC)
DORSEY, Douglas (17.1, 93-100), 86 yrs., house (FL via MD)
DORSEY, George (16.2, 52-57), 76 yrs. (KY)
DORSEY, Nelson (S1 - 2.3, 105-07), 89 yrs., house (MN via AR and MS)
DORTCH, Charles Green (8.2, 169-79), 81 yrs. (AR)
DORUM, Fannie (8.2, 180-84), 94 yrs., field (AR via NC)
DOTHRUM, Silas (8.2, 185-88), c. 83 yrs. (AR)
DOUGLASS, Alice (7.1, 73-75), 77 yrs., house (OK via TN)
DOUGLAS, Ambrose Hilliard (17.1, 101-04), 92 yrs., field and house
    (FL via MI, NC, and VA)
DOUGLAS, Hattie (S2 - 1.3, 62-65), 71 yrs., free (AR via TN)
DOUGLAS, Sarah (8.2, 189-92), c. 82 yrs., field (AR via AL)
DOUGLAS, Sebert (8.2, 204-05), 82 yrs. (AR via KY)
DOUGLAS, Steve (S2 - 4.3, 1225-29), 75 yrs. (TX via AR)
DOUGLAS, Tom (8.2, 193-203), 91 yrs., field (AR via LA)
DOUTHIT, Mrs. Charles (11.8, 107), 72 yrs. (MO)
DOWD, Rev. Squire (14.1, 263-69), 82 yrs., house (NC)
DOWDY, Doc Daniel (7.1, 76-80), 81 yrs., house (OK via GA)
DOWNING, Laurence (2.1, 329), 80 yrs. (SC)
DOYL, Henry (8.2, 206-07), 74 yrs. (AR via TN)
DOYLD, Willie (8.2, 208-11), 78 yrs. (AR via MS)
DOZIER, Washington (2.1, 330-35), 90 yrs. (SC)
DRAKE, Ann (S1 - 7.2, 642-52), 82 yrs., field (MS)
DRAPER, Johanna (7.1, 81-87), 83 yrs., house (OK via MS)
DRIVER, Fannie McCullough (S2 - 4.3, 1230-37), 80 yrs. (TX)
DUCK, Mama (17.1, 105-19), 110 yrs., nursemaid (FL)
DUDLEY, Wade (8.2, 212-13), 73 yrs. (AR via MS)
DUHON, Victor (4.1, 307-08) (S2 - 4.3, 1238-41), 97 yrs., coachman
    (TX via LA)
DUKE, Alice (2.1, 336), 72 yrs. (SC)
DUKE, Isabella (8.2, 214-16), 62 yrs., free (AR)
DUKE, Tillie (S2 - 4.3, 1242-43), 75 yrs. (TX via VA)
DUKES, Wash (8.2, 217-20), 83 yrs. (AR via GA)
DUKES, Willis (17.1, 120-25), 83 yrs., chores and errands (FL via GA)
DUNCAN, Rachael (S1 - 5.1, 67-68), 79 yrs., house (IN via KY)
DUNN, Fannie (14.1, 270-74) (NC)
DUNN, Jennylin (14.1, 275-77), 87 yrs. (NC)
DUNN, Lizzie (8.2, 221-22), 88 yrs., house (AR via MS)
DUNN, Lucy Ann (14.1, 278-83), 90 yrs., house (NC)
DUNNE, Nellie (8.2, 223-24), 78 yrs. (AR via MS)
DUNWOODY, William L. (8.2, 225-33), 98 yrs. (AR via SC)
DURANT, Sylvia (2.1, 337-48), 72 yrs. (SC)

DURDEN, John (S1 - 7.2, 653) (MS)
DURHAM, Tempie Herndon (14.1, 284-90) c. 103 yrs., spinning and
    weaving wool (NC)
DURR, Simon (S1 - 7.2, 654-58), 90 yrs., carriage driver (MS)
DURRELL, Betsy (S1 - 7.2, 659-60), 80 yrs., cook (MS)

EARLE, George (S2 - 4.3, 1244-49), 87 yrs., chores (TX)
EARLY, Sarah (S1 - 1.1, 126-29), c. 60 yrs., free (AL)
EASON, George (12.1, 300-04), field (GA)
EAST, Nancy (16.4, 35-41) (OH via VA)
EASTER, Aunt (13.4, 218-19), house (GA)
EASTER, Esther (7.1, 88-91), 85 yrs., house (OK via TN and MO)
EASTER, Willis (4.2, 1-4) (S2 - 4.3, 1200-58). 85 yrs., field (TX)
EATMAN, George (14.1, 291-94), 93 yrs., house (NC)
EAVES, Nannie (16.2, 60-61), 91 yrs. (KY)
EBENEZER, Mr. (S1 - 1.1, 130-34) (AL)
EDDINGTON, Harriet (2.2, 1), 86 yrs., free (SC)
EDMONDS, Mollie (S1 - 7.2, 661-74), c. 81 yrs., carried water (MS)
EDMONDSON, Manda (S1 - 7.2, 675-77), c. 95 yrs., field and weaver (MS)
EDMUNDS, (Rev.) H.H. (6.2, 64-66), 87 yrs., field (IN via TN, MS and VA)
EDWARDS, Anderson (4.2, 5-9) (S2 - 4.3, 1259-68), 93 yrs., field (TX)
    See Edwards, Minerva (TX)
EDWARDS, Ann J. (4.2, 10-14) (S2 - 4.3, 1269-77), 81 yrs., (TX via DC
    and VA)
EDWARDS, Doc (14.1, 295-97), 84 yrs., house (NC)
EDWARDS, Lucius (8.2, 234), 72 yrs., free (AR via LA)
EDWARDS, Malinda (S1 - 7.2, 678-80), 111 yrs., field and nurse
    (MS via AL)
EDWARDS, Mary (2.2, 2), 79 yrs. (SC)
EDWARDS, Mary (S2 - 4.3, 1282-84), 84 yrs., hired out (nurse)
    (TX via NC)
EDWARDS, Mary Kincheon (4.2, 15-16) (S2 - 4.3, 1278-81), c. 127 yrs.,
    house (TX via LA)
EDWARDS, Minerva (4.2, 5-9) (S2 - 4.3, 1259-68), 87 yrs. (TX)
    See Edwards, Anderson (TX)
ELDER, Callie (12.1, 305-15), 78 yrs. (GA)
ELDER, John C. (S2 - 1.10, 314-15), 90 yrs. (NE via TN)
ELDER, Lucinda (4.2, 17-20) (S2 - 4.3, 1285-91), 86 yrs., nursemaid
    (TX via VA)
ELGIN, Tempe (S2 - 4.3, 1292-98), 75 yrs. (TX via AR)
ELKINS, Fairy (S1 - 11.2, 115-16), 78 yrs., house (SC)
ELLERBE, Mary (S1 - 11.2, 117-20) (SC)
    See Ellerbe, Richmond (SC)
ELLERBE, Richmond (S1 - 11.2, 117-20) (SC)
    See Ellerbe, Mary (SC)
ELLIOTT, John (8.2, 235-39), 80 yrs. (AR via NC)
ELLIOTT, (Rev.) John B. (2.2, 3-5) (SC via NC)
ELLIS, John (4.2, 21-24), 85 yrs., laborer (TX)
ELMORE, Emanuel (2.2, 6-10), 77 yrs. (SC)
ELSE, Amy (S2 - 4.3, 1299-1305), 99 yrs. (TX)
EMANUEL, Gabe (7.2, 44-48) (S1 - 7.2, 681-86), 85 yrs., house (MS)
EMBERS, Charley (S2 - 1.2, 17-18), c. 86 yrs., free (AZ via CA)
EMMANUEL, (Mom) Ryer (2.2, 11-26), 78 yrs. (SC)
EMMONS, William (S1 - 5.2, 326-31), 93 yrs., field (OH via KY)

EPPES, Katherine (6.1, 119-21), 87 yrs., house (AL)
ERWING, Cynthia (S1 - 1.1, 135-39), 87 yrs., house (AL via GA)
ESTELL, John (11.8, 108), 85 yrs., field (MO)
EUBANKS, Jerry (S1 - 7.2, 687-701), 91 yrs., carriage driver and house
   (MS via GA)
EUBANKS, John (6.2, 67-76), 98 yrs., field (IN via KY)
EUBANKS, "Uncle Pen" (2.2, 27-29), 83 yrs. (SC)
EUGENE (13.4, 213-15), non-slave (GA)
EULENBERG, Smoky (11.8, 109-12), 83 yrs. (MO)
EVANS, Ann Ulrich (11.8, 113-19), 94 yrs., field (MO via AL)
EVANS, Eliza (7.1, 92-96), 87 yrs., house (OK via AL)
EVANS, Emma (S1 - 7.2, 702), 80 yrs., house (MS)
EVANS, John (14.1, 298-301), 78 yrs. (NC)
EVANS, Lawrence (S1 - 7.2, 703-06), 79 yrs. (MS)
EVANS, Lewis (2.2, 30-33), 96 yrs., field (SC)
EVANS, Louis (S2 - 4.3, 1306-16), 85 yrs. (TX via LA)
EVANS, Louise J. (S1 - 11.1, 15-20), c. 85 yrs. (NC)
EVANS, Millie (8.2, 240-51), 89 yrs. (AR via NC)
EVANS, Minerva (S1 - 7.2, 707-09), c. 80 yrs. (MS via LA)
EVANS, Mose (8.2, 252-57), 76 yrs. (AR)
EVANS, Phillip (2.2, 34-37), 85 yrs., fed animals; picked fruit (SC)
EVERETT, Louisa (17.1, 126-31), 90 yrs., field (FL via VA and GA)
EVERETT, Sam (17.1, 126-31), 86 yrs., field (FL via VA and GA)
EVERETTE, Martha (12.1, 316-17) (S1 - 3.1, 236-42), 88 yrs., farm
   work; house (GA)
EZELL, Lorenza (4.2, 25-32) (S2 - 4.3, 1317-29), c. 86 yrs., field
   (TX via SC)

FAIR, Eugenia (2.2, 38), 76 yrs. (SC)
FAIRBANKS, Calvin (S1 - 5.1, 240-42), over 80 yrs., free (IN via NY)
FAIRLEY, I.W. (S1 - 7.2, 710-11), field and hired out (MS)
FAIRLEY, Rachel (8.2, 258-61), 75 yrs., house (AR via MS)
FAKES, Pauline (8.2, 262-63), 74 yrs. (AR)
FALLS, Robert (16.6, 11-16), 97 yrs. (TN via NC)
FAMBRO, Hanna (S1 - 5.2, 332-47), 94 yrs., field (OH via GA)
FANNEN, Mattie (8.2, 264-68), 87 yrs. (AR via GA)
FARMER, Lizzie (7.1, 97-101), 80 yrs., house (OK via TX)
FARMER, Robert (8.2, 269-75), 84 yrs. (AR via NC)
FARNANDIS, Ben (S1 - 7.2, 712) (MS)
FARROW, Betty (4.2, 33-34) (S2 - 4.3, 1330-33), 90 yrs., house
   (TX via VA)
FARROW, Caroline (2.2, 39-42), 80 yrs., house (SC)
FAUCETTE, Lindsey (14.1, 302-06), 86 yrs., cared for cows (NC)
FAVOR, Lewis (12.1, 318-25), 82 yrs., waited table (GA)
FAVORS, Mr. (13.4, 266) (GA)
FAYMAN, Mrs. M.S. (16.3, 10-13), 87 yrs., tutor (MD via LA and KY)
FEASTER, Gus (2.2, 43-71), 97 yrs., field (SC)
FELDER, Sara (S1 - 7.2, 713-24), c. 84 yrs., field (MS)
FENNELS, Archie (S2 - 4.3, 1334-37) (TX)
FERGUSON, Ann (2.2, 72-73), 74 yrs. (SC)
FERGUSON, Mary (12.1, 326-31), 90 yrs., cared for children (GA via MD)
FERGUSSON, Mrs. Lou (8.2, 276-81), 91 yrs., field (AR)
FERRELL, Jennie (8.2, 282), 65 yrs., free (AR via MS)
FIELD, Sally (S1 - 2.1, 5-7), 105 yrs. (AR via AL)

FIELDER, Hampton (S1 - 11.2, 121-23), 65 yrs., free (SC)
FIELDS, Alphonse (S2 - 4.3, 1338-40), c. 83 yrs. (TX via LA)
FIELDS, John W. (6.2, 77-83), 89 yrs., field (IN via KY)
FIKES, Frank (8.2, 283-85), 88 yrs., house (AR via VA)
FILER, J.E. (8.2, 286), 76 yrs. (AR via GA)
FINGER, Orleans (8.2, 287-91), 79 yrs. (AR via MS)
FINLEY, Elizabeth (S1 - 7.2, 725-30), 88 yrs., house (MS)
FINLEY, Molly (8.2, 292-95), 75 yrs. (AR)
FINNELY, John (4.2, 35-40) (S2 - 4.3, 1341-50), 86 yrs., field
   (TX via AL)
FINNEY, Fanny (8.2, 296-99), over 74 yrs. (AR via MS)
FISHER, "Gate-Eye" (8.2, 300-02), over 71 yrs. (AR)
FISHER, George (S1 - 7.2, 731), c. 88 yrs., field (MS via Africa)
FITTS, Jennie (S2 - 4.3, 1351-53), over 80 yrs., house (TX)
FITZGERALD, Ellen (8.2, 303-04), 74 yrs. (AR)
FITZHUGH, Henry (8.2, 305-11), 90 yrs. (AR)
FITZPATRICK, Reuben (6.1, 122), 83 yrs., house (AL)
FLAGG, Mary (8.2, 312-14), 89 yrs., house (AR via MS)
FLAGG, Ora M. (14.1, 307-10), 77 yrs. (NC)
FLAGG, Randell (S1 - 3.1, 243-46), 87 yrs., mill work (GA via AL)
FLANNAGAN, William (S1 - 7.2, 732-35), 92 yrs., field and personal
servant (MS)
FLANNIGAN, Lula (S1 - 3.1, 247-49), 76 yrs. (GA)
FLEMING, George (S1 - 11.2, 126-39), 83 yrs., field (SC)
FLINT, Edmond (S1 - 12.1, 128-29) (OK)
FLOURNEY, Georgia (S1-1.1, 140-44), 90 yrs., nursemaid (AL)
FLOURNEY, Lou (S1 - 1.1, 145-48), 87 yrs., house (AL)
FLOWERS, Mrs. Cornelia J. (S1 - 2.6, 286-89), free (WA via MS)
FLOWERS, Doc (8.2, 315-18), c. 85 yrs. (AR via TN)
FLOYD, Angie (S1 - 7.2, 736-40), 76 yrs. (MS)
FLOYD, Fletcher (S1 - 11.2, 140) (SC)
FLOYD, Lydia (S1 - 11.2, 141-42) (SC)
FLOYD, Sylvia (S1 - 7.2, 741-46), 85 yrs. (MS)
FLOYD, Tom (S1 - 7.2, 747-51), c. 95 yrs., field (MS via MO)
FLUKER, Frances (8.2, 319-21), 77 yrs. (AR via MS)
FLUKER, Ida May (8.2, 322-23), 83 yrs. (AR via AL)
FOLTZ, Sally (S1 - 7.2, 752-54), 77 yrs., house (MS via VA and TN)
FOOTE, Thomas (16.3, 14-16), 70 yrs., free (MD)
FORBES, Fred (S2 - 1.10, 316-17), 72 yrs., free (NE via MO)
FORCE, Tinie (16.2, 112-15) (KY)
FORD, Aaron (2.2, 74-79), 88 yrs., field (SC)
FORD, Ellen Nora (S2 - 4.3, 1354-57) (TX via MS)
FORD, Heywood (6.1, 123-25), c. 80 yrs., field (AL)
FORD, Laura (S1 - 7.2, 755-58), 85 yrs., field (MS)
FORD, Sanford (S1 - 9.4, 1413) (MS)
   See McMurty, Uncle Sanford (MS)
FORD, Sarah (4.2, 41-46) (S2 - 4.3, 1358-69), c. 87 yrs., nursemaid
   (TX)
FORD, Violet (S1 - 7.2, 759), 88 yrs., field (MS)
FORD, Wash (8.2, 324-27), c. 74 yrs. (AR)
FORGE, Sam (S2 - 4.3, 1370-76) (TX)
FORREST, Susan (S2 - 4.3, 1377-80) (TX via GA)
FORTENBURY, Judia (8.2, 328-30), 75 yrs., field (AR)
FORTMAN, George (6.2, 84-95), field (IN via KY and AL)
FORTUNE, ____ (S1 - 9.4, 1844) (MS)
FORWARD, Millie (4.2, 47-49) (S2 - 4.3, 1381-85), c. 95 yrs., field (TX)

FOSTER, Analiza (14.1, 311-13), 68 yrs. (NC)
FOSTER, Charlotte (2.2, 80-83), 98 yrs., field (SC)
FOSTER, Emma (8.2, 331-33), 80 yrs., house (AR via LA)
FOSTER, Georgianna (14.1, 314-17), 76 yrs. (NC)
FOSTER, Ira (8.2, 334-35), 76 yrs. (AR via AL)
FOSTER, Viney (S1 - 7.2, 760-62), 77 yrs. (MS)
FOUNTAIN, Della (7.1, 102-07), 69 yrs., free (OK via LA)
FOWLER, Alex (S1 - 5.1, 70), over 85 yrs. (IN)
FOWLER, Louis (4.2, 50-54) (S2 - 4.3, 1386-95), 84 yrs. (TX via GA)
FOWLER, M. (S1 - 1.1, 155-63), house (AL via VA)
FOWLER, M. (S1 - 1.1, 149-54), c. 100 yrs., nursemaid (AL via VA, GA
    and LA)
FOWLER, Mat (S2 - 4.3, 1390-1401), c. 87 yrs., chores (TX via GA)
FOX, Hannah (S1 - 7.2, 281), 84 yrs. (MS)
    See Fox, Turner (MS)
FOX, Phillis (S1 - 7.2, 763-68), 101 yrs., house and field (MS)
FOX, Ruben (S1 - 7.2, 769-80), c. 84 yrs., field (MS via KY)
FOX, Turner (S1 - 7.2, 281), 97 yrs. (MS)
    See Fox, Hannah (MS)
FRANKLIN, B.C. (S1 - 12.1, 130-31), over 80 yrs. (OK via MS)
FRANKLIN, Chris (4.2, 55-59) (S2 - 4.3, 1402-14), c. 81 yrs.
    (TX via LA)
FRANKLIN, Jim (S2 - 4.3, 1415-17), 75 yrs., free (TX via AL)
FRANKLIN, John (2.2, 84-86), 84 yrs. (SC)
FRANKLIN, Leonard (8.2, 336-39), 70 yrs. (AR)
FRANKLIN, Richard (S1 - 12.1, 132-36), 81 yrs., field (OK)
FRANKLIN, Robert (S2 - 4.3, 1418-21), 86 yrs. (TX via MS)
FRANKS, Donna (7.2, 49-55) (S1 - 7.2, 782-92), c. 100 yrs., house (MS)
FRANKS, Orelia Alexie (4.2, 60-62) (S2 - 4.3, 1422-26), 90 yrs., weaver
    (TX via LA)
FRANKS, Pet (7.2, 56-60) (S1 - 7.2, 793-800), c. 92 yrs., field (MS)
FRASER, Emma (2.2, 87), 80 yrs. (SC)
FRAZIER, Eliza (8.2, 340-42), c. 88 yrs. (AR via SC)
FRAZIER, Mary (8.2, 343), 60 yrs., free (AR via MS)
FRAZIER, Rosanna (4.2, 63-65) (S2 - 4.3, 1427-31), 85-90 yrs., field
    (TX via MS)
FRAZIER, Tyler (8.2, 344-45), 75 yrs. (AR)
FREDERICK, Bert (6.1, 126-28) (S1 - 1.1, 164-65), 84 yrs., cow driver
    (AL)
FREEMAN, Alice (S1 - 2.5, 284-86) (S2 - 1.16, 397-98), c. 74 yrs.,
    free (WA via MO)
FREEMAN, Frank (14.1, 318-22), 76 yrs. (NC)
FREEMAN, Henry (S2 - 4.3, 1432-36) (TX via AL)
FREEMAN, (Aunt) Mittie (8.2, 346-52), 86 yrs. (AR via MS)
FRITZ, Mattie (8.2, 353-54), 79 yrs. (AR)
FROST, Adele (2.2, 88-90), 93 yrs., house (SC)
FRYER, Carrie Nancy (12.1, 332-43), 72 yrs. (GA)
FULCHER, Fannie (S1 - 3.1, 250-53), 75 yrs. (GA)
FULKES, Minnie (16.5, 11-14A), 77 yrs. (VA)
FULLER, Mrs. Sarah   (S2 - 4.3, 1437-39), 78 yrs. (TX)
FURR, Anderson (12.1, 344-52), 87 yrs. (GA)

GADSDEN, Amos (2.2, 91-96), 88 yrs. (SC)
GADSON, Charlie (9.3, 1), 67 yrs. (AR via SC)

GAFFNEY, Mary (S2 - 5.4, 1441-57), 92 yrs., chores (TX via MS)
GAIL, Annie (17.1, 375), 75 yrs. (FL via AL)
GAINES, Dr. D.B. (9.3, 2-6), 75 yrs. (AR via SC)
GAINES, Duncan (17.1, 132-38), 83 yrs., errands (FL via VA)
GAINES, Mary (9.3, 7-10), 65 yrs. (AR via AL)
GAINES, Rachel (16.6, 17-18), 95-100 yrs. (TN via KY)
GALLMAN, Janie (2.2, 97-99), 84 yrs. (SC)
GALLMAN, Lucy (2.2, 100-02), 80 yrs., field (SC)
GALLMAN, Simon (2.2, 103-05), 80 yrs. (SC)
GALLOWAY, Lucy (S1 - 8.3, 801-10), 74 yrs. (MS)
GANTLING, Clayborn (17.1, 139-45), 89 yrs., field (FL via GA)
GARDNER, Emma (S2 - 1.3, 66-67), 76 yrs. (AR via AL)
GARDNER, Nancy (7.1, 108-10), 79 yrs., house (OK via TN)
GAREY, Elisha (Doc) (12.2, 1-10), 76 yrs., house (GA via MS and GA)
GARLIC, Delia (6.1, 129-32), c. 100 yrs., house (AL via VA and LA)
GARRETT, Angie (6.1, 133-36), c. 92 yrs., house (AL)
GARRETT, Leah (12.2, 11-16) (GA)
GARRY, Henry (6.1, 137-43) (AL)
GARY, Laurence (2.2, 106), 76 yrs. (SC)
GASSAWAY, Menellis (16.3, 17-18), c. 86 yrs. (MD)
GATES, Hattie (S2 - 5.4, 1458-66) (TX)
GAULDING, Cicero (S1 - 8.3, 811-12), 90 yrs., house (MS)
GAUSE, Louisa (2.2,107-12), 70's (SC)
GENT, William (9.3, 11-14), 101 yrs., field (AR via TN)
GEORGE, Octavia (7.1, 111-14), 85 yrs., house (OK via LA)
GEORGIA (6.1, 144), over 90 yrs., house (AL)
GHOLSON, Letha (S1 - 8.3, 813-14) (MS)
GIBBS, Henry (S1 - 8.3, 815-36), 85 yrs. (MS)
GIBBS, Lizzie (S1 - 8.3, 837-38), 97 yrs., bodyguard (MS)
GIBON, Fannie (S1 - 3.1, 254-56), 87 yrs., house (GA via AL)
GIBSON, Fannie (6.1, 145-47), c. 87 yrs., house and field (AL)
GIBSON, Gracie (2.2, 113-14), 86 yrs. (SC)
GIBSON, Jennie Wormly (9.3, 17-18), 49 yrs., free (AR)
GIBSON, John Henry (6.2, 96-97), field (IN via NC)
GIBSON, Mandy (16.2, 74) (KY)
GIBSON, Mary Anne (S2 - 5.4, 1467-72), 76 yrs. (TX)
GIBSON, Priscilla (4.2, 66-67) (S2 - 5.4, 1473-76), c. 81 yrs.,
    weaver (TX via MS)
GILBERT, Gabriel (4.2, 68-70) (S2 - 5.4, 1477-82), field (TX via LA)
GILBERT,Taylor (17.1, 55-57, 223-24), 91 yrs., field (FL via GA)
GILES, Charlie (2.2, 115-16), 100 yrs., (SC)
GILL, Andrew Jackson (S1 - 8.3, 839-47), 82 yrs., house (MS)
GILL, Andy (14.1, 323-27), 74 yrs. (NC)
GILL, Frank (6.1, 148-53), c. 90 yrs., house (AL)
GILL, James (9.3, 19-26), 86 yrs., house (AR via AL)
GILLAM, Cora (9.3, 27-33), 86 yrs., house (AR via MS)
GILLARD, Jim (6.1, 154-56) (S1 - 1.1, 166-68), 87 yrs., house
    (AL via SC and GA)
GILLIAM, (Uncle) George (S2 - 1.1, 1-2) (AL)
GILLESPIE, J.N. (9.3, 34-37), 75 yrs., house (AR via TX)
GILLISON, Willis (2.2, 117-19), 75 yrs. (SC)
GILMER, Titus (S1 - 8.3, 848) (MS)
GILMORE, Brawley (2.2, 120-23) (SC)
GILMORE, Mattie (4.2, 71-73) (S2 - 5.4, 1483-99), field and house
    (TX via AL)
GILSTROP, John (S1 - 8.3, 849-51) (MS)

GIWBS, Georgina (16.5, 15-16), field (VA)
GLADDENY, Pick (2.2, 124-28), 81 yrs., house (SC)
GLADDY, Mary (12.2, 17-20, 22-27) (S1-3.1,   257-62), c. 84 yrs.,
   field (GA)
GLADNEY, Henry (2.2, 129-33), 82 yrs., field (SC)
GLASGOW, Emoline (2.2, 134-35), 78 yrs. (SC)
GLASKER, George (S2 - 5.4, 1500-08) (TX)
GLASS, Will (9.3, 38-41), 50 yrs., free (AR)
GLEED, Robert (S1 - 8.3, 852-54), field (MS via VA)
GLEN, Scot (S2 - 5.4, 1509-12) (TX)
GLENN, Frank William (9.3, 42-43), 75 yrs. (AR)
GLENN, Robert (14.1, 328-39), 87 yrs., field (NC)
GLENN, Silas (2.2, 136-37), 79 yrs. (SC)
GLENN, Wade (16.4, 38) (S1 - 5.2, 348-49), over 80 yrs., field
   (OH via NC)
GLISPIE, Ellis (9.3, 44-46), 71 yrs. (AR via MS)
GLOVER, John (2.2, 138-42), 77 yrs., house (SC)
GLOVER, Julia (S1 - 3.1, 263-64), over 80 yrs., house (GA)
GLOVER, Mary (S2 - 5.4, 1513-21), 83 yrs., field and house (TX)
GODBOLD, Hector (2.2, 143-48) (S1 - 11.2, 143-47), 87 yrs. (SC)
GODDARD, Daniel (2.2, 149-52), 74 yrs. (SC)
GODFREY, Ellen (2.2, 153-65) (S1 - 11.2, 148-49), c. 100 yrs. (SC)
GOHAGEN, Peter (S1 - 5.1, 71-75), 90 yrs. (IN via KY)
GOINGS, James (11.8, 120), carried wood and water (MO)
GOINGS, Rachal (11.8, 121-25), field (MO)
GOLDEN, Joe (9.3, 47-52), 86 yrs., field (AR)
GOLDER, Jennie (17.1, 365), field (FL via GA)
GONES, Mike (9.3, 15-16), 72 yrs. (AR)
GOOCH, Henrietta (S1 - 8.3, 854), 83 yrs., field (MS)
GOODMAN, Andrew (4.2, 74-80) (S2 - 5.4, 1522-29), c. 96 yrs., house
   (TX via AL)
GOODMAN, Ellen (S2 - 5.4, 1530-31), carding and spinning (TX via GA)
GOODRIDGE, Jane (9.3, 53-55), 87 yrs., field (AR via TN)
GOODSON John (9.3, 56-57), 72 yrs. (AR)
GOODWATER, Thomas (2.2, 166-70), 82 yrs., house (SC)
GOODWIN, Candis (16.5, 17-20), 80 yrs., house (VA)
GOODWIN, Nora (S1 - 8.3, 855-57), 73 yrs. (MS)
GOOLIE, Frank (16.6, 19-23), 85 yrs. (TN)
GOSS, Margaret (S1 - 8.3, 858-59), c. 113 yrs. (MS)
GOVAN, George (9.3, 63-64), 52 yrs, free (AR via SC)
GRACE, Julia (9.3, 65-66), 75 yrs., field (AR via TX)
GRAGSTON, Arnold (17.1, 146-55), 97 yrs., field (FL via KY and MI)
GRAHAM, Charles (9.3, 67-69), 79 yrs. (AR via TN)
GRAHAM, James (9.3, 70), 75 yrs. (AR via SC)
GRAHAM, Martin (S1 - 1.1, 169-71), 87 yrs., field (AL via SC)
GRAHAM, Sidney (S1 - 5.1, 76-77), over 85 yrs. (IN)
GRAHAM, Sidney (S2 - 1.7, 282-83) (TN)
GRAND, Austin (4.2, 81-86), 89 yrs., hired out (TX via MS)
GRANDBERRY, Mary Ella (6.1, 157-64), c. 90 yrs., field (AL)
GRANDY, Charles (16.5, 21-23), 95 yrs. (VA via MS)
GRANT, Anna (13.4, 255-56) (S1 - 3.1, 265-69) (GA)
GRANT, Austin (S2 - 5.4, 1532-45), hired out (farm hand) (TX via MS)
GRANT, Charlie (2.2, 171-76) (S1 - 11.2, 150-78), c. 84 yrs.,
   animal herder (SC)
GRANT, Dennis (S2 - 5.4, 1546-52), c. 80 yrs. (TX)
GRANT, Lizzie (S2 - 5.4, 1553-70), 91 yrs. (TX via WV)

GRANT, Marthala (9.3, 71-72), 77 yrs. (AR via NC)
GRANT, Rebecca Jane (2.2, 177-86), 92 yrs., house (SC)
GRANT, Sarah A. (S2 - 1.10, 318-21), 84 yrs. (NE via KY)
GRAVES, John (2.2, 187-89), 86 yrs. (SC via KY)
GRAVES, Sarah Frances Shaw (11.8, 126-38), 87 yrs., field (MO via KY)
GRAVES, Wesley (9.3, 73-76), 70 yrs. (AR via TN)
GRAY, Ambus (9.3, 77-79), 80 yrs., field (AR via AL)
GRAY, Callie (S1 - 8.3, 860-76), 80 yrs., house (MS)
GRAY, Green (9.3, 80-81), lower 70's, free (AR via AL)
GRAY, Neely or Nely (9.3, 82-86), 84 or 87 yrs. (AR via VA)
GRAY, Precilla (16.6, 24-26), 107 yrs., field and house (TN)
GRAY, Sarah (12.2, 28-30), house (GA)
GRAYSON, Mary (7.1, 115-23), 83 yrs., field (OK)
GREELEY, Sim (2.2, 190-94), 82 yrs. (SC)
GREEN, Alice (12.2, 31-47), 76 yrs. (GA)
GREEN, Benjamin T. (S1 - 8.3, 877-78), 83 yrs. (MS)
GREEN, Catherine (S2 - 5.4,, 1571-76), 84 yrs. (TX)
GREEN, Charles (S1 - 5.2, 350-52), 78 yrs. (OH via KY)
GREEN, Emily Camster (11.8, 139-42), maid (MO)
GREEN, Elijah (2.2, 195-99), 94 yrs. (SC)
GREEN, Esther (6.1, 165-67) (S1 - 1.1, 172-74), 82 yrs., house
    (AL via MS)
GREEN, Florence (S1 - 8.3, 879-81), 76 yrs., house (MS via NC)
GREEN, Frank (9.3, 102-03), 78 yrs., field (AR via SC)
GREEN, Granny (S1 - 8.3, 882-84), c. 100 yrs., house (MS)
GREEN, Henry (9.3, 87-101), c. 90 yrs., house (AR via AL)
GREEN, Isaiah (12.2, 48-59), 81 yrs., field (GA)
GREEN, Jake (6.1, 168-70), 85 yrs., field (AL)
GREEN, James (4.2, 87-89) (S2 - 5.4, 1577-83), 97 yrs., field
    (TX via VA)
GREEN, L. (S1 - 5.1, 78), over 70 yrs. (IN via KY)
GREEN, Margaret (12.2, 60-63), 82 yrs. (GA via SC)
GREEN, Marie Avrelia (S2 - 5.4, 1584-86) (TX via LA)
GREEN, Minnie (12.2, 64-65), 72 yrs. (GA)
GREEN, O.W. (4.2, 90-93), 88 yrs. (TX via AR)
GREEN, Phyllis (S1 - 11.2, 179-81) (SC)
GREEN, Rosa (4.2, 94-95) (S2 - 5.4, 1587-93), 85 yrs., house
    (TX via LA)
GREEN, Sara (S1 - 8.3, 885-89), 101 yrs., nurse (MS)
GREEN, Sarah Anne (14.1, 340-45), 78 yrs., worked around the house (NC)
GREEN, W.M. (2.2, 200-02), 71 yrs. (SC)
GREEN, William (4.2, 96-97) (S2 - 5.4, 1594-98), 87 yrs., cowboy
    (TX via MS)
GREENE, George (7.3, 104-11), c. 85 yrs., house and field (AR via MS)
GREER, Jenny (16.6, 27), 84 yrs. (TN via AL)
GREGORY, Andrew (9.3, 112), 74 yrs., field (AR via TN)
GREGORY, John (S1 - 8.3, 890) c. 89 yrs., field (MS via NC)
GRESHAM, Harriett (17.1, 156-64), 98 yrs., house (FL via SC)
GRESHAM, Wheeler (12.2, 66-71), 82 yrs. (GA)
GREY, Adeline (2.2, 203-08), 82 yrs. (SC)
GRICE, Pauline (4.2, 98-101) (S2 - 5.4, 1599-1606), 81 yrs. (TX via GA)
GRIEGG, Annie (9.3, 113-16), 84 yrs., house (AR via TN)
GRIFFIN, Lucendy (S2 - 5.4, 1607-13), c. 80 yrs. (TX via NC)
GRIFFETH, Dorcas (14.1, 346-49), 80 yrs., field (NC)
GRIFFIN, Abner (S1 - 3.1, 270-75), 88 yrs., field (GA)
GRIFFIN, Fannie (2.2, 209-11), 94 yrs., house (SC)

GRIFFIN, Heard (12.2, 72-77), 86 yrs., field (GA)
GRIFFIN, Lou (11.8, 143-44), over 90 yrs. (MO)
GRIFFIN, Madison (2.2, 212-14), 84 yrs. (SC)
GRIGSBY, Charity (6.1, 171-73), c. 85 yrs., house (AL)
GRIGSBY, Peggy (2.2, 215), 106 yrs., field (SC)
GRINSTEAD, Robert E. (7.1, 124-27), 80 yrs., field (OK via MS)
GRISHAM, Emma (16.6, 28-30), over 90 yrs. (TN)
GRUBBS, Minerva (S1 - 8.3, 891-94), c. 80 yrs., nursemaid and field
   (MS)
GRUMBLES, James (S2 - 5.4, 1614-20), 80 yrs. (TX)
GUDGEL, Ann (16.2, 28) (KY)
GUDGER, Sarah (14.1, 350-58), 121 yrs., field (NC)
GUESS, Charlotte (9.3, 117-18), 66 yrs. (AR via TX)
GUESS, William (9.3, 117), 68 yrs. (AR)
GUIDON, Lee (9.3, 119-26), 89 yrs., field (AR via MS)
GULLAGE, Phillip Davenport (S1 - 8.3, 895), 83 yrs. (MS)
GULLINS, David G. (12.2, 78-90), 82 yrs., house and yard work (GA)
GUNTHARPE, Violet (2.2, 216-20), 82 yrs. (SC)
GURDNER, Julia (S1 - 5.2, 353-54), 82 yrs. (OH via TN)
GUWN, Betty (6.2, 98-100), 105 yrs., house and field (IN via KY)

HADLEY, Linley (9.3, 127-28), 77 yrs. (AR via MS)
HADNOT, Josh (S2 - 5.4, 1621-25), house (TX)
HADNOT, Mandy (4.2, 102-05) (S2 - 5.4, 1626-30), cook (TX)
HADNOT, Maria (S2 - 5.4, 1631-32), 75 yrs. (TX)
HAIRSTON, Davey (S1 - 8.3, 896), carriage driver (MS via VA)
HALFEN, July Ann (S1 - 8.3, 897-906), field (MS)
HALL, Anna (9.3, 129-30), 68 yrs. (AR via MS)
HALL, Bolden (17.1, 165-66), 83 yrs., field (FL)
HALL, David A. (16.4, 39-41), 90 yrs. (OH via NC)
HALL, Minnie (S1 - 8.3, 907), 80 yrs. (MS)
HALL, Thomas (14.1, 359-62), 81 yrs. (NC)
HAMILTON, Albert (S1 - 8.3, 908-09), c. 116 yrs., field (MS)
HAMILTON, Ellie (9.3, 131-32), 75 yrs., field (AR via MS)
HAMILTON, Hecter (14.1, 363-69), 90 yrs., personal servant (NC via VA)
HAMILTON, Jeff (S2 - 5.4, 1633-35), 97 yrs., personal servant and
   shepherd (TX via KY)
HAMILTON, John (2.2, 221-22), 80 yrs. (SC)
HAMILTON, Josephine (9.3, 133-34), 77 yrs., house (AR via MS)
HAMILTON, Louis (11.8, 145-46), 90 yrs. (MO)
HAMILTON, Peter (9.3, 137-38), 68 yrs. (AR via MS)
HAMILTON, William (4.2, 106-08) (S2 - 5.4, 1636-41), 77 yrs. (TX)
HAMLIN, Susan (2.2, 223-36), 104 yrs. (SC)
HAMMOND, Caroline (16.3, 19-21), 95 yrs. (MD)
HAMMOND, Milton (12.2, 91-96), 84 yrs., town slave (GA)
HAMPTON, Lawrence (9.3, 139-41), 78 yrs., field (AR via SC)
HAMPTON, Wade D. (S1 - 11.2, 182-85) (SC)
HANCOCK, Filmore (11.8, 147-61) (S1 - 2.4, 178-91), 86 yrs. (MO)
HANCOCK, George (S1 - 2.4, 192) (MO)
HANCOCK, Hannah (9.3, 142-47), over 80 yrs., house (AR via SC)
HANEY, Julia E. (9.3, 149-53), 78 yrs. (AR via TN)
HANNA, Moses (S1 - 2.2, 40-46), 93 yrs., seaman (CO via FL)
HARDIN, Matilda (S1 - 8.3, 910-11), 103 yrs., nurse (MS)
HARDMAN, Mattie (7.1, 128-30), 78 yrs., house (OK via TX)

HARDRICK, Eliza (S1 - 12.1, 137-40), 77 yrs. (OK)
HARDRIDGE, Mary Jane (9.3, 157-60), 85 yrs. (AR)
HARDY, Mrs. Allie O. (S2 - 1.10, 322-24), 68 yrs., free (NE via IL)
HARDY, O.C. (9.3, 161-62), 69 yrs., field (AR via LA)
HARDY, Rosa (9.3, 163), c. 80 yrs. (AR via TN)
HARE, Simon (S1 - 8.3, 912-23), 88 yrs. (MS via NC)
HARMON, George W. (S1 - 12.1, 141-44), 83 yrs. (OK via TX)
HARMON, Jane Smith Hill (12.2, 97-102), 88 yrs., house (GA)
HARP, Anson (2.2, 237-39), 87 yrs. (SC via MS)
HARPER, Dave (11.8, 162-68), 87 yrs., field (MO)
HARPER, Eda (9.3, 164-67), 93 yrs., field (AR via MS)
HARPER, Pierce (4.2, 109-14) (S2 - 5.4, 1642-51), c. 87 yrs., errands
   (TX via NC)
HARPER, (Rev.) Thomas (2.2, 240-41), 84 yrs. (SC)
HARRELL, Clara (11.8, 169), c. 81 yrs. (MO)
HARRELL, Molly (4.2, 115-17) (S2 - 5.4, 1658-64), house (TX)
HARRIS, Abe (2.2, 242-43), 74 yrs. (SC)
HARRIS, Abram (9.3, 168-75), 93 yrs., house (AR via SC)
HARRIS, Betty (9.3, 176), 45-50 yrs., free (AR)
HARRIS, Charles (S1 - 2.2, 47-51), 67 yrs., free (CO via KS)
HARRIS, Della (16.5, 24-26), 85 yrs., house (VA via NC)
HARRIS, Dosia (12.2, 103-14), 78 yrs. (GA)
HARRIS, Eliza (Uncle Tom's Cabin) (S1 - 5.1, 245-48) (OH via KY)
HARRIS, Ella (S1 - 1.1, 175-76), 82 yrs., house (AL)
HARRIS, George (S1 - 8.3, 924), 90 yrs. (MS)
HARRIS, George W. (14.1, 370-74), 82 yrs., field (NC)
HARRIS, John (S1 - 3.1, 276-304), 70 yrs. (GA)
HARRIS, Lancy (S2 - 1.4, 255-57), 84 yrs. (DC via NC)
HARRIS, Mary (9.3, 177-78), 82 yrs., house (AR)
HARRIS, Maston (S1 - 5.1, 79) (IN)
HARRIS, Orris (S1 - 8.3, 925-35), c. 79 yrs. (MS)
HARRIS, Page (16.3, 22-25), 79 yrs., nurse (MD)
HARRIS, Rachel (9.3, 179-82), 90 yrs., field (AR via MS)
HARRIS, Sarah (14.1, 375-78), 76 yrs. (NC)
HARRIS, "Uncle Shang" (12.2, 117-25), 97 yrs., played with master's
   children (GA)
HARRIS, Squire (S1 - 3.1, 305-10), 96 yrs., tended stock animals
   (GA via NC)
HARRIS, Susan (S1 - 2.2, 52-55), 65 yrs., free (CO)
HARRIS, Sybella (S1 - 8.3, 936), nurse (MS)
HARRIS, Virginia (S1 - 8.3, 937-48) (MS via LA)
HARRIS, William (9.3, 183-84), 75-80 yrs., house (AR via TN)
HARRISON, Eli (2.2, 244-46), 87 yrs. (SC)
HARRISON, Ethel (S1 - 3.1, 311-14) (GA)
HARRISON, Jack (S2 - 5.4, 1652-57), field (TX)
HARRISON, John (S1 - 12.1, 145-68), 80 yrs. (OK)
HARRISON, William H. (9.3, 185-89), over 100 yrs. (AR via VA and TN)
HARSHAW, Plomer (S1 - 12.1, 169-72), 86 yrs. (OK via MS and TX)
HART, Cy (14.1, 379-81), 78 yrs., field (NC)
HART, Laura (9.3, 190-92), 85 yrs., field (AR)
HARVEY, Charlie Jeff (2.2, 247-51), 82 yrs. (SC)
HARVEY, Nealy (S1 - 5.1, 80-81), free (IN)
HARWELL, Alice (S2 - 5.4, 1665-74) (TX)
HASKELL, Hetty (9.3, 193-94), field (AR via TN)
HASTY, Eliza (2.2, 252-57), 85 yrs. (SC)
HATCHETT, Matilda (9.3, 195-201), c. 100 yrs., field (AR)

HATFIELD, Mollie (S1 - 8.3, 949-55), 77 yrs. (MS via AL)
HATLEY, Sarah (S2 - 5.4, 1675-81), c. 77 yrs. (TX)
HATTIE, Thomas (17.1, 377-78), 77 yrs., helped care for children
   (FL via GA)
HAWES, William (S2 - 1.10, 325-26), 54 yrs., free (NE via KY)
HAWKENS, John G. (9.3, 202-04), 71 yrs. (AR via MS)
HAWKENS, Lizzie (9.3, 205-08), 65 yrs. (AR)
HAWKINS, Annie (7.1, 131-33), 90 yrs., field (OK via TX and GA)
HAWKINS, Ella (S1 - 3.1, 315-18), 81 yrs. (GA via SC)
HAWKINS, G.W. (9.3, 212-20), 75 yrs. (AR via AL)
HAWKINS, Joe (S1 - 8.3, 956-61), c. 83 yrs. (MS via AL)
HAWKINS, Packy (9.3, 209-11), 75 yrs. (AR via AL)
HAWKINS, Rachel (9.3, 154-56), 88 yrs., field (AR via AL)
HAWKINS, Susan (S1 - 5.2, 355-56), 79 yrs. (OH via NC)
HAWKINS, Tap (S1 - 5.2, 357-58), 87 yrs., field (OH via NC)
HAWKINS, Tom (12.2, 126-35), 75 yrs., house (GA)
HAWTHORNE, Ann (4.2, 118-25), c. 83 yrs., work around house (TX)
HAYES, Charles (6.1, 174-75) (S2 - 1.1, 3-4), 77 yrs. (AL)
HAYES, Dorah (S1 - 8.3, 962), 87 yrs., house (MS)
HAYES, James (4.2, 126-29) (S2 - 5.4, 1682-87), c. 101 yrs., errands,
   chores, and field (TX)
HAYES, Tom (9.3, 227-28), 80 yrs., house (AR)
HAYES, Wash (S1 - 8.3, 963-68), c. 77 yrs. (MS)
HAYGOOD, Burt (S1 - 11.2, 186-87), 84 yrs. (d. 1924) (SC)
HAYNES, Dolly (2.2, 258-60), 91 yrs. (SC)
HAYNES, Jack (S1 - 8.3, 969-70), c. 100 yrs., field (MS)
HAYS, Elisa (9.3, 221-26), 77 yrs. (AR)
HAYS, Mose (S1 - 8.3, 971), 91 yrs., carriage driver (MS via AL)
HAYWOOD, Alonzo (14.1, 382-84), 67 yrs. (NC)
HAYWOOD, Barbara (14.1, 385-88), 85 yrs., weaving (NC)
HAYWOOD, Felix (4.2, 130-34) (S2 - 5.4, 1688-95), c. 93 yrs., shepherd
   and cowboy (TX)
HAYWOOD, Joe (9.3, 229-30), 76 yrs. (AR via MS, LA, and TX)
HEAD, _____ (11.8, 170-72), 75 yrs. (MO via LA)
HEARD, Bill (12.2, 136-46), 73 yrs. (GA)
HEARD, Clark (S1 - 5.2, 359-64), 86 yrs., field (OH via GA)
HEARD, Emmaline (12.1, 32-36; 147-64) (13.4, 245-50; 256-60), c. 77 yrs.
   (GA)
HEARD, Mildred (12.2, 165-69), non-slave (GA)
HEARD, Robert (12.2, 170-72), 96 yrs., field (GA)
HEMMETT, London Law (S1 - 12.1, 173-76), 89 yrs., field (OK via GA)
HENDERSON, Albert (S2 - 5.4, 1696-1701), 95 yrs., field (TX via KY)
HENDERSON, Benjamin (12.2, 173-77), 79 yrs., yard work (GA)
HENDERSON, Celia (16.4, 42-43) (S1 - 5.2, 365-77), 88 yrs., house
   (OH via KY and LA)
HENDERSON, George (16.2, 5-8), c. 77 yrs., field (KY)
HENDERSON, Harris (12.2, 115-16), 79 yrs., light field and yard work
   (GA)
HENDERSON, Henry (S1 - 12.1, 177-80), 95 yrs. (OK via AR and FL)
HENDERSON, Isabell (14.1, 389-92), 83 yrs. (NC)
HENDERSON, Isabelle (S1 - 2.4, 193-95), over 90 yrs., house (MO)
HENDERSON, Julia (S1 - 3.1, 319-28), over 85 yrs., house (GA)
HENDERSON, Liney (2.2, 261-65), 70 yrs. (SC)
HENDERSON, Mack (S1 - 8.3, 972-73) (MS)
HENDERSON, Phoebe (4.2, 135-36) (S2 - 5.4, 1702-05), c. 105 yrs.,
   field (TX via GA)

HENRY, Essex (14.1, 393-98), tended animals (NC)
HENRY, Francis (S1 - 8.3, 974), free (MS via LA)
HENRY, Ida (7.1, 134-37), 83 yrs., field (OK via TX)
HENRY, Jefferson Franklin (12.2, 178-93), 78 yrs. (GA)
HENRY, Jim (2.2, 266-70), 77 yrs. (SC)
HENRY, Milly (14.1, 399-404), 82 yrs., house (NC via MS)
HENRY, Nettie (7.2, 61-67) (S1 - 8.3, 975-87), 82 yrs., house
   (MS via AL)
HENRY, Robert (S2 - 5.4, 1706-12), 84 yrs. (TX)
HENRY, "Uncle Robert" (12.2, 194-99), 82 yrs., waited table (GA)
HENSON, Annie Young (16.3, 26-28), 86 yrs. (MD via VA)
HERNDON, Jack (2.2, 271-75), 93 yrs., house (SC)
HERRIN, Evie (S1 - 8.3, 988-91) (MS)
HERRINGTON, Harriet (S1 - 5.1, 82-83), over 85 yrs. (IN via AL)
HERVEY, Marie E. (9.3, 231-34), 62 yrs., free (AR via TN)
HEWITT, Florida (S1 - 8.3, 992-1006), 107 yrs., house (MS)
HEWS, Chaney (14.1, 405-08), 80 yrs., swept yards (NC)
HEYWARD, Lavinia (2.2, 276-78), 67 yrs. (SC)
HEYWARD, Lucretia (2.2, 279-81), 96 yrs., house (SC)
HEYWOOD, Maria (S1 - 11.2, 188) (SC)
HEYWOOD, Mariah (2.2, 282-88), 82 yrs. (SC)
HICKMAN, (Rev.) Robert (S1 - 2.3, 108-14), 74 yrs. (MN via MS)
HICKS, Phyllis (9.3, 235-37), 71 yrs. (AR via TN)
HICKS, (Dr.) S. (S1 - 5.1, 84-88), free (IN via KY)
HIGGERSON, Joe (11.8, 173-78), 92 yrs. (MO)
HIGGINS, Bert (9.3, 238-40), 88 yrs., field (AR via MS)
HIGH, Joe (14.1, 409-16), 80 yrs., house (NC)
HIGH, Susan (14.1, 417-21), 70 yrs. (NC)
HIGHTOWER, Jim Polk (S1 - 8.3, 1007-14) (MS)
HILL, Albert (4.2, 137-40) (S2 - 5.4, 1713-24), 81 yrs., field
   (TX via GA)
HILL, Annie (9.3, 241-46), 60 yrs., free (AR via TN)
HILL, Clark (9.3, 247-51), c. 83 yrs., house (AR via GA)
HILL, Delia (11.8, 179-83), over 90 yrs. (MO via MS)
HILL, Elmira (9.3, 252-55), 97 yrs., house (AR via VA)
HILL, Gillie (9.3, 256-57), 45 yrs., free (AR)
   See Jones, Evelyn (AR)
HILL, Harriet (9.3, 258-61), 84 yrs., house (AR via GA)
HILL, Hattie (9.3, 262-63), 85 yrs., house (AR via GA)
HILL, James (S1 - 8.3, 1015-21), 91 yrs., field and hired out (MS)
HILL, Jerry (2.2, 289-90), 85 yrs. (SC)
HILL, John (12.2, 200-07), c. 74 yrs., odd jobs (GA)
HILL, Kitty (14.1, 422-26), 76 yrs. (NC via VA)
HILL, Laura (S1 - 1.1, 177-78), 83 yrs. (AL)
HILL, Lizzie (6.1, 176-77) (S1 - 1.1, 179), 94 yrs., house (AL via GA)
HILL, Louis (11.8, 184-90), 79 yrs. (MO)
HILL, Nellie (S2 - 5.4, 1725-29), mid-80's (TX)
HILL, Oliver (9.3, 264-66), 94 yrs., field (AR via MS)
HILL, P.M.E. (S2 - 1.10, 327-29), 68 yrs., free (NE via NY)
HILL, Rebecca Brown (9.3, 267-71), field (AR via MS)
HILL, Sarah Laws (S2 - 1.16, 389-402) (WA)
HILL, Tanny (9.3, 272), 56 yrs., free (AR)
HILLY, Joanna (S1 - 8.3, 1022-23), 90 yrs., field (MS)
HILLYER, Morris (7.1, 138-44), 84 yrs., house (OK via GA)
HILYARD, Della Bess (17.1, 54-55, 222), 78 yrs., field (FL via SC and
   GA)

HINES, Elizabeth (9.3, 273-75) (AR via LA)
HINES, Gabe (6.1, 178-80) (S1 - 1.1, 180-81), c. 100 yrs., carried
  water (AL via GA)
HINES, Marriah (16.5, 27-30), 102 yrs. (VA)
HINTON, Charlie (9.3, 276-80), 89 yrs., field (AR via NC)
HINTON, Jerry (14.1, 427-32), 82 yrs. (NC)
HINTON, Martha Adeline (14.1, 433-35), 76 yrs. (NC)
HINTON, Robert (14.1, 436-40), 81 yrs., light house work (NC)
HINTON, William George (14.1, 441-45), 78 yrs. (NC)
HITE, Ben (9.3, 281), 74 yrs. (AR via TN)
HOARD, Rosina (4.2, 141-43) (S2 - 5.4, 1730-38), 78 yrs. (TX)
HOBBS, W.E. (S2 - 10.9, 4342-48), 79 yrs., white (TX via TN)
HOBBY, Lee (S2 - 5.4, 1739-54) (TX via KY)
HOCKADAY, Mrs. (6.2, 101-04), middle-aged (IN)
HODGE (or HODGES), Adeline (6.1, 181-84) (S1 - 1.1, 182-86), field and
  house (AL via MS)
HODGE, Betty (9.3, 282-84), 63 yrs., free (AR via VA)
HODGES, Adeline (AL via MS)
  See Hodge, Adeline (AL via MS)
HODGES, Eustace (14.1, 446-48), 76 yrs. (NC)
HODGES, Fanny Smith (7.2, 68-71) (S1 - 8.3, 1024-28), house (MS)
HOGAN, Nelson (S2 - 5.4, 1755-57), c. 82 yrs. (TX)
HOGUE, William P. (S1 - 5.2, 378-79), 76 yrs. (OH via VA)
HOLBERT, Clayton (16.1, 1-7) (S2 - 1.8, 285-91), 86 yrs., field
  (KS via TN)
HOLLAND, Benjamin (S2 - 5.4, 1758-59), 75 yrs. (d. 1900), slave driver
  (TX via AL)
  See Holland, Margaret (TX)
HOLLAND, Caroline (6.1, 185-87), 88 yrs., house (AL)
HOLLAND, Margaret (S2 - 5.4, 1758-59), 74 yrs. (d. 1909), house
  (TX via VA)
  See Holland, Benjamin (TX)
HOLLAND, Tom (4.2, 144-47) (S2 - 5.4, 1760-69), 97 yrs., field (TX)
HOLLIDAY, Wayne (7.2, 72-75) (S1 - 8.3, 1029-32), 84 yrs., house (MS)
HOLLINS, Jane (2.2, 291-93), 97 yrs., field (SC)
HOLLOMON, Minnie (9.3, 285-86), 75 yrs., house (AR via SC)
HOLLOWAY, H.B. (9.3, 287-305), 89 yrs., house (AR via GA)
HOLLOWAY, Jane (6.1, 188-89) (S1 - 1.1, 187-88), 85 yrs., field (AL)
HOLLY, Pink (9.3, 306), 70 yrs. (AR via SC)
HOLMAN, Charles (S1 - 8.3, 1033-36), 83 yrs. (MS)
HOLMAN, Eliza (4.2, 148-50) (S2 - 5.4, 1770-78), 82 yrs. (TX via MS)
HOLMAN, Gillam (S1 - 11.2, 189-91), 72 yrs. (SC)
HOLMAN, Rose (S1 - 8.3, 1037-41), c. 84 yrs., carried water (MS)
HOLMES, Augustus (S1 - 8.3, 1043-47), 94 yrs., tended cows and house
  (MS)
HOLMES, (Rev.) B.R. (S1 - 4.2, 671-73), free, founder of the Ex-Slave
  Association (GA)
HOLMES, Charlie (S1 - 8.3, 1042), 92 yrs. (MS)
HOLMES, Cornelius (2.2, 294-97), 82 yrs. (SC)
HOLMES, Dora (9.3, 307), 60 yrs., free (AR)
HOLMES, Henry (13.4, 265-67) (GA)
HOLMES, Joseph (6.1, 190-200) (S2 - 1.1, 5-12), 81 yrs., field (AL
  via GA and VA)
HOLMES, Mundy (S1 - 11.2, 192-93), 80's (SC)
HOLSELL, Rhody (11.8, 191-202), 89 yrs., field (MO)
HOLT, John A. (S1 - 2.4, 196-98), 91 yrs., field (MO via AR)

HOLT, Larnce (4.2, 151-52) (S2 - 5.4, 1779-82), 79 yrs. (TX)
HOMER, Bill (4.2, 153-56) (S2 - 5.4, 1783-89), 87 yrs., coachman
   (TX via LA)
HOMER, Mary (S2 - 5.4, 1790-96), 81 yrs. (TX via TN)
HOMES, Walter (S1 - 2.1, 8) (S2 - 1.3, 94-95), c. 67 yrs., free (AR)
HOOD, Laura (12.2, 208-10), c. 107 yrs., house (GA)
HOOD, Willis (S1 - 2.2, 56-58), over 70 yrs. (CO via MS)
HOOKS, Rebecca (17.1, 171-77), 90 yrs., house (FL via GA)
HOOPER, Scott (4.2, 157-58) (S2 - 5.4, 1797-1802), 81 yrs. (TX)
HOOVER, Silvia (S1 - 8.3, 1048-49), 111 yrs., nurse (LA via MS and TN)
HOPKINS, Elijah Henry (9.3, 308-16), 81 yrs., field (AR via GA and SC)
HOPSON, Moble (16.5, 31-41), 85 yrs. (VA)
HOPSON, Nattie (9.3, 317), over 80 yrs. (AR via AL)
HORN, Josh (6.1, 201-10) (S1 - 1.1, 189-99), field (AL)
HORN, Molly (9.3, 318-20), 77 yrs. (AR via NC)
HORRY, Ben (2.2, 298-326) (S1 - 11.2, 194-203), c. 88 yrs. (SC)
HORRY, Stella (S1 - 11.2, 204), 60's, free (SC)
HORTON, Cora L. (9.3, 321-24), 55 yrs., free (AR via GA)
HOUGH (or HOUSE), Samantha (S1 - 5.1, 92-93), 93 yrs. (IN via KY)
HOUSE, Laura (9.3, 325), 75 yrs. (AR)
HOUSE, Samantha (IN)
   See Hough, Samantha (IN)
HOUSEAL, William P. (S1 - 11.2, 205-07), 81 yrs. (SC)
HOUSTON, Alice (4.2, 159-62), 78 yrs., house (TX)
HOUSTON, (Aunt) Carolina (S2 - 5.4, 1803-05), 81 yrs. (TX via GA)
HOWARD, Emma L. (6.1, 211-14), c. 85 yrs., house (AL)
HOWARD, Josephine (4.2, 163-65) (S2 - 5.4, 1806-11), field (TX via AL)
HOWARD, Perry W. (S1 - 8.3, 1050) (MS)
HOWARD, Pinkie (9.3, 326-40), 85 yrs., house (AR via LA)
HOWARD, R.H. (S1 - 8.3, 1051), 84 yrs. (MS)
HOWARD, Robert (6.2, 105-06), 85 yrs. (IN via KY)
HOWELL, Jerry (S1 - 8.3, 1052), 85 yrs. (MS)
HOWELL, Pauline (9.3, 341-44), 65-70 yrs. (AR via TN)
HUBBARD, Clara (S1 - 8.3, 1054), 76 yrs. (MS via AL)
   See Hubbard, James Nelson (MS)
HUBBARD, James Nelson (S1 - 8.3, 1053-54), 95 yrs., house (MS via AL)
   See Hubbard, Clara (MS)
HUDDLESTON, Mr. (18.1, 3042)
HUDESPETH, Esther (16.2, 117-18) (KY)
HUDGENS, Molly (9.3, 345-46), 69 yrs. (AR via NC)
HUDSON, Carrie (12.2, 211-19), 75 yrs., cared for young children (GA)
HUDSON, Charlie (12.2, 220-32), 80 yrs., hauling and message boy (GA)
HUDSON, Measy (16.6, 31-32), 90 yrs. (TN via NC)
HUFF, Bryant (12.2, 238-43), chores (GA)
HUFF, Charlie (9.3, 347-48), 64 yrs., free (AR via NC and VA)
HUFF, Esther (12.2, 244-51) (GA)
HUFF, Louvenia (9.3, 349-50), 64 yrs., free (AR via MS)
HUFF, Mary (12.2, 233-37), 87 yrs., yard work and spinning (GA)
HUGGINS, Alex (14.1, 449-52), 87 yrs. (NC)
HUGGINS, Anna (9.3, 251-56), c. 50 yrs., free (AR)
HUGHES, Emanuel (S1 - 8.3, 1055-56), 84 yrs. (MS)
HUGHES, "Aunt Fanny" (S1 - 3.1, 328-34), house (GA)
HUGHES, Frank (S1 - 8.3, 1057-66), 79 yrs. (MS via AL)
HUGHES, Lizzie (4.2, 166-68) (S2 - 5.4, 1812-20), 89 yrs., house (TX)
HUGHES, Margaret (2.2, 327-30), 82 yrs., house (SC)
HULM, Margaret (9.3, 357-58), 97 yrs., house (AR)

HUME, Matthew (6.2, 107-10), field (IN via KY)
HUMPHREY, Alex (S2 - 5.4, 1821-24), 73 yrs. (TX)
HUMPHREY, Anna (S2 - 5.4, 1825-31), c. 88 yrs., house (TX via AL)
HUNLEY, Tom ("Hambone") (S1 - 8.3, 1067-74), c. 77 yrs. (MS)
HUNT, Betty (S1 - 3.1, 335), c. 79 yrs. (GA)
HUNT, Rhoda (S1 - 8.3, 1075-77), 83 yrs. (MS)
HUNTER, Charlie H. (14.1, 453-56), 80 yrs., errands (NC)
HUNTER, Elbert (14.1, 457-60), 93 yrs., field (NC)
HUNTER, Forrest (S1 - 11.2, 208-09) (S2 - 1.15, 379-80), 73 yrs. (SC)
HUNTER, Hester (2.2, 331-46), 85 yrs. (SC)
HUNTER, John (9.3, 359-66), 74 yrs. (AR via NC)
HUNTER, Lillian (S1 - 5.1, 94-95), free (IN)
HUNTER, Lina (12.2, 252-72), c. 90 yrs., cared for children (GA)
HUNTER, William (9.3, 367-68), 70 yrs. (AR via MS)
HURLEY, Emma (12.2, 273-80), over 80 yrs. (GA)
HURSEY, Mose (4.2, 169-71)(S2 - 5.4, 1832-36), c. 82 yrs. (TX via LA)
HURST, Pattie (S1 - 8.3, 1078), 122 yrs. (d. 1886) (MS via VA)
HURT, Charley (4.2, 172-76) (S2 - 5.4, 1837-46), 85 yrs., chores and
   meat packing (TX via GA)
HUTCHESON, Alice (12.2, 281-88), 76 yrs. (GA)
HUTCHINSON, Cassie (S1 - 3.1, 336-37), 81 yrs. (GA via AL)
HUTCHINSON, Ida Blackshear (9.3, 369-78), 73 yrs. (AR via AL)
HUTCHISON, Jemima (S1 - 3.1, 338-41), 96 yrs., house (GA)
HUSTON, Hal (7.1, 145-47), 90 yrs., field (OK via TN)
HUTSON, William (7.1, 148-51), 98 yrs., house (OK via GA)
HYDE, Patsy (16.6, 33-36) (TN)

INGRAM, Addison (S1 - 1.1, 200-02), 107 yrs., field (AL)
INGRAM, Everett (6.1, 215-17) (S1 - 1.1, 203-05) (AL)
INGRAM, Mary (S2 - 5.4, 1847-51), 86 yrs., house (TX via LA)
INGRAM, Wash (4.2, 177-79) (S2 - 5.4, 1852-55), 93 yrs., field
   (TX via VA)
IRBY, Bettie White (S2 - 5.4, 1856-63), 80 yrs. (TX)
IRVIN, Squire (S1 - 8.3, 1079-90), 88 yrs., odd jobs (MS via TN)
IRVING, William (S2 - 5.4, 1864-75), 87 yrs., chores (TX via GA)
IRWIN, Hannah (6.1, 218-19) (S1 - 1.1, 206), 84 yrs. (AL)
ISAAC, (Uncle)   (S1 - 1.1, 423-24), coachman (AL)
ISABELLE (11.8, 203-04), 87 yrs., nursemaid (MO)
ISHMON, Cornelia (9.3, 379), 73 yrs. (AR)
ISLAND, (Uncle) Jack (9.3, 380-88), 73 yrs. (AR via LA)
ISLAND, Mary (9.3, 389-93), 80 yrs., house (AR via LA)
ISOM, Henrietta (9.3, 391-93), 81 yrs. (AR via MS)
ISOM, Joanna Thompson (S1 - 8.3, 1091-1106), 81 yrs. (MS)

"ARMY JACK" (S1 - 8.3, 1107-08) (MS)
JACKSON, Adeline (3.3, 1-4), 88 yrs., field (SC)
JACKSON, Alex (S2 - 5.4, 1876-82), 80 yrs. (TX)
JACKSON, Amanda (12.2, 289-93), yard work and fed animals (GA)
JACKSON, Camilla (12.2, 294-98) (13.4, 254-55), 80 yrs., field (GA)
JACKSON, Carter (4.2, 180-81) (S2 - 5.4, 1883-87), 85 yrs., chores
   (TX via AL)
JACKSON, Clarice (9.4, 1-4) (S1 - 2.1, 9) (S2 - 1.3, 96), 82 yrs, (AR)

JACKSON, Cordelia (3.3, 5-7), 78 yrs. (SC)
JACKSON, Dora (S1 - 8.3, 1109-11), 79 yrs. (MS)
JACKSON, (Aunt) Easter (12.2, 299-302) (GA)
JACKSON, Ed (S2 - 5.4, 1888-90), upper 70's (TX)
JACKSON, Edna (S1 - 5.2, 380-85), 97 yrs., house (OH via KY)
JACKSON, Frank (S1 - 12.1, 181-84), 95 yrs., field (OK via LA and AL)
JACKSON, G.W. (S1 - 1.1, 207-11), c. 90 yrs. (AL)
JACKSON, George (16.4, 45-49), 79 yrs., garden work (OH via VA)
JACKSON, George (S1 - 11.2, 210-12), c. 70 yrs. (SC)
JACKSON, Gus (S2 - 5.4, 1891-94), 73 yrs., free (TX)
JACKSON, Henrietta (6.2, 111-12), c. 105 yrs., field and house (IN via
  AL and VA)
JACKSON, Isabella (7.1, 152-54), 79 yrs., field (OK via LA)
JACKSON, Israel (9.4, 5-8), 78 yrs., house (AR via MS)
JACKSON, J.F. (S1 - 1.1, 212-13), 96 yrs., house (AL)
JACKSON, James (4.2, 182-84) (S2 - 5.4, 1895-99), 87 yrs., house and
  shepherd (TX via LA)
JACKSON, James W. (S1 - 2.2, 59-61), 78 yrs. (CO via KY)
JACKSON, John H. (15.2, 1-7), 86 yrs., field (NC)
JACKSON, Laura Jane (S1 - 8.3, 1112-13), 86 yrs., carried water (MS)
JACKSON, Lizzie (S1 - 12.1, 185-88), 88 yrs., house (OK via MS)
JACKSON, Lula (9.4, 9-19), 79 yrs., house (AR via AL)
JACKSON, Maggie (4.2, 185-86) (S2 - 5.4, 1900-01), 80 yrs., house (TX)
JACKSON, Maria (S2 - 1.6, 267-74), 79 yrs. (GA via AL)
JACKSON, Martha (6.1, 220-23), 87 yrs., field (AL)
JACKSON, Martin (4.2, 187-92) (S2 - 5.4, 1902-09), c. 91 yrs., house
  (TX)
JACKSON, Mary (9.4, 20-21), 75 yrs. (AR via TX)
JACKSON, Nancy (4.2, 193-94) (S2 - 5.4, 1910-14), c. 106 yrs. (TX via
  TN)
JACKSON, Richard (4.2, 195-97) (S2 - 5.4, 1915-18), c. 79 yrs. (TX)
JACKSON, (Rev.) Silas (16.3, 29-33), c. 90 yrs., field (MD via VA)
JACKSON, (Aunt) Snovey (12.2, 303-09), c. 80 yrs. (GA via VA)
JACKSON, Solomon (S1 - 1.1, 214-18), 90 yrs., house (AL)
JACKSON, (Rev.) Squires (17.1, 178-83), 96 yrs., field (FL)
JACKSON, Taylor (9.4, 22-25), 88 yrs., field (AR via MD and VA)
JACKSON, Virginia (9.4, 26-27), 74 yrs. (AR via MS)
JACKSON, William (9.4, 28-29), 84 yrs., field (AR via TN)
JACOBS, Turner (S1 - 8.3, 1114-21), 82 yrs., field (MS)
JAKE, "Uncle" (12.2, 310-14) (S1 - 4.2, 616-22), over 90 yrs., field
  and house (GA)
JAMAR, Lawson (9.4, 30-31), 66 yrs., free (AR via AL)
JAMES, Agnes (3.3, 8-13), 80 yrs., house (SC)
JAMES, Arena (S1 - 8.3, 1122-23), 110 yrs. (d. 1939) (MS)
JAMES, Fred (3.3, 14-16), 81 yrs., field (SC)
JAMES, James Calhart (16.3, 34-36), 91 yrs. (MD via VA)
JAMES, John (4.2, 198-200) (S2 - 5.4, 1919-25), 78 yrs. (TX via MO
  and LA)
JAMES, Joseph ("Tobe") (S2 - 6.5, 1927-32), 92 yrs., field (TX via LA)
JAMES, Julia A. (S1 - 5.2, 386-89), 83 yrs., house (OH via NC)
JAMES, Mary Moriah Anne Susanna (16.3, 37-40), field (MD via VA)
JAMES, Nellie (9.4, 32-33), 72 yrs. (AR via MS)
JAMES, Robert (9.4, 34-35), 66 yrs., free (AR via MS)
JAMES, Thomas W. (S1 - 5.2, 390), 81 yrs., free (OH via VA)
JAMES, Tippett (S1 - 5.2, 391) (OH via VA)
JAMES, Wash (S1 - 8.3, 1124-26), 74 yrs. (MS)

JAMESON, Hannah (S2 - 6.5, 1933-38), c. 88 yrs., chores (TX via AR)
JANE (6.1, 224-26), 86 yrs., house (AL)
JARMAGIN, Andrew (S1 - 8.3, 1127-30), 84 yrs. (MS)
JEFFRIES, Isiah (3.3, 17-19), 86 yrs., field (SC)
JEFFERSON, Ellis (Uncle Jeff) (9.4, 36-37), 77 yrs. (AR via VA and MS)
JEFFERSON, Hattie (S1 - 8.3, 1131-36), 81 yrs. (MS)
JEFFERSON, Lewis (S1 - 8.3, 1137-47), c. 84 yrs., house and field (MS)
JEFFERSON, Lydia (S2 - 6.5, 1939-47), 86 yrs. (TX via LA)
JEFFERSON, Thomas (3.3, 20-22), 102 yrs., field (SC)
JEFFRIES, Moses E. (9.4, 38-42), 81 yrs., field (AR via LA)
JEFSON, Ellis (9.4, 43-46), 77 yrs. (AR via MS)
JEMISON, Perry Sid (16.4, 50-56), 79 yrs., field (OH via AL)
JEMISON, Ophelia (S1 - 11.2, 213-28), c. 69 yrs., free (SC)
JEMISON, Rube (S1 - 8.3, 1148), wheelwright and blacksmith (MS)
JENKINS, Absolom (9.4, 47-49), 80 yrs., house (AR via TN)
JENKINS, Henry D. (3.3, 23-26), 87 yrs., field (SC)
JENKINS, Lewis (S1 - 12.1, 189-96), 93 yrs., house (OK via AL and TX)
JENKINS, Maria (3.3, 27-29), 90 yrs., field (SC)
JENKINS, Nep (S1 - 8.3, 1149-50), 84 yrs. (MS via AL)
JENKINS, Paul (3.3, 30-32), 70 yrs., free (SC)
JERMAN, Dora (9.4, 50-51), 60 yrs., free (AR)
JETER, Emma (3.3, 33-34) (SC)
JEWEL, Mahala (12.2, 315-21), 76 yrs., yard work (GA)
JIMMERSON, Amanda (S1 - 1.1, 219-20), 94 yrs., field (AL)
JOE (13.4, 264), non-slave (GA)
JOHN, Zeno (S2 - 6.5, 1948-51), 76 yrs. (TX via LA)
JOHNS, Thomas (4.2, 201-04) (S2 - 6.5, 1952-72), 90 yrs., field and
    weaver (TX via AL)
JOHNS, Mrs. Thomas (4.2, 205-07) (S2 - 6.5, 1973-76), 73 yrs. (TX)
JOHNSON, Adaline (9.4, 52-58), 96 yrs., field (AR via MS and NC)
JOHNSON, Addie (S1 - 3.1, 342), c. 82 yrs. (GA)
JOHNSON, Adeline (3.3, 35-39), 93 yrs., house (SC)
JOHNSON, Alice (9.4, 56-62), 77 yrs., house (AR via MS)
JOHNSON, Allen (9.4, 63-66), 82 yrs., house (AR via GA)
JOHNSON, Allen (S1 - 11.2, 229-32) (SC)
JOHNSON, Anna (3.3, 40), 75 yrs. (SC)
JOHNSON, Annie (9.4, 67-69), 78 yrs. (AR via MS and IL)
JOHNSON, Ben (9.4, 70-72), 73 or 84 yrs. (AR via TN)
JOHNSON, Ben (15.2, 8-13), 85 yrs. (NC)
JOHNSON, Benjamin (12.2, 322-26), field (GA)
JOHNSON, Betty (9.4, 73-75), 83 yrs., free (AR via AL)
JOHNSON, Callie (S1 - 8.3, 1151), 97 yrs., field (MS via SC)
JOHNSON, Charles (S1 - 2.4, 199-201), 95 yrs. (MO via VA)
JOHNSON, Charley (S2 - 6.5, 1977-87), 87 yrs. (TX)
JOHNSON, Cinda (9.4, 76), 83 yrs. (AR via AL)
JOHNSON, Eliza (S1 - 8.3, 1152), house (MS)
JOHNSON, Ella (9.4, 77-84), 85 yrs., field (AR)
JOHNSON, Ella (S1 - 4.2, 343-48), 80 yrs., house (GA via SC)
JOHNSON, Emma (S1 - 8.3, 1153), 83 yrs., house and field (MS)
JOHNSON, Fanny (9.4, 84-90), 76 yrs., field (AR via TN)
JOHNSON, George (9.4, 91-93), 75 yrs. (AR via VA)
JOHNSON, George (S1 - 2.3, 115-17), 76 yrs. (MN via MO)
JOHNSON, George (S1 - 8.3, 1158-60), 111 yrs. (d. 1926) (MS via NC)
JOHNSON, Georgia (12.2, 327-36), 74 yrs. (GA via SC, MS, AR, and TN)
JOHNSON, Gus (4.2, 208-11) (S2 - 6.5, 1988-93), c. 90 yrs., field
    (TX via AL)

JOHNSTON, Wiley (S1 - 8.3, 1184) (MS)
JONES, Aaron (S1 - 8.3, 1185-89), 92 yrs., field (MS)
JONES, Abraham (6.1, 233-35), 112 yrs., field (AL)
JONES, Albert (16.5, 42-43), 95 yrs., house (VA)
JONES, Alfred (S1 - 1.1, 221-25), 104 yrs., yard work (AL)
JONES, Amelia (16.2, 38-39), 88 yrs. (KY)
JONES, Anderson (S2 - 6.5, 2064-76), c. 85 yrs. (TX)
JONES, Angeline (9.4, 134-35), 79 yrs. (AR via TN)
JONES, Austin (S1 - 8.3, 1190-91), house (MS)
JONES, Betty (6.2, 116-17), field (IN via KY)
JONES, Bob (15.2, 24-26), 86 yrs. (NC)
JONES, Bud (S2 - 6.5, 2077-92), c. 85 yrs., house (TX via AFRICA, KY,
  and VA)
JONES, Charity (S1 - 8.3, 1192-1202), c. 84 yrs., house and chores (MS)
JONES, Charlie (9.4, 136-37), 76 yrs. (AR via MS)
JONES, Clara (15.2, 28-33), c. 89 yrs., field (NC)
JONES, Cynthia (9.4, 138-40), 88 yrs., house (AR)
JONES, Ed (17.1, 10), 86 yrs. (GA)
JONES, Edmond (9.4, 141-42), 75 yrs. (AR)
JONES, Edward (S1 - 8.3, 1203-09), 82 yrs., field (MS via AL)
JONES, Eliza (9.4, 143-44) (S1 - 2.1, 10) (S2 - 1.3, 97), c. 89 yrs.,
  house (AR via TN and IL)
JONES, Emma (6.1, 236-37) (S1 - 1.1, 226-28), 83 yrs., house (AL via GA)
JONES, Estella (12.2, 345-50) (GA)
JONES, Ester (S1 - 4.2, 349-51), over 85 yrs. (GA)
JONES, Evelyn (9.4, 145-47), c. 70 yrs. (AR)
JONES, Fannie (12.2, 351-55), 85 yrs. (GA)
JONES, George (16.3, 44-45), 84 yrs. (MD)
JONES, Green (S2 - 6.5, 2093-94) (TX via LA)
JONES, Hannah (6.1, 238-40), over 90 yrs., house (AL via VA)
JONES, Hannah (11.8, 214-17), 87 yrs. (MO)
JONES, Harriet (4.2, 231-36) (S2 - 6.5, 2095-2107), 93 yrs., house
  (TX via NC)
JONES, Ira (S1 - 5.1, 99-101), free (IN via KY)
JONES, Isam (S1 - 8.3, 1210-11), c. 85 yrs. (MS via AL)
JONES, Jack (S1 - 8.3, 1212-14), c. 89 yrs. (MS)
JONES, John (9.4, 149-50), 82 yrs., house (AR)
JONES, John (9.4, 148), 71 yrs. (AR via TN)
JONES, Julius (S1 - 8.3, 1215-25), field (MS via AR and TN)
JONES, Lark (S2 - 17, 275-77) (IN)
JONES, Lewis (4.2, 237-40) (S2 - 6.5, 2108-2114), 86 yrs., coachman (TX)
JONES, Lidia (9.4, 151-54) (S2 - 1.3, 98), 94 yrs., house (AR via MS)
JONES, Liza (9.4, 155-57), 88 yrs., house (AR via TN)
JONES, Liza (4.2, 241-45) (S2 - 6.5, 2115-22), 81 yrs., cared for
  children (TX)
JONES, Lizzie (4.2, 246-48) (S2 - 6.5, 2123-26), 86 yrs., cook (TX)
JONES, Lottie (S2 - 6.5, 2127-29), c. 87 yrs., carver and cook (TX via
  AL)
JONES, Lucy (9.4, 158), 72 yrs. (AR via MS)
JONES, Mandy (S1 - 8.3, 1226-42), c. 80 yrs., field (MS)
JONES, Martha (16.2, 47-48), 89 yrs. (KY via VA and WV)
JONES, Martha (S2 - 6.5, 2130-34), 77 yrs. (TX via VA)
JONES, Mary (9.4, 159-62), 72 yrs., free (AR)
JONES, Mary (9.4, 163), 78 yrs. (AR via SC)
JONES, Mary Jane (S1 - 8.3, 1243-46), c. 88 yrs., field (MS)
JONES, Myra (S1 - 8.3, 1247-51), 88 yrs., field (MS)

JONES, Nannie (9.4, 164-65), 81 yrs. (AR)
JONES, Nathan (6.2, 118-19), 78 yrs., field (IN via MO and TN)
JONES, Oliver (S1 - 8.3, 1252-55), 79 yrs. (MS)
JONES, Praise de Lawd Rilla Patterson (S2 - 1.12, 363-70) (NC)
JONES, Rastus (12.2, 356-57), c. 107-110 yrs. (GA via NC and MS)
JONES, Reuben (9.4, 166-68), 85 yrs., field (AR via MS)
JONES, Richard (3.3, 63-71), 93 yrs., field (SC)
JONES, Royal Allen (S1 - 5.2, 393-94), 91 yrs. (OH via VA)
JONES, Steve (S2 - 6.5, 2135-42), c. 89 yrs., field (TX via SC)
JONES, Susan (S1 - 8.3, 1256-59), 95 yrs., house (MS)
JONES, Toby (4.2, 249-52) (S2 - 6.5, 2143-54), 87 yrs., field (TX via SC)
JONES, Vergil (9.4, 169-70), 70 yrs. (AR)
JONES, Walter (9.4, 171-72), 72 yrs. (AR via TN and MS)
JONES, Wesley (3.3, 72-73), 97 yrs., field (SC)
JORDAN, Abner (15.2, 35-36), 95 yrs., house (NC)
JORDAN, Dempsey (S2 - 6.5, 2155-66), c. 100 yrs., house (TX via LA)
JORDAN, Jonce (S1 - 8.3, 1260), c. 91 yrs. (MS via AL)
JORDAN, Josie (7.1, 160-64), 75 yrs., house (OK via TN)
JORDAN, Sam (S1 - 12.1, 197-201), 88 yrs. (OK via AL)
JORDAN, Watt (S1 - 5.2, 395-97), 80 yrs., field (OH via KY)
JORDAN, Charlie (S1 - 8.3, 1261-63), 88 yrs . (MS)
JOSEPHINE, Aunt (6.1, 241), 94 yrs., house (AL)
JULIA, Aunt (S2 - 10.9, 4374-77), home manager (TX)
    See Dave, Uncle (TX)
    See Woorling, James G. (TX)
JUNELL, Oscar Felix (9.4, 173-74), 60 yrs., free (AR)
JURDON, Lucindy (6.1, 242-43) (S2 - 1.1, 13-15), 79 yrs. (AL via GA)
JUSTICE, Mollie (S1 - 2.1, 11), 79 yrs. (AR via TN)

KANNON, Ellis Ken (16.6, 37-39) (TN)
KATES, Ralph (S1 - 5.1, 102-03), 68 yrs., free (IN via TN)
KATHERINE, Aunt (S1 - 8.3, 1264-65) (MS)
KEATON, Sam (9.4, 175-76), 78 yrs. (AR)
KEENAN, Sallie (3.3, 74-79), 80 yrs. (SC via MS)
KELLEY, Abe (S1 - 8.3, 1266-70), 101 yrs., chores and field (MS)
KELLEY, Alexander (S1 - 5.1, 104-05), 82 yrs. (IN via NC)
KELLEY, Bell (S1 - 5.1, 106-07), 80 yrs. (IN via KY)
KELLEY, Mary Jane (3.3, 89-90), 85 yrs., field (SC)
KELLEY, (Aunt) Pinkie (4.2, 253-54) (S2 - 6.5, 2167-70), field (TX)
KELLY, C.H. (S1 - 4.2, 352-54), 70 yrs. (GA)
KELLY, Ella (3.3, 80-82), 81 yrs., house (SC)
KELLY, Ellen (S2 - 6.5, 2171-77), 90 yrs., nursemaid (TX)
KELLY, Martha (3.3, 83-88), 71 yrs. (SC)
KELLY, (Aunt) Pinkie (TX)
    See Kelley, (Aunt) Pinkie (TX)
KELLY, Susan (16.5, 44), 100 yrs., house (VA)
KEMP, ("Prophet") John Henry (17.1, 184-89), 80 yrs., field (FL via MS)
KENDRICKS, Jennie (13.3, 1-7), 82 yrs., house (GA)
KENDRICKS, Tines (9.4, 177-88), 104 yrs., field (AR via GA)
KENNARD, Calvin (S2 - 6.5, 2178-80), 80 yrs., chores (TX via LA)
KENNEDY, Frank (9.4, 189-90), 65-70 yrs. (AR via MS)
KENNEDY, Hamp (S1 - 8.3, 1271-77), 78 yrs. (MS)
KENNELL, Henderson (S1 - 8.3, 1278-79), c. 87 yrs. (MS)

KERNS, Adrianna (9.4, 191-95), 85 yrs., field (AR via TX)
KEY, George (9.4, 196-97), over 70 yrs. (AR via TN)
KEY, Lucy (9.4, 198-200), over 70 yrs. (AR via MS)
KEYS, Susan (S1 - 8.3, 1280), 111 yrs. (MS via VA via DC)
KILGORE, Sam (4.2, 255-59) (S2 - 6.5, 2181-92), 92 yrs., personal
    servant (TX via TN)
KILPATRICK, Emmaline (13.3, 8-13), 74 yrs. (GA)
KIMBALL, Lucy (6.1, 244-47) (S1 - 1.1, 229-32), c. 86 yrs., house (AL)
KIMBROUGH, Frances (13.3, 14-15) (S1 - 4.2, 355-56), c. 82 yrs. (GA)
KIMBROUGH, Robert (S1 - 4.2, 357-67), 99 yrs., carriage driver (GA)
KIMMONS, Richard (S2 - 6.5, 2193-98), c. 93 yrs., farm work (TX via MO)
KINCHLOW, Ben (4.2, 260-84), 91 yrs., cook and ranch hand (TX)
KINDRED, Mary (4.2, 285-87) (S2 - 6.5, 2199-2210), c. 80 yrs., child's
    nurse; field (TX)
KING, Anna (9.4, 201- 06), 80 yrs., house (AR via NC)
KING, Charlie (13.3, 16-20), c. 86 yrs (GA)
KING, Ellen (6.1, 248-50) (S1 - 1.1, 233-35), 86 yrs., field (AL via
    MS)
KING, (Uncle) George G. (7.1, 165-68), 83 yrs., field (OK via SC)
KING, Horace (S1 - 4.2, 368-71), 80 yrs. (d. 1926), free (GA via AL)
KING, J.W. (John) (S2 - 6.5, 2211-18), 83 yrs., chores (TX via MO)
KING, Julia (16.4, 57-61), c. 80 yrs. (OH via KY)
KING, Martha (7.1, 169-71), 85 yrs., house (OK via AL)
KING, Mose (9.4, 207-09), 81 yrs. (AR via VA)
KING, Nancy (4.2, 288-89) (S2 - 6.5, 2219-23), 93 yrs., child's nurse
    and field (TX)
KING, Silvia (4.2, 290-95) (S2 - 6.5, 2224-39), claimed 133 yrs., cook
    and weaver (TX via MOROCCO, FRANCE, and LA)
KING, (Aunt) Susie (9.4, 210-13), 93 yrs., house (AR)
KINNEY, Nicey (13.3, 21-33), 86 yrs. (GA)
KINSEY, Cindy (17.1, 190-93), 85 yrs., field (FL via AR)
KINSEY, Mollie (S1 - 4.2, 372-86), 82 yrs., house (GA)
KIRK, Jeff (S1 - 8.3, 1281), carpenter (MS)
KIRK, William (9.4, 214-15), 84 yrs., field (AR)
KIRKLAND, Mollie (S2 - 6.5, 2240-49), 85 yrs. (TX via AL)
KITCHENS, Mary Ann (S1 - 8.3, 1282-85), c. 85 yrs., carried water and
    chores (MS)
KLUGH, Henry G. (S1 - 11.2, 233), 76 yrs. (SC)
KNIGHT, Emma (11.8, 218-21) (S1 - 2.4, 202-04), over 90 yrs., yard work
    (MO via FL)
KNOWLES, Merton (S1 - 5.1, 69; 108-09) (IN)
KNOX, Lillie (S1 - 11.2, 234-36), 35 yrs., non-slave (SC)
KNOX, Lonie (S1 - 11.2, 237) (SC)
KNOX, Silas (S1 - 8.3, 1286-88), 78 yrs. (MS)
KRUMP, Betty (9.4, 216-19), c. 60 yrs., free (AR)
KYE, George (7.1, 172-75), 100 yrs., field (OK via AR)
KYLES, Preston (9.4, 220-22), 81 yrs. (AR)

LACKEY, Milton (S1 - 8.3, 1289-90), 77 yrs., field (MS)
LACY, Alex (S2 - 6.5, 2250-52), 79 yrs. (TX via KY)
LACY, Anthony (S2 - 6.5, 2253-55), 75 yrs. (TX)
LADLY, Ann (S2 - 6.5, 2256-62), 87 yrs., carried water and nurse
    (TX via TN)
LAGRONE, Susan (9.4, 223-24), 79 yrs., house (AR via MS)

LAIRD, Barney (9.4, 225-27), 79 yrs. (AR via MS)
LAIRD, Robert (S1 - 8.3, 1291-95), 83 yrs., field (MS)
LAIRD, Ruben (S1 - 8.3, 1296-1301), 87 yrs. (MS)
LAMAR, Arey (9.4, 228), 78 yrs. (AR via MS)
LAMB, Alice (S1 - 2.2, 62-64), 66 yrs. (CO via MO)
LAMBERT, Solomon (9.4, 229-34), 89 yrs., hired out field slave (AR)
LANDRUM, Janey (S2 - 6.5, 2263-64), 87 yrs. (TX)
LANE, Gabe (3.3, 91-93), 77 yrs., field (SC)
LARKEN, Julia (13.3, 34-46), 76 yrs., field (GA)
LARKIN, Frank (9.4, 235-38), 77 yrs. (AR via VA)
LARKIN, Frank (9.4, 239-41), 85 yrs., carded wool (AR via VA)
LASSITER, Jane (15.2, 38-42), 80 yrs., house (NC)
LATTIMORE, William (9.4, 242-43), 78 yrs. (AR via MS)
LAURA (13.4, 216-17), c. 75 yrs. (GA)
LAWRENCE, Ephraim (3.3, 94-99), 81 yrs., field (SC)
LAWS, Sarah (S1 - 2.5, 281-83), field (WA via KS and MO)
LAWSOM, Bessie (9.4, 244-46), 76 yrs. (AR via GA)
LAWSON, Ben (7.1, 176-77), 84 yrs., field (OK via IL and KY)
LAWSON, Dave (15.2, 14-50), c. 60 yrs., free (NC)
LAWSON, Victoria (S1 - 8.3, 1302-08), c. 87 yrs., house and field (MS)
LEBBY, R. Bee (S1 - 11.2, 238) (SC)
LEE, Anna (S2 - 6.5, 2272-90), 88 yrs., field and cook (TX via TN)
LEE, David (17.1, 378-79), drove buggy (FL via GA)
LEE, Elvira (S1 - 5.1, 110-11), 88 yrs., house (IN via KY)
LEE, Florence (S1 - 5.2, 398-401), over 80 yrs., house (OH via KY)
LEE, Harriet (11.8, 222-23) (MO via TN)
LEE, Henry (9.4, 247-49), 87 yrs., field (AR via AL)
LEE, Jane (15.2, 52-53), 81 yrs. (NC)
LEE, Lu (S2 - 6.5, 2291-2312), c. 88 yrs., field (TX)
LEE, Mandy (9.4, 250), 85 yrs., house (AR)
LEE, Mary (9.4, 251), 74 yrs (AR via TX)
LEE, Mattie (11.8, 224-26), 75 yrs. (MO via LA, TX, and LA)
LEE, Randall (17.1, 194-203), 77 yrs., errands (FL via SC)
LEE, Sarah (S2 - 6.5, 2313-18), 94 yrs., nursemaid (TX)
LEE, Wes (11.8, 227-29) (MO)
LEGGETT, Walter (S2 - 6.5, 2319-24), c. 82 yrs. (TX via NC)
LEITNER, Ben (3.3, 100-02), 85 yrs. (SC)
LENNOX, Adeline (6.2, 120-22) (S1 - 5.1, 112-14), c. 87 yrs., field
    (IN via TN)
LEONARD, George (13.4, 261,67), non-slave (GA)
LESLIE, Mandy (6.1, 251-54), 77 yrs., field (AL)
LESTER, Angeline (16.4, 62-63), c. 90 yrs. (OH via GA)
LEWIS, Alice (16.3, 46-48), 84 yrs., house (MD via GA and NC)
LEWIS, Ben (S1 - 8.3, 1309-12), 77 yrs. (MS)
LEWIS, (Uncle) Cinto (5.3, 1-3) (S2 - 6.5, 2325-29), over 100 yrs.,
    field (TX)
LEWIS, Cudjoe (S1 - 1.1, 236-41), 99 yrs. (AL)
LEWIS, Dellie (6.1, 255-57) (S1 - 1.1, 242-47), field (AL)
LEWIS, Mrs. E. (S1 - 5.1, 115), 84 yrs. (IN via KY)
LEWIS, Eddie (S1 - 8.3, 1313-14), 77 yrs. (MS via AL)
LEWIS, Ellen (S1 - 8.3, 1315), over 90 yrs. (MS via AL)
LEWIS, Elvira (16.2, 112-15) (KY)
LEWIS, Ezekiel (S1 - 5.1, 243-44), tanner (IN via VA)
LEWIS, George (13.3, 47-50), 88 yrs. (GA via FL)
LEWIS, Hagar (5.3, 4-7) (S2 - 6.5, 2330-35), 82 yrs. (TX)
LEWIS, Henry (5.3, 8-13) (S2 - 6.5, 2336-48), c. 101 yrs., cowboy (TX)

LEWIS, John H. (S1 - 2.2, 65-68), 69 yrs., free (CO via KY)
LEWIS, Lavinia (S2 - 6.5, 2349-60) (TX)
LEWIS, Lucy (5.3, 14-16) (S2 - 6.5, 2361-68), personal servant (TX)
LEWIS, Perry (16.3, 49-50) (MD)
LEWIS, Tabitha (9.4, 252-54), 86 yrs. (AR via NC)
LEWIS, Thomas (6.2, 123-27), 80 yrs., field (IN via KY)
LEWIS, William (S1 - 4.2, 387-88), 83 yrs. (GA)
'LIGHTNIN' (6.1, 258-59) (S1 - 1.1, 248-49), 88 yrs., field (AL)
LINCOLN, Amos (5.3, 17-19) (S2 - 6.5, 2369-72), 85 yrs. (TX via LA)
LINDSAY, Abbie (9.4, 255-59), 84 yrs. (AR via LA)
LINDSAY, Mary (7.1, 178-86), 91 yrs., house (OK)
LINDSEY, Felix L. (S2 - 6.5, 2373-86), 90 yrs. (TX via KY)
LINDSEY, Rosa (9.4, 260-61), 83 yrs., house (AR via GA)
LIPSCOMB, Mary (3.3, 103-04), white (SC)
LITTLE, Annie (5.3, 20-23) (S2 - 6.5, 2387-98), 81 yrs. (TX via MS and
    MO)
LITTLE, Kate (S1 - 2.2, 69-71), 81 yrs. (CO via GA)
LITTLE, Westly (S1 - 8.3, 1316-23), c. 91 yrs., field (MS)
LITTLEJOHN, Chana (15.2, 55-59), 87 yrs. (NC)
LITTLEJOHN, Govan (3.3, 105-07), 87 yrs., field (SC)
LIVINGSTON, Abe (5.3, 24-25) (S2 - 6.5, 2399-2402), 83 yrs. (TX)
LOCKE, Sarah H. (6.2, 128-30), 78 yrs., field (IN via KY)
LOCKHART, Easter (3.3, 108-11), 80 yrs., field (SC)
LOCKLIER, Gable (3.3, 112-17), 86 yrs., field (SC)
LOCKRIDGE, Sue (S2 - 6.5, 2403-06), upper 70's (TX)
LOFTON, (Aunt) Minerva (9.4, 264-66), 69 yrs. (AR)
LOFTON, Robert (9.4, 267-73), 88 yrs., house (AR via GA)
LOGAN, John H. (9.4, 274-80), 88 yrs., house (AR)
LOGAN, Mattie (7.1, 187-91), 79 yrs., house (OK via MS)
LOMACK, Elvie (9.4, 281-83), 78 yrs., house (AR via TN)
LONG, Amos (S1 - 11.1, 27-32), c. 100 yrs., house (NC)
LONG, Ellen (WA via KY)
    See Miller, Mrs. Ellen (WA via KY)
LONG, Henry (9.4, 284-89), 71 yrs. (AR via KY)
LONG, Walter (3.3, 118-23), 83 yrs., field (SC)
LONG, Will (S2 - 6.5, 2407-15), 85 yrs., hired out (riverboat enter-
    tainer) (TX via TN)
LONGSLAUGHTER, Billy Abraham (6.1, 260-62) (S1 - 1.1, 250-53), 80 yrs.
    (AL via VA)
LONIAN, Moses (S1 - 12.1, 202-12), 80 yrs. (OK)
LOPER, Frank (S1 - 2.2, 72-73), over 85 yrs. (CO via TN)
LOUIS, Jane (S1 - 8.3, 1324-25), 86 yrs., house (MS)
LOUIS, Uncle (6.1, 263-67), field (AL)
LOVE, Annie (9.4, 290-91), c. 85 yrs., field (AR via VA and MS)
LOVE, John (5.3, 26-28) (S2 - 6.5, 2416-29); 7.6, 2431-43), 76 yrs.
    (TX)
LOVE, Kiziah (7.1, 192-99), 93 yrs., field (OK)
LOVE, Louis (5.3, 29-31) (S2 - 7.6, 2444-50), 91 yrs., house (TX via LA)
LOVE, Maria (S1 - 5.1, 116), free (IN via TN)
LOVE, Needham (9.4, 292-96), over 80 yrs., field (AR via MS)
LOVELY, Henry (S1 - 8.3, 1326), carpenter (MS via SC)
LOWDEN, Gillam (3.3, 124), 75 yrs., small child (SC)
LOWE, Sally (S1 - 8.3, 1327), over 100 yrs. (MS via VA)
LOWERY, Martha (S1 - 11.2, 239-43), 84 yrs., free (SC)
LOWRAN, Emma (3.3, 125), c. 80 yrs. (SC)
LOYD, Nellie (3.3, 126-29), 91 yrs., house (SC)

LUCAS, Daniel William (7.1, 200-02), 94 yrs., field (OK)
LUCAS, James (7.2, 91-99) (S1 - 8.3, 1328-48), 104 yrs., house (MS)
LUCAS, Louis (9.4, 297-303), 83 yrs. (AR via LA)
LUCKADO, Lizzie (9.4, 304-05), 71 yrs. (AR via MS)
LUCKETT, John(9.4, 306), 83 yrs., field (AR via MS)
LUMPKIN, Amie (3.3, 130-33), 88 yrs. (SC)
LUSTER, Bert (7.1, 203-06), 85 yrs., field (OK via TX and TN)
LYCURGAS, Edward (17.1, 204-11), 64 yrs., free (FL)
LYLES, Baalam (3.3, 134-35) (S1 - 11.2, 244-45), 74 yrs. (SC)
LYLES, Eison (3.3, 136-38), 73 yrs. (SC)
LYLES, Moses (3.3, 139-41), 81 yrs., field (SC)
LYNCH, John (9.4, 307-09), 69 yrs. (AR via TN)
LYNCH, John R. (S1 - 8.3, 1349), 90 yrs.(MS via LA)
LYNCH, Josephine Scott (9.4, 310), 69 yrs. (AR via TN)
LYONS, Phoebe (S1 - 5.2, 402-04), 83 yrs., field (OH via GA)
LYONS, Samuel (S1 - 5.2, 405-07), c. 90 yrs., field (OH via KY)

MCADAMS, Andy (S2 - 7.6, 2451-59) (TX)
MCADAMS, John (S2 - 7.6, 2460-77), c. 89 yrs., field (TX via TN)
MCALLILLEY, George (3.3, 142-45), 84 yrs. (SC)
MCALLISTER, Charity (15.2, 61-63), 95 yrs., field (NC)
MCALLUM, Sam (7.2, 100-12) (S1 - 9.4, 1350-66), 95 yrs., house (MS)
MCALPIN, Tom (6.1, 268-71), over 90 yrs., house (AL)
MCBEE, Lucy Pulliam (S1 - 9.4, 1367-69) (MS)
MCBLACKWELL, Elenora Lee (S1 - 9.4, 1370), 77 yrs. (MS via MD and VA)
MCCARTY, William H. (S1 - 9.4, 1371-79), 100 yrs., errands, chores,
    and house (MS)
MCCASTLE, Duncan (S1 - 9.4, 1380-82), 77 yrs. (MS)
MCCAY, Fannie (17.1, 377), 73 yrs. (FL)
MCCHRISTIAN, Bell (S1 - 9.4, 1383-86), c. 90 yrs., field (MS)
MCCINNEY, Alex (S1 - 9.4, 1387-92), 76 yrs., chores (MS)
MCCLAIN, Hettie (S1 - 5.1, 117-19), field (IN via KY)
MCCLENDON, Charlie (10.5, 1-3), 77 yrs., field (AR via VA)
MCCLENDON, Prince (S1 - 9.4, 1393), 87 yrs. (MS)
MCCLOUD, Lizzie (10.5, 4-8) (S1 - 2.1, 12) (S2 - 1.3, 99), c. 103 yrs.,
    field (AR via TN)
MCCOMMONS, Mirriam (13.3, 51-55), 76 yrs., field (GA)
MCCONICO, Dualena (10.5, 9-11), 49 yrs., free (AR)
MCCORMICK, Joe (S1 - 4.2, 389-93), over 85 yrs., house and field (GA)
MCCOWAN, Samuel (S2 - 1.10, 330-32), 79 yrs. (NE via MO)
MCCOY, Clara Cotton (15.2, 65-71), 82 yrs., house (NC)
MCCOY, Ike (10.5, 12-14), 68 yrs. (AR via NC)
MCCOY, John (5.3, 32-34) (S2 - 7.6, 2481-84), 99 yrs., field (TX)
MCCOY, Rachel (S1 - 4.2, 394-400), 74 yrs. (GA)
MCCRAY, Amanda (17.1, 212-17), c. 95 yrs., house (FL)
MCCRAY, Bill (5.3, 38-39) (S2 - 7.6, 2478-80), 86 yrs., cared for
    children (TX via FL)
MCCRAY, C.B. (5.3, 40-42), 76 yrs. (TX)
MCCRAY, Stephen (7.1, 207-09), 88 yrs., house (OK via AL)
MCCREE, Ed (13.3, 56-65), 76 yrs. (GA)
MCCROREY, Ed (3.3, 146-50), 82 yrs., field (SC)
MCCRORY, Henry Lawrence (S1 - 11.1, 33) (S2 - 1.15, 381-82), c. 73 yrs.
    (NC via SC)
MCCULLERS, Henrietta (15.2, 73-75), 87 yrs., field (NC)

MCCULLOUGH, Lucy (13.3, 66-70), 79 yrs., house (GA)
MCCULLOUGH, Willie (15.2, 77-81), 68 yrs., free (NC via SC)
MCDANIEL, Amanda (13.3, 71-75), 87 yrs., field (GA)
MCDANIEL, Richard W. (10.5, 15-16), 73 yrs. (AR via MS)
MCDONALD, Kate (S1 - 2.2, 74-76), 69 yrs. (CO via TN)
MCDONALD, John (S2 - 7.6, 2485-86), 77 yrs. (TX)
MCDONALD, William M. (S2 - 7.6, 2487-88), 75 yrs. (TX)
MCFARLAND, Hannah (7.1, 210-11), 85 yrs., house (OK via SC)
MCGADE, "Curley" (S2 - 7.6, 2490-91) (TX)
MCGAFFEY, Henry Louis (S1 - 9.4, 1394-1401), 84 yrs., house (MS via LA)
MCGEE, Perry (11.8, 230-37), 87 yrs., field (MO)
MCGHEE, Liza (S1 - 9.4, 1402-04), c. 90 yrs., spinning and weaving;
    field (MS)
MCGILLERY, Lee (S2 - 7.6, 2492-98), c. 105 yrs., field (TX via SC)
MCGILLERY, Rosie (S2 - 7.6, 2499-2505), c. 90 yrs., field (TX via SC)
MCGRUDER, Tom (13.3, 76-77), 102 yrs. (GA via VA)
MCGUIRE, John (11.8, 238-40), 74 yrs. (MO)
MCINTIRE, Thomas (S1 - 5.2, 408-13), 90 yrs., field (OH via VA)
MCINTOSH, Susan (13.3, 78-87), 87 yrs., house (GA)
MCINTOSH, Waters (10.5, 17-24), 76 yrs., field (AR via SC)
MCKAY, Martha (S1 - 9.4, 1405) (MS)
MCKEE, Jenny (16.2, 41-42), 85 yrs. (KY via TX)
MCKEEVER, Duncan (S2 - 10.9, 4349-52), 94 yrs., white (TX via NC)
MCKIMM, Kisey (16.4, 64-65), 83 yrs. (OH via KY)
MCKINLEY, Robert (6.2, 131-33), 88 yrs., field (IN via NC)
MCKINNEY, John (S1 - 9.4, 1406), personal servant (MS)
MCKINNEY, Matilda (13.3, 88-90), house (GA via TX)
MCKINNEY, Warren (10.5, 27-31), 85 yrs., field (AR via SC)
MCKLENNAN, Abe (S1 - 9.4, 1407-11), 90 yrs., heavy farm work (MS)
MCLEAN, James Turner (15.2, 83-89), 79 yrs. (NC)
MCLEOD, Jake (3.3, 157-63), 83 yrs., field (SC)
MCMILLAN, Thomas (16.4, 66-69) (OH via AL)
MCMULLEN, Mimy (S1 - 9.4, 1412), house (MS)
MCMULLEN, Victoria (10.5, 32-38) (S2 - 1.3, 100), 54 yrs., free
    (AR via LA)
MCMURTY, Uncle Sanford (Sanford Ford) (S1 - 9.4, 1413), 74 yrs. (MS)
MCNAIR, Chaney (S1 - 12.1, 213-28), 85 yrs., field (OK via GA)
MCNARY, Winfield (S2 - 1.3, 101), c. 108 yrs. (AR via TN)
MCNEESE, Marshall (S1 - 9.4, 1414) (MS)
MCNEIL, Bill (3.3, 164-66), 82 yrs. (SC)
MCQUEEN, Nap (5.3, 35-37) (S2 - 7.6, 2506-14), 80 yrs. (TX via TN)
MCRAY, Calvin Bell (S2 - 7.6, 2515-20), 76 yrs. (TX)
MCWHORTER, William (13.3, 91-103), 78 yrs. (GA)
MACK, Chaney (Chanie) (S1 - 9.4, 1415-29), 74 yrs. (MS)
MACK, Cresa (10.5, 25-26), 85 yrs., field (AR)
MACK, Marshall (7.1, 212-14), 83 yrs., house (OK via VA)
MACK, Richard (3.3, 151-56) (S2 - 1.15, 383-91), 104 yrs., spinner
    (SC via VA)
MACKS, Richard (16.3, 51-56), 87 yrs., field and stable work (MD)
MADDEN, Mannie P. (10.5, 39), 69 yrs., free (AR)
MADDEN, Perry (10.5, 40-46), 79 yrs., house (AR via AL)
MADDOX, Anne (6.1, 272-74), 113 yrs., field (AL via VA)
MADDOX, Jack (S2 - 7.6, 2521-50), 89 yrs., field (TX via GA)
    See Maddox, Rosa (TX)
MADDOX, Rosa (S2 - 7.6, 2521-50), 90 yrs., house (TX via MS)
    See Maddox, Jack (TX)

MADISON, Eliza (11.8, 241-42), 75 yrs. (MO)
MAGEE, Primous (S1 - 9.4, 1430-33), 78 yrs., light work around house
    (MS)
MAGRUDER, Tom (S1 - 5.1, 120-25) (IN via VA and KY)
MAGWOOD, Frank (15.2, 91-94), 73 yrs. (NC via SC)
MAJORS, John (S2 - 7.6, 2551-59), c. 85 yrs., house (TX via MS)
MALINDA (13.4, 219-20), house (GA)
MALLOY, Caroline (S1 - 4.2, 410-17), 96 yrs., house (GA)
MALONE, Julia (5.3, 43-44) (S2 - 7.6, 2560-65), 79 yrs., house (TX)
MALONE, Melea (S2 - 7.6, 2566-67), field (TX)
MALONE, Mollie (13.3, 104-07), c. 90 yrs., house (GA)
MANDY (6.1, 275-77), field (AL)
MANGUM, Rosa (S1 - 9.4, 1434-35), c. 106 yrs., house and field (MS)
MANN, Lewis (10.5, 47-48), 81 yrs., field (AR via TX)
MANN, Sarah (16.4, 70-71), 76 yrs. (OH via VA)
MANNING, Allen V. (7.1, 215-220), 87 yrs., field (OK via TX)
MANSON, Jacob (15.2, 96-99), 86 yrs. (NC)
MANSON, Roberta (15.2, 101-04), 74 yrs. (NC)
MANUEL, James J. (S1 - 2.2, 77-79), over 80 yrs. (CO via AR)
MANUEL, Millie (S2 - 7.6, 2568-71), c. 90 yrs. (TX)
MAPLES, Ella (S2 - 7.6, 2572-75), c. 72 yrs. (TX)
MARION, Andy (3.3, 167-71), 92 yrs., carriage driver (SC)
MARION, "Uncle" (S2 - 1.3, 142-77) (AR)
MARKHAM, Millie (15.2, 106-08), 82 yrs. (NC)
MARSH, O.A. (S2 - 10.9, 4353-58), 77 yrs., white (TX via MS)
MARSHAL, Ed (S1 - 4.2, 418-19), 89 yrs. (GA)
MARSHALL, Adeline (5.3, 45-47) (S2 - 7.6, 2576-80), field (TX via SC)
MARSHALL, Alonzo (S1 - 9.4, 1436-37) (MS)
MARSHALL, Milton (3.3, 172-75), 82 yrs., field (SC)
MARTIN, Angeline (10.5, 49-50), 80 yrs., field (AR via GA)
MARTIN, Charlotte (17.1, 166-67), 82 yrs. (FL)
MARTIN, Drucilla (11.8, 243-48), 102 yrs., carded wool and cotton (MO)
MARTIN, Dulcinda (S1 - 5.2, 414-17), 78 yrs. (OH via KY)
MARTIN, Eva (S2 - 7.6, 2581-88), 82 yrs., field (TX via LA)
MARTIN, Isaac (5.3, 48-61) (TX)
MARTIN, James (5.3, 62-64) (S2 - 7.6, 7589-94), 90 yrs., free
    (TX via VA)
MARTIN, Jim (S1 - 9.4, 1438-44), 80 yrs., carried water and milked
    cows (MS)
MARTIN, John (S1 - 9.4, 1445-47), personal servant and blacksmith (MS)
MARTIN, Josie (10.5, 51-52), 86 yrs., field (AR)
MARTIN, Marvel (S1 - 9.4, 1448), sheriff's trusted slave (MS)
MARTIN, Richard (11.8, 243-48), 92 yrs. (MO)
    See Martin, Drucilla (MO)
MARTIN, Scott (16.6, 40-42), 90 yrs., house (TN)
MARY (13.4, 215-16), 90 yrs. (GA)
MASON, Carrie (13.3, 108-14) (S1 - 4.2, 420-25), 90 yrs., field (GA)
MASON, Harriet (16.2, 9-11; 31-32), 90-100 yrs., house (KY)
MASON, Sam Meredith (S2 - 7.6, 2595-2601), 79 yrs. (TX)
MASON, Tom (S1 - 9.4, 1449), c. 74 yrs. (MS)
MATHEUS, John Williams (16.4, 72-73), 77 yrs. (OH via WV)
MATHEWS, Louis (5.3, 65-66) (S2 - 7.6, 2602-09), 83 yrs. (TX)
MATHEWS, Tom (S1 - 4.2, 426-27), over 85 yrs. (GA)
MATHEWS, William (5.3, 67-71) (S2 - 7.6, 2610-20), 89 yrs., house;
    carriage driver (TX via LA)
MATHIS, Beth (10.5, 53-54), 82 yrs., house (AR via MS)

MATHIS, E.M. (S1 - 1.1, 254), 81 yrs. (AL)
MATILDA (13.4, 217-18), c. 90 yrs., field (GA)
MATTHEWS, Ann (16.6, 43-46) (TN)
MATTHEWS, Caroline (10.5, 55-56), 79 yrs., field (AR via TX and MS)
MATTHEWS, Hattie (11.8, 249-51), 58 yrs., free (MO)
MATTHEWS, John (S1 - 9.4, 1450-60), 85 yrs., carried water and yard
   work (MS)
MATTHEWS, Maggie Whitehead (S2 - 7.6, 2621-26), 80 yrs. (TX)
MATTHEWS, Susan (13.3, 115-17), 84 yrs., house (GA)
MATTHEWS, Z.D. (S1 - 11.1, 34-35) (NC)
   See Rufe (NC)
MAUCHISON, Lucy C.F. (S2 - 7.6, 2627-33), 66 yrs., free (TX)
MAXWELL, Henry (17.1, 218-19), 77 yrs. (FL via GA)
MAXWELL, Malindy (10.5, 57-63), 80's, field (AR via MS)
MAXWELL, Nellie (10.5, 64-65), 63 yrs., free (AR)
MAY, Ann (10.5, 66-67), 82 yrs., house (AR)
MAY, Ann (S1 - 9.4, 1461-66), 90's, house (MS)
MAYES, Hiram (5.3, 72-74) (S2 - 7.6, 2634-38), c. 75 yrs. (TX)
MAYES, Joe (10.5, 68-69), 74 yrs. (AR via KY)
MAYFIELD, Bert (16.2, 13-17), c. 85 yrs., field (KY)
MAYNARD, Bob (7.1, 223-26), 79 yrs., house (OK via TX)
MAYS, Emily (13.3, 118-20), 75 yrs. (GA)
MAYS, Martha (S1 - 9.4, 1467-70), c. 84 yrs., house (MS via GA)
MAZIQUE, Alex (S1 - 9.4, 1471), house (MS)
MAZIQUE, (Dr.) J.C. (S1 - 9.4, 1471), non-slave (MS)
MEAD, William (S1 - 4.2, 428-32), 71 yrs. (GA)
MEADOW, Charlie (3.3, 176-81), 83 yrs. (SC)
MEADOWS, Louis (S1 - 1.1, 255-57), 84 yrs., field (AL via GA)
MEADOWS, Minerva (S1 - 1.1, 258-59), over 80 yrs., field (AL)
MEANS, Albert (3.3, 182-84), 91 yrs., field (SC)
MEANS, Andrew (3.3, 185-87), c. 80 yrs., young child (SC)
MEEK, Ned (S1 - 9.4, 1472) (MS)
MEEKS, Jesse (10.5, 70-71), 76 yrs. (AR)
MEEKS, Letha Taylor (11.8, 252-55) (MO via MS)
MELTON, Perry (S1 - 9.4, 1473), free (MS)
MENEFEE, Frank (6.1, 278-81), 84 yrs., field (AL)
MENTION, Liza (13.3, 121-25), 73 yrs. (GA)
MERCER, Rose (S1 - 12.1, 229), c. 118 yrs., house (OK via GA and LA)
MERCHANT, Harvey (S2 - 1.2, 18), c. 77 yrs. (AZ via TX)
MERRILL, Sarah E. (S1 - 5.1, 126-30), free (IN)
MERRIMAN, Frank (S1 - 9.4, 1474), 84 yrs. (MS)
MERRITT, Susan (5.3, 75-78) (S2 - 7.6, 2639-45), 87 yrs., spinning
   and loom work (TX)
MESSERSMITH, August (S1 - 2.4, 240-65), 92 yrs., house (MO)
   See Smith, August (MO)
METCALF, Jeff (10.5, 72-73), 75 yrs. (AR via MS)
METTS, Susan (S1 - 9.4, 1475), personal servant (MS)
MIALS, Maggie (15.2, 110-12), 78 yrs., house (NC)
MICKEY, Ann (S2 - 7.6, 2646-49), c. 90 yrs., house (TX)
MIDDLETON, Cassie (S2 - 7.6, 2650-53), field and spinning (TX)
MIDDLETON, (Uncle) John (S1 - 9.4, 1476-79), c. 120 yrs. (d. 1934)
   house (MS)
MIDDLETON, Kisanna (S1 - 9.4, 1480-81), c. 103 yrs., house (MS)
MIKE, Uncle (S1 - 11.2, 246-51) (SC)
MILES, Josh (5.3, 79-81) (S2 - 7.6, 2654-80), 78 yrs. (TX via VA)
MILES, July (S2 - 1.10, 333-37), 90 yrs. (NE via AL)

MILLEDGE, Annette (S1 - 4.2,, 433-37), 83 yrs., house (GA)
MILLEGAN, Jasper (13.4, 251-53) (GA)
   See Millegan, Rosa
MILLEGAN, Rosa (13.4, 251-53) (GA)
   See Millegan, Jasper
MILLER, Anna (5.3, 82-84) (S2 - 7.6, 2681-86), 85 yrs., chores
   (TX via KY and MO)
MILLER, Mrs. Ellen (Ellen Long) (S1 - 2.6, 283-84), c. 89 yrs.
   (WA via KY)
MILLER, George Washington (S1 - 9.4, 1482-97), 81 yrs., tended animals
   (MS via SC)
MILLER, Hardy (10.5, 74-77), 85 yrs., field and house (AR via GA)
MILLER, Harriet (13.3, 126-32), c. 100 yrs. (GA)
MILLER, Harriet (S1 - 9.4, 1498-1507), c. 78 yrs., house (MS)
MILLER, Henry Kink (10.5, 78-89), 86 yrs., field (AR via GA)
MILLER, Jason (3.3, 188-90), 77 yrs., young child (SC)
MILLER, Jeremiah (S1 - 9.4, 1508-09), 115 yrs., personal servant (MS)
MILLER, Lucinda (3.3, 191-93), 82 yrs., house (SC)
MILLER, Matilda (10.5, 90-92), 79 yrs., house (AR)
MILLER, Mintie Maria (5.3, 85-87) (S2 - 7.6, 2687-93), c. 86 yrs.,
   cook (TX via AL)
MILLER, Nathan (10.5, 93-94), 75 yrs. (AR)
MILLER, Richard (6.2, 134-36), 94 yrs., field (IN via KY)
MILLER, Sallie C. (10.5, 177-78), 83 yrs., field (AR via TN)
MILLER, Sam (10.5, 95-96), 98 yrs., field (AR via TX)
MILLER, Thomas Ezekiel (S2 - 1.15, 392-96), c. 89 yrs. (SC)
MILLER, W.D. (10.5, 97-99), 65 yrs., free (AR via NC)
MILLER, Wylie (11.8, 256-57), 83 yrs. (MO)
MILLETT, Harriet (S2 - 7.6, 2694-2701), 83 yrs., house (TX via MS)
MILLIE, Aunt (S1 - 1.1, 22-24) (AL)
MILLING, Cureton (3.3, 194-96), 80 yrs., house (SC)
MILLION, Eliza (S1 - 5.1, 131-32), 85 yrs., house (IN via KY)
MILLS, Tom (5.3, 88-106), 79 yrs. (TX via AL)
MILTON, Julia (S1 - 4.2, 438), 87 yrs. (GA)
MINGO, Sam (S1 - 9.4, 1806), field (MS)
   See Ree, Henry R. (MS)
MINTER, Fannie (S1 - 9.4, 1510), 94 yrs., house (MS)
MINTON, Gip (10.5, 100-02), 84 yrs., field (AR via AL)
MIRE, La San (5.3, 107-09) (S2 - 7.6, 2702-09), 86 yrs., oxcart
   driver (TX via LA)
MISHOW, Abbey (3.3, 197-99), c. 80 yrs., house (SC)
MITCHEL, Anna (15.2, 114-15), 76 yrs. (NC)
MITCHELL, A.J. (10.5, 103-10), 78 yrs., field (AR)
MITCHELL, Ann (S1 - 2.1, 13) (S2 - 1.3, 102), 68 yrs., free (AR via MS)
MITCHELL, Charley (5.3, 110-13) (S2 - 7.6, 2710-16), 85 yrs., house
   hired out (TX via VA)
MITCHELL, Christine Drummel (17.1, 226-28), 84 yrs. (FL)
MITCHELL, Cindy (S1 - 9.4, 1511), house (MS)
MITCHELL, Hattie (10.5, 111-12), 69 yrs. (AR via TN)
MITCHELL, Jeff (S1 - 9.4, 1512), 82 yrs. (d. 1936) (MS)
MITCHELL, John (S2 - 1.3, 103-04), 70 yrs., free (AR via TN)
MITCHELL, May (10.5, 113-19), 60 yrs., free (AR via TN)
MITCHELL, Melinda (S1 - 4.2, 439-44), over 85 yrs., house (GA)
MITCHELL, Mollie (13.3, 133-35), 85 yrs. (GA)
MITCHELL, Peter (5.3, 114-15) (S2 - 7.6, 2717-20), c. 76 yrs. (TX)
MITCHELL, Priscilla (17.1, 376), 78 yrs., field (FL)

MITCHELL, Sam (3.3, 200-04), 87 yrs., field (SC)
MITCHELL, Scott (16.2, 76-77), 70's, house (KY)
MITCHNER, Patsy (15.2, 117-23), 84 yrs. (NC)
MOBLEY, Bob (13.3, 136-38) (S1 - 4.2, 445-52), c. 90 yrs., house (GA)
MONROE, Roy (S1 - 5.1, 133-34), over 80 yrs. (IN via LA)
MONROE, Woodford (S1 - 5.1, 135-37), over 70 yrs., free (IN via KY)
MONTGOMERY, Adeline (S1 - 9.4, 1513-21), c. 78 yrs., house (MS via AL)
MONTGOMERY, Alex (S1 - 9.4, 1522-31), 80 yrs., field helper (MS via GA)
MONTGOMERY, Isaiah T. (S1 - 9.4, 1532-47), 77 yrs. (d. 1924), office
   work (MS)
MONTGOMERY, J.P.T. (S1 - 9.4, 1548-49), 59 yrs. (d.1913) (MS)
MONTGOMERY, Jane (7.1, 227-29), 80 yrs., house (OK via LA)
MONTGOMERY, Laura (S1 - 9.4, 1550-59), c. 87 yrs., weaving and spinning
   (MS)
MONTGOMERY, Rube (S1 - 9.4, 1560-64), 86 yrs., house and field (MS)
MOODY, Andrew (5.3, 116-17) (S2 - 7.6, 2721-25), c. 82 yrs., field (TX)
MOODY, Dave (S1 - 9.4, 1565) (MS via VA)
MOODY, Tildy (S2 - 7.6, 2726-28), c. 78 yrs. (TX)
MOORE, Almont M. ("Mount") (5.3, 118-20) (S2 - 7.6, 2729-35), c. 91
   yrs., field (TX)
MOORE, Ben (S1 - 5.1, 138-40) (IN)
MOORE, Charity (3.3, 205-08), 75 yrs. (SC)
MOORE, Charlotte (S1 - 9.4, 1566), house (MS)
MOORE, Crozier ("Crow") (S1 - 9.4, 1567-68), 88 yrs., house (MS)
MOORE, Emeline (15.2, 125-26), 80 yrs., field (NC)
MOORE, Emma (10.5, 120-22), 80 yrs. (AR)
MOORE, Fannie (15.2, 128-37), 88 yrs. (NC)
MOORE, Jerry (5.3, 121-24), 89 yrs. (TX)
MOORE, John (S1 - 5.1, 141-45), 89 yrs. (IN via TN)
MOORE, John (5.3, 125-27) (S2 - 7.6, 2736-42), 84 yrs. (TX via LA)
MOORE, (Rev.) John (16.6, 47-48) (TN via GA)
MOORE, Laura (S2 - 7.6, 2743-47), 86 yrs., loom work (TX)
MOORE, Lindsey (17.1, 229-33), 87 yrs., cleaning and spinning cotton
   (FL via GA)
MOORE, Mrs. (18.1, 36, 38-40)
MOORE, Patsy (10.5, 123-24), 74 yrs. (AR via TN)
MOORE, Riley (S1 - 9.4, 1569-72), c. 85 yrs. (MS)
MOORE, Sena (3.3, 209-12), 83 yrs. (SC)
MOORE, Van (5.3, 128-31) (S2 - 7.6, 2748-53), c. 79 yrs. (TX via VA)
MOORE, Vina (S2 - 7.6, 2754-63), c. 92 yrs., cook (TX via MS)
MOORE, William (5.3, 132-37) (S2 - 7.6, 2764-73), c. 82 yrs., shepherd
   (TX via AL)
MOOREHEAD, Ada (10.5, 125-26), 82 yrs. (AR via AL)
MOOREMAN, Mattie (10.5, 127-35), 90 yrs., house (AR via KY)
MOORMAN, (Rev.) Henry Clay (6.2, 137-40), 83 yrs., field (IN via KY)
MORELAND, Elsie (S1 - 4.2, 453-51), 85 yrs. (GA)
MORGAN, America (6.2, 141-44), 85 yrs., house (IN via KY)
MORGAN, Anna (S1 - 11.2, 252) (SC)
MORGAN, Annie (16.2, 103-04), 65 yrs. (KY)
MORGAN, Evelina (10.5, 136-40), 81 yrs., house (AR via NC)
MORGAN, Isaam (6.1, 282-85) (S1 - 1.1, 260-65), 84 or 102 yrs., house
   (AL via MS)
MORGAN, Jane (10.5, 141-44), 65 yrs., free (AR)
MORGAN, (Aunt) Jane (S1 - 9.4, 1573-78), 106 yrs., house (MS)
MORGAN, Olivia (10.5, 145-47), 62 yrs., free (AR)
MORGAN, Tom (10.5, 148-51), 71 yrs. free (AR)

MORGAN, (Uncle) Tony (6.1, 286-88) (S1 - 1.1, 471-75), c. 105 yrs.
  (1884), (AL)
MORING, Richard (15.2, 139-42), 86 yrs. (NC)
MORRIS, Charlie (10.5, 219-20), 81 yrs., house (AR)
MORRIS, Emma (10.5, 152-54), 71 yrs. (AR)
MORRIS, Joe (S1 - 11.2, 253-57) (SC)
MORRIS, Tom (S1 - 9.4, 1579-91), c. 82 yrs., house (MS via VA)
MORRISON, George (6.2, 145-46A) (S1 - 5.1, 146-47), over 80 yrs.,
  house and field (IN via KY)
MORROW, Mandy (5.3, 138-41) (S2 - 7.6, 2774-79), 80 yrs. (TX)
MORSE, Peyton (S1 - 9.4, 1592-94) (MS via VA)
  See Morse, Rose (MS)
MORSE, Rose (S1 - 9.4, 1592-94) (MS)
  See Morse, Peyton (MS via VA)
MOSE, Uncle (6.1, 289-93), over 80 yrs., house (AL)
MOSELEY, Mrs. Alex (S2 - 1.1, 105-06), 75 yrs. (AR)
MOSELEY, John Archie (S1 - 9.4, 1595-96), 73 yrs. (MS)
MOSES, Charlie (7.2, 113-18) (S1 - 9.4, 1597-1603), 84 yrs., field (MS)
MOSES, Mary (S2 - 3.2, 933-36) (TX)
  See Cormier, Valmar (TX via LA)
MOSES, Patsy (5.3, 142-44) (S2 - 7.6, 2780-94), 74 yrs. (TX)
MOSLEY, John (S2 - 7.6, 2795-2809), 87 yrs., field and carriage
  driver (TX)
MOSELY, Joseph (6.2, 147-49), 84 yrs., field (IN via KY)
MOSLEY, Rose (S1 - 2.1, 14-16), 70 yrs. (AR via KY)
MOSLEY, Sam (S1 - 9.4, 1604-05), 75 yrs. (MS)
MOSS, Andrew (16.6, 49-54) (TN via GA)
MOSS, Claiborne (10.5, 155-66), 81 yrs., field (AR via GA)
MOSS, Frozie (10.5, 167-68), 69 yrs. (AR via MS)
MOSS, Mollie (16.6, 55-59), c. 83 yrs., field (TN)
MOSS, Mose (10.5, 169), 65 yrs., free (AR)
MOUTON, Leo (S2 - 7.6, 2810-15), 73 yrs. (TX via LA)
MOYE, Calvin (S2 - 7.6, 2816-73), 95 yrs., blacksmith (TX via GA)
MULLEN, Mack (17.1, 234-41), 79 yrs. (FL via GA)
MULLINS, Hannah (S2 - 7.6, 2874-79), 81 yrs. (TX)
MULLINS, S.O. (10.5, 170-72), 80 yrs., field (AR via AL)
MUMFORD, Matilda (S1 - 4.2, 462-64), 92 yrs., field (GA)
MUNDY, Lewis (11.8, 258-60) (S1 - 2.4, 205-07), over 85 yrs., field
  (MO via VA)
MUNSON, Melissa (S1 - 9.4, 1606-07), 101 yrs. (MS)
MURDOCK, Alex (10.5, 173-74), 65 yrs., free (AR via MS)
MURPHY, Hannah (S1 - 4.2, 465-69), 80 yrs., field (GA)
MURPHY, Malinda (11.8, 261-62), 80 yrs., field (MO)
MURPHY, Sally (6.1, 294-96) (S1 - 1.1, 266-69), c. 82 yrs., house (AL)
MURRAY, George W. (S1 - 11.2, 258-60) (SC)
MURRAY, Henrietta (S1 - 9.4, 1608-12), 84 yrs., helped care for slave
  children (MS)
MURRAY, Henry (S1 - 9.4, 1613-17), 97 yrs., keep birds from crops
  (MS via AL)
MYERS, Bessie (10.5, 175-76), c. 50 yrs., free (AR)
MYERS, Betty (S1 - 2.1, 17-18) (S2 - 1.3, 107-08) (AR)
MYERS, Elbert (S1 - 9.4, 1618-21), 86 yrs., house and yard work (MS)
MYLES, Nettie (S1 - 4.2, 470), 92 yrs. (GA via AL)
MYREX, Griffin (10.5, 179-83), 77 yrs. (AR via OK)

NANCE, Sara (S1 - 4.2, 471-72), 84 yrs. (GA)
NAPIER, Florence (S2 - 7.6, 2880-83), 79 yrs. (TX)
NAPOLEON, Louis (17.1, 242-48), 79 yrs., gathered eggs (FL)
NASH, Joe (S1 - 2.4, 208-11), 78 yrs. (MO via KS)
NAVE, Cornelius Neely (S1 - 12.1, 234-37), 69 yrs., free (OK)
NEAL, Peter (S1 - 5.1, 148-49), 83 yrs. (IN via KY)
NEALY, Sally (10.5, 184-87), 91 yrs., house (AR via TX)
NEALY, Wylie (10.5, 188-93), 85 yrs., field (AR via SC)
NECAISE, Henri (Henry) (7.2, 119-24) (S1 - 9.4, 1622-35), 105 yrs.,
  tended animals (MS)
NEEDHAM, W.S., Jr. (S2 - 10.9, 4359-70), 83 yrs., white (TX via AL)
NEELY, Sally (S2 - 7.6, 2884-89), c. 94 yrs., field and house (TX via
  MS)
NEIGHTON, William (17.1, 366-67), field (FL)
NEILL, Louis (S2 - 7.6, 2890-91), 77 yrs. (TX)
NELSON, Andy (5.3, 145-47) (S2 - 7.6, 2892-96), 76 yrs. (TX)
NELSON, Arch Wesley (S2 - 1.3, 109-11), 85 yrs. (AR via AL)
NELSON, Bell (S2 - 7.6, 2897-99), 76 yrs. (TX)
NELSON, Fran (10.5, 203-04), 77 yrs., house (AR via MS)
NELSON, Henry (10.5, 197-202), 70 yrs. (AR via TN)
NELSON, Ida (S2 - 7.6, 2900-01), 71 yrs., free (TX)
NELSON, James Henry (10.5, 205-07), 83 yrs., house (AR via AL)
NELSON, John (10.5, 208), 76 yrs. (AR)
NELSON, Julius (15.2, 144-46), 77 yrs., field (NC)
NELSON, Lottie (10.5, 209), 55 yrs., free (AR)
NELSON, Mattie (10.5, 210), 72 yrs. (AR)
NELSON, (Rev.) Oliver (S1 - 5.1, 150), free (IN)
NELSON, Silas (3.3, 213), 74 yrs. (SC)
NELSON, Susan (3.3, 214-16), 80 yrs., house (SC)
NELSON, William (16.4, 74-76), 88 yrs. (OH via MO)
NESBITT, Israel (S1 - 11.2, 261-63), free (SC)
NETTLES, Hattie Anne (6.1, 297-98) (S1 - 1.1, 270-71), 80 yrs.
  (AL via GA)
NEWBORN, Dan (10.5, 211-12), 78 yrs. (AR via TN)
NEWELL, Tom (S1 - 9.4, 1636-37), 104 yrs. (MS)
NEWMAN, Virginia (5.3, 148-51) (S2 - 7.6, 2902-08), c. 113 yrs., free
  (TX via LA)
NEWSOM, Sallie (10.5, 213-15), c. 75 yrs. (AR via MS and GA)
NEWTON, George (S2 - 7.6, 2909-10), c. 71 yrs., free (TX via AR and LA)
NEWTON, Pete (10.5, 216-18), 83 yrs., field (AR via TX)
NICHOLS, Lila (15.2, 148-50), 89 yrs., field (NC)
NICHOLS, Pierce (S2 - 7.6, 2911-14) (TX)
NICKENS, Margaret (11.8, 263-65) (S1 - 2.4, 213-14), c. 85 yrs.,
  nursemaid (MO)
NICKERSON, Jim (S1 - 9.4, 1638) (MS)
  See Nickerson, Sally (MS)
NICKERSON, Margaret (17.1, 250-56), c. 90 yrs., field (FL)
NICKERSON, Mary (S2 - 8.7, 2915-19), upper 90's, dairy helper
  (TX via LA)
NICKERSON, Sally (S1 - 9.4, 1638) (MS)
  See Nickerson, Jim (MS)
NILLIN, Margrett (5.3, 152-53) (S2 - 8.7, 2920-26), 90 yrs., personal
  servant (TX)

NIX, Fanny (13.3, 139-42), c. 87 yrs., house (GA)

NIX, Henry (13.3, 143-45), 89 yrs. (GA)

NORFLEET, Lizzie (S1 - 9.4, 1639-51), carried water and helped gin cotton (MS)

NORMAN, Fannie (S2 - 8.7, 2927-31), 78 yrs. (TX)

NORRIS, Isom (S2 - 8.7, 2932-38), c. 90 yrs., tannery work and house (TX via SC)

NORRIS, Mr. (S1 - 2.3, 118-21), over 80 yrs., field (MN)

NORTHCROSS, Rev. W.E. (6.1, 299-305), 97 yrs., field (AL)

NORTON, Annie (S2 - 8.7, 2939-42), 84 yrs. (TX via GA)

NORTON, Hester (S1 - 9.4, 1652-54), 80 yrs., fed chickens; waited table; helped weave (MS)

NORWOOD, Glascow (S1 - 9.4, 1655-58), c. 85 yrs., odd jobs (MS)

NORWOOD, Isaiah (S2 - 8.7, 2943-52), 85 yrs., field; herdsman (TX via TN)

NUNN, Aaron (S2 - 8.7, 2953-58), 81 yrs., house (TX)

NUNN, (General) Jefferson Davis (S1 - 1.1, 278-85), 75 yrs. (AL via VA)

OATS, Emma (10.5, 221-25), over 90 yrs., house (AR via MO)

OATS, Will (16.2, 18-20), 84 yrs., yard chores (KY)

OCKLBARY, Julia Grimes Jones (S2 - 8.7, 2959-67), 82 yrs. (TX)

ODELL, Andy (16.6, 60-61), c. 96 yrs. (TN)

ODOM, Charley (S2 - 8.7, 2968-71), 84 yrs., field (TX)

ODOM, Helen (10.5, 226-27), 30 yrs., free (AR)

ODOM, Sara
    See Odom, Helen (AR)

O'DONNELL, (Mrs.) James (S2 - 1.10, 338-39), 74 yrs. (NE via MO)

O'DONNELL, Sarah (S1 - 5.1, 151-52), 107 yrs., field (IN via KY)

OGEE, John (5.3, 154-56) (S2 - 8.7, 2972-77), 96 yrs., field (TX via LA)

OGLETREE, Lewis (13.3, 146-48), 88 yrs., house (GA)

O'HARA, Cynthia (S1 - 5.1, 153-54) (IN via KY)

"OLE BILL" (female) (S2 - 1.3, 112-14), nursemaid (AR)

OLIVER, Amanda (7.1, 230-32), 80 yrs., house (OK via MO and TX)

OLIVER, Jane (10.5, 228-29), 81 yrs., house (AL via MS)

OLIVER, Joe (S2 - 8.7, 2978-88), c. 90 yrs., mill helper (TX)

OLIVER, Mark (S1 - 9.4, 1659-71), 81 yrs., tended cows (MS)

OLIVER, Solomon (7.1, 233-35), 78 yrs., field (OK via MS)

OLIVER, William (3.3, 217-20) (SC)

ORFORD, Richard (13.3, 149-52), 95 yrs., house (GA)

ORGAN, Martha (15.2, 152-54), 61 yrs., free (NC)

OSBORNE, Annie (5.3, 157-59) (S2 - 8.7, 2989-95), 81 yrs., house (TX via GA)

OSBORNE, (Uncle) Harve (S2 - 1.3, 115-16), 101 yrs. (1926), livestock work (AR via NC)

OSBORNE, Ivory (10.5, 230-31), 85 yrs., field (AR via TX)

OSBROOK, Jane (10.5, 232-33), 90 yrs., house (AR)

OVERSTREET, Horace (5.3, 160-61) (S2 - 8.7, 2996-99), c. 82 yrs., ranch hand (TX)

OVERTON, Eliza (11.8, 266-68) (S1 - 2.4, 215-18), c. 88 yrs. (MO via TN)

OVERTON, Mary (5.3, 162-64) (S2 - 8.7, 3000-05), over 100 yrs., house (TX via TN)

OWEN, George (S1-4.2, 476-77), 81 yrs. (GA)
OWENS, A.F. (S1-1.1, 286-88), 73 yrs. (AL)
OWENS, George (5.3, 165-70), 84 yrs. (TX)
OWENS, Henry (S2 - 8.7, 3006-13), 94 yrs., field (TX)
OWENS, Joana (16.2, 46-47), c. 90 yrs., field (KY)
OWENS, (Rev.) Wade (6.1, 306-08), 74 yrs. (AL)
OXNER, Albert (3.3, 221-22), 75 yrs. (SC)

PAGE, Annie (10.5, 234-39), 85 yrs., house (AR)
PAGE, Sid (S1 - 9.4, 1672) (MS)
PALMER, Ann (3.3, 223-25), 90 yrs. (SC)
PARHAM, Dolph (S1 - 1.1, 289), 85 yrs., cow driver (AL)
PARHAM, Maria (S1 - 9.4, 1673-76), hired out for field work (MS via
  TN)
PARISH, Douglas (17.1, 257-62), 86 yrs., field and stable boy (FL)
PARKER, Ann (15.2, 156-57), c. 104 yrs. (NC)
PARKER, Caesar (S1 - 9.4, 1677), c. 99 yrs. (1913), cook (MS)
PARKER, Fannie (10.5, 240-41), 90 yrs., field (AR)
PARKER, J.M. (10.5, 242-48), 76 yrs. (AR via SC)
PARKER, Jim (S2 - 8.7, 3014-16), over 100 yrs., field (TX)
PARKER, Judy (10.5, 249-54), 77 yrs. (AR)
PARKER, Laura Ramsey (16.6, 62-63), 87 yrs. (TN)
PARKER, Molly (6.1, 309-10) (S1 - 1.1, 290-91), 85 yrs., house (AL via
  VA)
PARKER, R.F. (10.5, 255-56), 76 yrs. (AR)
PARKER, Will (S2 - 8.7, 3017-21), 95 yrs., house and shepherd (TX via
  GA)
PARKES, Anna (13.3, 153-64), 86 yrs. (GA)
PARKS, Annie (10.5, 257-61), 80 yrs., field (AR via LA)
PARNELL, Austin   (10.5, 262-72), 73 yrs. (AR via MS)
PARR, Ben (10.5, 273-75), 85 yrs., house (AR via TN)
PARROTT, Richard (S1 - 5.1, 155-58), over 80 yrs. (IN via KY)
PATE, Charlotte (S1 - 5.2, 418-19), free (OH via VA)
PATTERSON, Amy Elizabeth (6.2, 150-52), 87 yrs., house (IN via KY)
PATTERSON, Delicia Ann Wiley (11.8, 269-76), 92 yrs., house (MO)
PATTERSON, Frances (S1 - 9.4, 1678-81), 84 yrs., carried food to field
  slaves (MS via GA)
PATTERSON, Frank A. (10.5, 276-83), 88 yrs., field (AR via NC)
PATTERSON, George (3.3 226-30), c. 90 yrs., field (SC)
PATTERSON, Haywood (S1 - 5.1, 159), free (IN)
PATTERSON, John (10.5, 284-85), 74 yrs. (AR via KY)
PATTERSON, Mrs. Mary Anne (5.3, 171-72) (S2 - 8.7, 3022-25), c. 100
  yrs., field; loom; wet nurse (TX via LA)
PATTERSON, Sam (S1 - 9.4, 1682-83), plowed (MS via NC)
PATTERSON, Sarah (S1 - 9.4, 1684-85), house (MS)
PATTERSON, Sarah Jane (10.5, 286-91), 90 yrs., house (AR via GA)
PATTILLE, Solomon P. (10.5, 292-96), 76 yrs. (AR)
PATTILLO, G.W. (13.3, 165-70), 85 yrs., field (GA)
PATTON, Carry Allen (10.5, 297-99), 71 yrs. (AR via TN)
PATTON, Grundy (S1 - 9.4, 1686), 70 yrs., non-slave (MS)
PATTON, Lindy (6.1, 311), 96 yrs., field (AL)
PATTON, Martha (5.3, 173-76), 91 yrs., field (TX via AL)
PATTON, Ned (S1 - 9.4, 1687), tanner (MS)
PAUL, Sallie (3.3, 231-47), 79 yrs., house (SC via NC)

PAULS, Jessie (S2 - 8.7, 3031-38), 79 yrs. (TX)
PAXTON, William (S2 - 8.7, 3026-30), 107 yrs., field (TX via TN)
PAYNE, Ellen (5.3, 177-79) (S2 - 8.7, 3039-43), 88 yrs., tended ani-
    mals (TX)
PAYNE, Elsie (S1 - 1.1, 292-94), over 90 yrs., house (AL via GA)
PAYNE, Harriet (10.5, 300-03), 83 yrs. (AR via TX)
PAYNE, Jack (S2 - 8.7, 3044-46), 93 yrs., field (TX)
PAYNE, John (10.5, 304-05), 74 yrs. (AR via GA)
PAYNE, Larkin (10.5, 306-07), 85 yrs., field (AR via NC)
PEALE, Andrew (S1 - 9.4, 1688-89) (MS)
PEARL, Billy (S1 - 9.4, 1690) (MS)
PEARSON, Bevelina (S1 - 11.2, 264-67) (SC)
PEEK, Anna (S1 - 4.2, 478-83), over 90 yrs., field (GA via NC)
PENDERGRASS, Lina Anne (3.3, 248-50), 82 yrs., house (SC)
PENNY, Amy (15.2, 159-61), field (NC via VA)
PERKINS, Cella (10.5, 308-10), 67 yrs., free (AR via GA)
PERKINS, Henderson (5.3, 180-82) (S2 - 8.7, 2047-53), c. 85 yrs.,
    mill worker (TX via TN)
PERKINS, Lu (S2 - 8.7, 3054-70), mid-80's, spinning (TX via MS)
PERKINS, Maggie (10.5, 311-14), c. 81 yrs. (AR)
PERKINS, Rachel (10.5, 315-17) (AR via AL)
PERKINS, Sarah (S2 - 8.7, 3071-77), 88 yrs. (TX via TN)
PERRIER, (Rev.) John (S2 - 8.7, 3078-81), mid-70's (TX via LA)
PERRY, Amy (3.3, 215-55), 82 yrs. (SC)
PERRY, Dinah (10.5, 318-21), 78 yrs. (AR via AL)
PERRY, Lily (15.2, 163-66), 84 yrs., house (NC)
PERRY, Noah (S1 - 12.1, 238-48), 81 yrs. (OK via GA)
PERRY, Rob (3.3, 256-59), 73 yrs. (SC)
PERRY, Valley (15.2, 168-72), 50 yrs., free (NC)
PERRY, Victoria (3.3, 260-62), 80 yrs. (SC)
PERRYMAN, Patsy (S1 - 12.1, 249-53), 80 yrs. (OK)
PETERS, Alfred (10.5, 322-23), 78 yrs. (AR)
PETERS, Mary Estes (10.5, 325-31), 78 yrs. (AR via MO)
PETERSON, John (10.5, 332-33), 80 yrs. (AR via LA)
PETHY, Marilda (11.8, 277-82), 80 yrs. (MO via VA)
PETITE, Phyllis (7.1, 236-41), 83 yrs., field (OK via TX)
PETTIS, Louise (10.5, 334-37), 59 yrs., free (AR)
PETTUS, Henry C. (10.5, 338-43), 80 yrs., field (AR via GA)
PETTUS, Joe (S1 - 9.4, 1691-92), c. 80 yrs., carriage driver (MS)
PETTY, John (3.3, 263-67), 87 yrs., field (SC)
PETTY, William (S1 - 9.4, 1693), carriage driver (MS)
PHILLIPS, Daniel (5.3, 183-84), 83 yrs. (TX)
PHILLIPS, Dolly, (10.5, 344), 67 yrs. (AR)
PHILLIPS, Rebecca (S1 - 9.4, 1694-98), house (MS)
PHILLIPS, Simon (6.1, 312-15), 90 yrs., house (AL)
PHOENIX, Katie (S2 - 8.7, 3082-86), 80 yrs., house (TX via LA)
PICKETT, Century (S1 - 9.4, 1699), c. 90 yrs. (MS via AL)
PICKETT, Lee (S2 - 8.7, 3087-91), c. 78 yrs. (TX via LA)
PIERCE, Lee (5.3, 185-87) (S2 - 8.7, 3092-97), 87 yrs., nurse (hired
    out) (TX)
PIERNAS, Louis Joseph (S1 - 9.4, 1700-09), 81 yrs., free (MS)
PIGGY, Tony (10.5, 345-46), 75 yrs. (AR via MS and AL)
PINKARD, Maggie (S1 - 12.1, 254-59), 80 yrs., house (OK via TN)
PINNACLE, (Rev.) Aaron (S1 - 11.2, 268-71), 45 yrs., free (SC)
PITMAN, Spear (S1 - 5.1, 160-64) (IN via NC)
    See Battle, Anthony (IN)

PITTMAN, Ella (10.5, 347-50), 85 yrs., house (AR via SC)
PITTMAN, Sarah (10.5, 351-54), 82 yrs., house (AR via LA)
PITTS, Celeste (S1 - 4.2, 484-85), 85 yrs., house (GA)
PITTS, Dempsey (S1 - 9.4, 1710-24), 106 yrs., carriage driver (MS via NC)
PITTS, Roxy (6.1, 316-17) (S1 - 1.1, 295-96), c. 82 yrs. (AL)
PITTS, Tempe (15.2, 174-76), 91 yrs. (NC)
PLEASANT, Louvinia Young (S2 - 8.7, 3098-3104), 86 yrs., house and field (TX)
PLUMMER, Hannah (15.2, 178-82), 81 yrs. (NC)
PLUMMER, Nat (S1 - 9.4, 1725-26), 96 yrs. (MS via TN)
POCHE, Cora (S1 - 9.4, 1727-30), 71 yrs., free (MS via LA)
POE, Mary (10.5, 355-56), 60 yrs., free (AR)
POE, Matilda (7.1, 242-44), 80 yrs., house (OK via INDIAN TERRITORY)
POINDEXTER, Allen (S1 - 9.4, 1731), 81 yrs., carpenter (MS)
POINDEXTER, Sarah (3.3, 268-70), 87 yrs. (SC)
POINSETTE, Fred (S1 - 11.2, 272-73), 75 yrs. (SC)
POLITE, Sam (3.3, 271-76), 93 yrs., field (SC)
POLK, Ellen (5.3, 188-89), 83 yrs. (TX)
POLK, James (S2 - 8.7, 3105-12), 87 yrs., field (TX)
POLK, Lizzie (S1 - 9.4, 1732-34), 87 yrs., house (MS)
POLK, Nelson (S1 - 5.1, 165-68), c. 108 yrs., field (IN via TN and NC)
POLLACKS, W.L. (10.5, 357-58), 68 yrs. (AR via TN)
POLLARD, Carrie (6.1, 318-19), 78 yrs. (AL)
POLLARD, Melinda (S2 - 8.7, 3113-16), house (TX via MS)
POLLARD, Rosa L. (S2 - 8.7, 3117-28), 93 yrs., house and field (TX via OH)
POMPEY, Nettie (S1 - 5.1, 169-70) (IN via LA)
POOL, Parker (15.2, 184-91), 91 yrs., house (NC)
POOLE, Irene (6.1, 320-22), 85 yrs., field (AL)
POPE, Alec (13.3, 171-77), 84 yrs., field (GA)
POPE, (Doc) John (10.5, 359-61), 87 yrs. (AR via MS)
PORTER, Ophelia (S2 - 8.7, 3129-33) (TX via AL)
PORTER, William (10.5, 362-63), 81 yrs. (AR via TN)
POSEY, Elsie (S1 - 9.4, 1735-38), 98 yrs. (MS)
POTTER, Bob (10.5, 364-66), 65 yrs., free (AR)
POTTER, Isaac (S1 - 9.4, 1739-46), c. 86 yrs., cared for animals (MS)
POWELL, Jim (S1 - 4.2, 486), 86 yrs., field (GA via NC)
POWELL, Salem (S1 - 9.4, 1747-49), c. 80 yrs., cared for animals (MS)
POWERS, Betty (5.3, 190-92) (S2 - 8.7, 3134-42), 80 yrs., house (TX)
POWERS, Charlie (S1 - 9.4, 1750-54), c. 86 yrs. (MS)
POWERS, Tillie R. (5.3, 193-94) (S2 - 8.7, 3143-48), 77 yrs. (TX via NC and OK)
PRATHER, Georgia A. (S1 - 4.2, 487-88), 82 yrs. (GA)
PRATT, William (3.3, 277-79), 77 yrs. (SC)
PRAYER, Louise (10.5, 367-68), 80 yrs. (AR)
PRESTON, Mrs. (6.2, 153-54), 83 yrs., house and field (IN via KY)
PRETTY, George (17.1, 262-78), 84 yrs., free (FL via PA)
PRICE, Allen (5.3, 195-96) (S2 - 8.7, 3149-60), 75 yrs. (TX)
PRICE, Andrew (S1 - 9.4, 1755-57), 76 yrs. (MS)
PRICE, Annie (13.3, 178-84), 82 yrs. (GA)
PRICE, Dick (S1 - 9.4, 1758), 88 yrs. (MS)
PRICE, John (5.3, 197-200) (S2 - 8.7, 3161-65), 80 yrs. (TX via LA)
PRICE, (Rev.) Lafayette (5.3, 201-04) (S2 - 8.7, 3166-83), upper 80's (TX via LA and AL)
PRINCE, John (S1 - 9.4, 1759), 104 yrs., personal servant (MS)

PRINGLE, "Uncle Ike" (S1 - 9.4, 1760-65), 96 yrs., personal servant
    (MS)
PRISTELL, Henry (3.3, 280-82), 83 yrs. (SC)
PROBASCO, Henry (5.3, 205-07) (S2 - 8.7, 3184-91), 79 yrs. (TX)
PROCTOR, Jenny (5.3, 208-17), 87 yrs., field (TX via AL)
PROUT, Robert (S2 - 8.7, 3192-99), 87 yrs., field (TX via AL)
PRUITT, A.C. (5.3, 218-21) (S2 - 8.7, 3200-06), 76 yrs. (TX via LA)
PRYOR, Elsie (S1 - 12.1, 260-64), 81 yrs. (OK)
PUGH, J.L. (S1 - 12.1, 265-66), 63 yrs., free (OK via MS)
PUGH, (Aunt) Nicey (6.1, 323-25) (S1 - 1.1, 297-304), 85 yrs., house
    (AL)
PULLEN, Andres (S2 - 8.7, 3207-12) (TX)
PULLIN, Beverly (S1 - 4.2, 489-94), over 90 yrs. (GA)
PYE, Charlie (13.3, 185-88), 81 yrs. (GA)
PYLES, Henry F. (7.1, 245-56), 81 yrs., field (OK via TN)
PYRON, Lula (S1 - 4.2, 495-96), over 85 yrs., field (GA)

QUARLS, Harre (5.3, 222-24) (S2 - 8.7, 3213-16), 96 yrs., field
    (TX via MO)
QUATTLEBAUM, Junius (3.3, 283-86), 84 yrs., field (SC)
QUESNESBERRY, Mrs. Betty (S2 - 1.3, 117-20), 77 yrs. (AR)
QUINN, Doc (10.6, 1-9) (S1 - 2.1, 19-20), 93 yrs. (AR via MS)
QUINN, James Hamilton (S1 - 9.4, 1766-67), 78 yrs. (MS)
QUINN, S.B. (S1 - 9.4, 1768), 88 yrs. (MS)
QUINN, Spart (S1 - 9.4, 1769-74), 88 yrs., carried water; house (MS)
QUINN, William M. (6.2, 155-57), 82 yrs., field (IN via KY)

RABB, Jack (S1 - 9.4, 1774) (MS)
RACHEL (13.4, 217), nursemaid (GA)
RACHEL, Aunt (S1 - 1.1, 25-27), over 90 yrs. (AL)
RAHLS, Mary (S2 - 8.7, 3217-20), 90's, house (TX)
RAINES, Charlotte (13.3, 189-93), over 75 yrs., house (GA)
RAINES, Mary (3.4, 1-2), 99 yrs., field (SC)
RAINES, Rena (15.2, 193-95), 75 yrs. (NC)
RAINS, Aunt Eda (5.3, 225-26) (S2 - 8.7, 322-26), 94 yrs., house
    (hired out) (TX via AR)
RALLS, Henrietta (10.6, 10-11), 88 yrs. (AR via MS)
RAMSEY, George Washington (S1 - 9.4, 1775-91), 83 yrs., minor house
    work (MS)
RAMSEY, Ella Belle (S2 - 8.7, 3227-37), 95 yrs., nursemaid (TX via VA)
RAMSEY, Filmore (S1 - 9.4, 1792-97), 86 yrs., house (MS)
RAMSEY, Lillian (S1 - 4.2, 497-99), 70 yrs. (GA)
RANDALL, Millie (5.3, 227-28) (S2 - 8.7, 3238-41), c. 78 yrs. (TX via
    LA and MS)
RANDALL, Tom (16.3, 57-59), 81 yrs., house (MD)
RANDOLPH, Fanny (13.3, 194-99), c. over 100 yrs., house (GA)
RANGE, Frank (3.4, 3-4), 103 yrs. (SC)
RANKINS, Diana (10.6, 12-13), 66 yrs., free (AR via TN)
RANSOM, Daniel (S2 - 8.7, 3242-47), 70 yrs., free (TX via JAMAICA)
RANSOM, Sycamore (S1 - 1.1, 305-09), over 95 yrs. (AL)
RANSOME, Anthony (15.2, 197), 80 yrs. (NC)
RATLIFF, Bunk (S1 - 9.4, 1798-99) (MS)

RAWLS, Joe (S2 - 8.7, 3248-53), over 90 yrs. (TX)
RAWLS, John (S1 - 4.2, 500-01), 84 yrs. (GA via AL)
RAWLS, Sam (3.4, 5-8), 84 yrs. (SC)
RAY, Aaron (S2 - 8.7, 3254-61), 70's (TX)
RAY, Laura (S2 - 8.7, 3262-64), 84 yrs., yard work (TX)
RAY, Morgan (S1 - 5.2, 420-29), 70 yrs. (OH via GA)
RAYFORD, Jeff (S1 - 9.4, 1800-05), 96 yrs., cook (MS)
REAVES, Clay (10.6, 17-20), 80 yrs. (AR via KY)
REDMOUN, Laura (5.3, 229-32) (S2 - 8.7, 3265-70), c. 82 yrs. (TX via
    TN)
REE, Henry R. (S1 - 9.4, 1806) (MS)
    See Mingo, Sam (MS)
REECE, Elsie (5.3, 233-35) (S2 - 8.7, 3271-79), 90 yrs., weaver; house
    (TX)
REECE, Jane (10.6, 21-22), 85 yrs., house and field (AR via NC)
REECE, Naisy (16.6, 64-65), c. 80 yrs. (TN)
REED, Annie (S1 - 1.1, 310-12), 80 yrs. (AL)
REED, Easter (S1 - 4.2, 502-09), 84 yrs. (GA)
REED, Frank (10.6, 23), 78 yrs. (AR via AL)
REED, (Uncle) George (S1 - 9.4, 1807-13), c. 84 yrs. (MS)
REED, Rachel Santee (S1 - 9.4, 1814-19), 80 yrs. (MS)
REESE, Bill (S1 - 4.2, 510-36), 74 yrs., free (GA)
REESE, Kitty (S2 - 8.7, 3280-83), c. 83 yrs. (TX via MO)
REEVES, James (10.6, 24-32), 68 yrs. (AR)
RESNICK, Ellen (3.4, 9), 79 yrs., field (SC)
REVELS, Hiram Rhodes (S1 - 9.4, 1820-37), 79 yrs. (d. 1901), free;
    Senator (MS)
REYNOLDS, Mary (5.3, 236-46) (S2 - 8.7, 3284-99), c. 100 yrs., field
    (TX via LA)
REYNOLDS, Sallie (6.1, 326-28), 75 yrs., house (AL via GA)
RHODES, Susan Davis (11.8, 283-89), over 100 yrs., house (MO via VA
    and NC)
RHONE, Shepherd (10.6, 33-34), 75 yrs. (AR)
RHYMES, Will (S2 - 8.7, 3300-02), 84 yrs., chores (TX via LA)
RICE, Anne (3.4, 10-11), 75 yrs., field (SC)
RICE, George Washington (S2 - 8.7, 3303-05), 77 yrs. (TX via AR)
RICE, Jesse (3.4, 12-16), 80 yrs. (SC)
RICE, Mary (6.1, 329-30) (S1 - 1.1, 313-14), 92 yrs., field (AL)
RICE, Phillip (3.4, 17-18), 75 yrs., field (SC)
RICE, Savannah (S1 - 1.1, 315-25), 80 yrs. (AL via GA)
RICHARD, Dora (10.6, 35-36), 76 yrs., house (AR via TN and SC)
RICHARDS, Shade (13.3, 200-05), 91 yrs., field (GA)
RICHARDSON, Ben (S1 - 9.4, 1838-43), hauled sugar cane (MS)
RICHARDSON, Candus (6.2, 158-61), 90 yrs., field (IN via KY and MS)
RICHARDSON, Caroline (15.2, 199-202), 60 yrs., free (NC)
RICHARDSON, Chaney (7.1, 257-62), 90 yrs., house (OK)
RICHARDSON, Charlie (11.8, 290-97), 86 yrs., carried water and wood
    (MO)
RICHARDSON, Henry J. (S2 - 8.7, 3306-08), 78 yrs. (TX)
RICHARDSON, Martha (3.4, 19-22), 78 yrs. (SC)
RICHARDSON, Red (7.1, 263-65), 75 yrs., field (OK via TX)
RICKS, Jim (10.6, 37-38), 79 yrs. (AR)
RIENSHAW, Adora (15.2, 213-15), 92 yrs., free (NC)
RIGGER, Charlie (10.6, 39-41), 85 yrs. (AR)
RIGLEY, Ida (10.6, 42-46), 82 yrs., house (AR via VA)
RILEY, Cicely (S1 - 9.4, 1844), c. 100 yrs. (MS)

See Riley, Ephraim (MS)
RILEY, Ephraim (S1 - 9.4, 1844), c. 100 yrs. (MS)
    See Riley, Cicely (MS)
RILEY, Jack (S2 - 10.9, 4371-73), 91 yrs., white (TX via OH)
RILEY, Mamie (3.4, 23-24), 80 yrs. (SC)
RIMM, Walter (5.3, 247-51) (S2 - 8.7, 3309-23), 80 yrs., chores (TX)
RINGO, Joseph (S1 - 5.2, 430-32), 86 yrs., tended cows (OH via KY)
RISER, Susie (3.4, 25), 80 yrs., field (SC)
RITCHIE (10.6, 47-50), 78 yrs. (AR via GA)
RIVERS, Alice (10.6, 51), 81 yrs. (AR via MS)
RIVERS, George (S2 - 8.7, 3324-30), dairy worker (TX)
RIVERS, Joshua (S1 - 11.2, 274-77), 50 yrs., free (SC)
ROBERSON, Uncle (S1 - 9.4, 1845), cook (MS)
ROBERTS, Charley (17.1, 364-65), tended animals (FL via SC)
ROBERTS, Dora (13.3, 206-08), 88 yrs., field (GA)
ROBERTS, Fanny (S1 - 4.2, 537), c. 71 yrs. (GA)
ROBERTS, Isom (13.4, 26-30), 80 yrs. (SC)
ROBERTS, Melvina (S1 - 4.2, 538-40), 80 yrs. (GA)
ROBERTS, Nancy (S1 - 5.1, 171-73), free (IN)
ROBERTSON, Alexander (3.4, 31-34), 84 yrs. (SC)
ROBERTSON, Betty (7.1, 266-69), 95 yrs., house (OK via CANADA)
ROBERTSON, (ROBINSON), George (10.6, 54) (AR via TN)
ROBERTSON, Irene (10.5, 194-96), 78 yrs., house (AR via TN)
ROBERTSON, Steve (S2 - 8.7, 3331-44), 79 yrs., field (TX)
ROBINSON, Albert L. (S1 - 1.1, 326-51), 72 yrs. (AL via VA)
ROBINSON, Augustus (10.6, 55-59), 78 yrs. (AR)
ROBINSON, Belle (16.2, 21-22), c. 85 yrs., house (KY)
ROBINSON, (Rev.) Ben J. (S1 - 9.4, 1846-48), 89 yrs. (MS)
ROBINSON, Celia (15.2, 217-19), c. 93 yrs., house (NC)
ROBINSON, Charlie (3.4, 35-37), 87 yrs., field (SC)
ROBINSON, Cornelia (6.1, 331-33) (S1 - 1.1, 352-54), 76 yrs. (AL)
ROBINSON, Ephriam (S1 - 9.4, 1849-53), 87 yrs., personal servant (MS)
ROBINSON, Fannie (S2 - 8.7, 3345-47), 82 yrs. (TX)
ROBINSON, George
    See Robertson, George (AR via TN)
ROBINSON, Harriet (7.1, 270-74), 95 yrs., house (OK via TX)
ROBINSON, Ibby Barnes (S1 - 9.4, 1845-55), 91 yrs., nurse and cook (MS)
ROBINSON, J.A. (S2 - 8.7, 3348-49), c. 81 yrs. (TX)
ROBINSON, Joe (6.2, 162-63), 83 yrs., field (IN via KY)
ROBINSON, Malindy (10.6, 60), 61 yrs., free (AR via MS)
ROBINSON, Manus (S1 - 9.4, 1856-60), c. 76 yrs. (MS via NC)
ROBINSON, Mariah (5.3, 252-55) (S2 - 8.7, 3350-58), c. 90 yrs., house
    (TX)
ROBINSON, Nancy (S1 - 9.4, 1861-62), 86 yrs., house (hired out) (MS)
ROBINSON, Tom (10.6, 61-68), 88 yrs., field (AR via NC)
ROBY, Edd (S1 - 9.4, 1863-68), 74 yrs. (MS)
ROCKET, Nettie (S1 - 9.4, 1869-74), yard work (MS)
RODGERS, Caroline (S1 - 9.4, 1874) (MS)
RODGERS, Isaac (S1 - 5.2, 433-36), over 75 yrs., field (OH via NC)
ROGERS, B.E. (S1 - 11.1, 54-55) (NC)
ROGERS, Ellen (S2 - 8.7, 3359-62), c. 100 yrs., field (TX via TN)
ROGERS, Ferebe (13.3, 209-16), c. 108 yrs., field (GA)
ROGERS, George (15.2, 221-25), 94 yrs. (NC)
ROGERS, Gus (6.1, 334-36), over 90 yrs., field (AL via NC)
ROGERS, Hattie (15.2, 227-31), 80 yrs. (NC)
ROGERS, Henry (13.3, 217-28), 73 yrs. (GA)

ROGERS, Isom (10.6, 69), 67 yrs. (AR via MS)
ROGERS, Jane (S1 - 9.4, 1875-76), 106 yrs., house (MS via AL)
ROGERS, John (S1 - 4.2, 541-42), 107 yrs., field (GA)
ROGERS, Noah (S1 - 9.4, 1877-82), 92 yrs., house (MS via AR)
ROGERS, Oscar (10.6, 70-72), over 70 yrs. (AR via NC)
ROGERS, Rosaline (6.2, 164-66), 110 yrs., field (IN via TN and SC)
ROGERS, Will Ann (10.6, 73-75), 70 yrs. (AR via MS)
ROLAND, Jennie (S1 - 9.4, 1883), 85 yrs., midwife (MS)
ROLLEY, Callie (S1 - 9.4, 1884-90), farm work (MS via TN)
ROLLINS, Joe (S1 - 9.4, 1891-1900), 87 yrs., tended children; field
   work (MS)
ROLLINS, Parthena (6.2, 167-68), 84 yrs., field (IN via KY)
RONE, Martin (S1 - 2.2, 80-82) (CO)
ROOKS, William Henry (10.6, 76-79), 84 yrs., field (AR via MS)
ROSBORO, Al (3.4, 38-41), 90 yrs., field (SC)
ROSBOROUGH, Ransom (S2 - 8.7, 3363-64), 76 yrs. (TX)
ROSBOROUGH, Reuben (3.4, 45-47), 82 yrs., field (SC via VA)
ROSE, Amanda (10.6, 80-85), 82 yrs., field (AR)
ROSE, "Cat" (10.6, 86-87), 70 yrs. (AR)
ROSE, Katie (S1 - 5.1, 174-78), c. 85 yrs., field (IN via KY)
ROSE, Mammie (S1 - 9.4, 1901), house (MS)
ROSE, William (3.4, 48-50), 80 yrs. (SC)
ROSIER, Mrs. Sarah (S2 - 1.10, 340-42), 80 yrs., free (NE via WI)
ROSS, Elsie (S1 - 5.2, 437-43), c. 86 yrs., field (OH via FL)
ROSS, Frederick (11.8, 298-300), 90 yrs., field (MO)
ROSS, Gertie (S1 - 2.2, 83-85), 58 yrs., free (CO via KS)
ROSS, Nimrod (S2 - 1.10, 343-45), 75 yrs. (NE via TN)
ROSS, Sarah (17.1, 168-69), 80 yrs., field (FL via MS)
ROSS, Susan (5.3, 256-57) (S2 - 8.7, 3365-67), c. 75 yrs. (TX)
ROSSBERRY, Senia (10.6, 14-16), 84 yrs., house (AR)
ROUNDTREE, Henry (15.2, 233-35), 103 yrs., field (NC)
ROW, Annie (5.3, 258-61) (S2 - 8.7, 3368-75), 86 yrs., wool worker (TX)
ROWE, Katie (7.1, 275-84), 88 yrs., field (OK)
ROWELL, Jessie (17.1, 375) (FL via MS)
ROWLAND, Laura (10.6, 90-91), 65 yrs., free (AR via MS)
ROXBORO, Tom (3.4, 42-44), 79 yrs. (SC)
RUCKER, Landy (10.6, 92-93), 83 yrs., field (AR via GA)
RUDD, John (6.2, 169-72), 83 yrs., field (IN via KY)
RUDDICK, Charity (15.2, 204-06), 80 yrs. (NC)
RUDDICK, Samuel (15.2, 208-11), 96 yrs., field (NC)
RUFE (S1 - 11.1, 34-35), 23 yrs. (d. 1863) (NC)
   See Matthews, Z.D. (NC)
RUFFIN, Gill (5.3, 262-64) (S2 - 8.7, 3376-79), 100 yrs., house and
   field (TX)
RUFFIN, Martha (10.6, 94-96), 80 yrs. (AR via NC)
RUFFIN, Martin (5.3, 265-67), 83 yrs. (TX)
RUFFIN, Thomas (10.6, 97-102), c. 82 yrs. (AR via NC)
RUFFIN, Tom (S1 - 1.1, 355-56), 84 yrs. (d. 1921) (AL)
RUFFINS, Florence (5.3, 268-69) (S2 - 8.7, 3380-85), 67 yrs., free (TX)
RULLERFORD, George (S1 - 1.1, 357-59), 83 yrs., field (AL)
RUMPLE, Caspar (10.6, 103-08), 78 yrs. (AR via SC)
RUSH, Julia (13.3, 229-31) (13.4, 263; 265-66; 267-68), 109 yrs. (GA)
RUSH, Mrs. (S1 - 4.2, 649-53), midwife (GA)
   See Womble, George (GA)
RUSSEAU, Lou (S1 - 1.1, 360), 84 yrs. (AL)
RUSSEL, Aaron (5.3, 270-73) (S2 - 8.7, 3386-93), 82 yrs. (TX via LA)

RUSSELL, Benjamin (3.4, 51-54), 88 yrs., field (SC)
RUSSELL, Elizabeth (S1 - 5.1, 179-86), 79 yrs. (IN via AR)
RUSSELL, Henry (10.6, 109-10), 72 yrs. (AR)
RUSSELL, Rose (S1 - 9.4, 1902-07), c. 98 yrs., house (MS)
RUTHERFORD, Joe (3.4, 55-56), 92 yrs., field (SC)
RUTHERFORD, Lila (3.4, 57-58), 86 yrs., house (SC)
RUTLEDGE, Sabe (3.4, 59-70), 76 yrs. (SC)
RYAN, Henry (3.4, 71-74), 83 yrs., field (SC)
RYAS, Peter (5.3, 274-77) (S2 - 8.7, 3394-3402), 77 yrs. (TX via LA)
RYE, Katie (10.6, 111-12), 82 yrs. (AR)
RYLES, Josephine (5.3, 278-79) (S2 - 9.8, 3403-06) (TX)

SADIE, Aunt (S1 - 3.1, 32-38), 77 yrs. (GA)
SADLER, Felix Grundy (S2 - 9.8, 3407-35), 73 yrs. (TX)
SIMPSON, Millie (17.1, 374-75), 74 yrs. (FL via SC)
SAMUEL, C.G. (S1 - 12.1, 267), 68 yrs., free (OK)
SAMUEL, Phil (S1 - 1.1, 383-96), over 60 yrs. (at death) (AL)
SAMUELS, Amanda Elizabeth (6.2, 173-74), c. 80 yrs., house (IN via KY
    and TN)
SAMUELS, Bob (10.6, 113-17), 92 yrs., field (AR)
SANCO, Mazique (5.4, 1-2) (S2 - 9.8, 3436-39), 88 yrs., personal ser-
    vant (TX via SC)
SANDERS, Harriet (S1 - 10.5, 1908-15), 70 yrs. (MS)
SANDERS, Mary (S1 - 11.2, 278-80), 75 yrs. (SC)
SANDERS, Susan Dale (16.2, 43-45), house (KY)
SANDERSON, Emma (10.6, 118-23), 75 yrs. (AR)
SANDLES, Charlie (S2 - 9.8, 3440-56), 80 yrs. (TX via TN)
SANTEE, Hamp (S1 - 10.5, 1916-19), 78 yrs., cobbler (MS)
SATTERWHITE, Emoline (3.4, 75), 82 yrs., field (SC)
SATTERWHITE, Janie (S1 - 4.2, 543-46), 84 yrs., field (GA via SC)
SCAIFE, Alexander (3.4, 76-77), 82 yrs., house (SC)
SCALES, Anderson (15.2, 236-43), 82 yrs., house (NC)
SCALES, Catherine (15.2, 244-51), 92 yrs. (NC)
SCALES, Clarissa (5.4, 3-5) (S2 - 9.8, 3457-64), 79 yrs. (TX)
SCALES, Porter (15.2, 252-58), 97 yrs. (NC)
SCANTLING , Eliza (3.4, 78-80), 87 yrs., field (SC)
SCARBER, Mrs. Mary Elizabeth   - 1.7, 278-79) (IN via AL)
SCOTT, Anna (17.1, 279-85), 91 yrs., house (FL via SC and LIBERIA)
SCOTT, Annie Groves (S1 - 12.1, 268-73), 93 yrs., house (OK via SC)
SCOTT, Dorsey (S2 - 9.8, 3465-71), 81 yrs., nursemaid (hired out)
    (TX via TN)
SCOTT, Hannah (5.4, 6-8) (S2 - 9.8, 3472-78), field (TX via AR and AL)
SCOTT, Janie (6.1, 337-39), 70 yrs., free (AL)
SCOTT, Lulu (S1 - 5.1, 187-90), c. 85 yrs., house (IN via KY)
SCOTT, Mary (10.6, 124-27) (AR)
SCOTT, Mary (3.4, 81-87), 90 yrs. (SC)
SCOTT, Mollie Hardy (10.6, 128-30), 90 yrs., field (AR via GA)
SCOTT, Nina (3.4, 88), 78 yrs. (SC via NC)
SCOTT, Sam (10.6, 131-33), 79 yrs. (AR)
SCOTT, Tom (S2 - 9.8, 3479-80) (TX)
SCOTT, William (15.2, 260-64), 77 yrs., free (NC)
SCRANTON, Mary (S2 - 9.8, 3481-83), 77 yrs. (TX via LA)
SCROGGINS, Cora (10.6, 134-35), 49 yrs., free (AR)
SCRUGGS, George (16.2, 29-30), 100 yrs., house; groom (KY)

SCURRY, Morgan (3.4, 89-90), 78 yrs., field (SC)
SELBY, Mrs. Carrie (S1 - 2.5, 289-92), 82 yrs. (WA via AL)
SELLERS, Fanny (S2 - 1.10, 346-48), free (NE via TN)
SELLERS, Mary (S1 - 2.3, 122-24), 82 yrs., field (MN via TN)
SELLS, Abram (5.4, 9-14) (S2 - 9.8, 3484-92), 80's (TX)
SELLS, George (S2 - 9.8, 3493-97), 74 yrs. (TX)
SELMAN, George (5.4, 15-16) (S2 - 9.8, 3498-3502), 85 yrs., house and
    field (TX)
SETTLES, Nancy (13.3, 232-35), 92 yrs., field (GA via SC)
SEWELL, Alice (11.8, 301-07), 86 yrs. (MO via AR and AL)
SEXTON, Sarah (10.6, 136-39), house (AR)
SHAVER, Roberta (10.6, 140), 50 yrs., free (AR via MS)
SHAW, Alice (S1 - 10.5, 1920-24), 86 yrs., house (MS)
SHAW, Fartheny (S1 - 4.2, 547-50), 76 yrs. (GA)
SHAW, Lucindy Hall (S1 - 10.5, 1925-31), c. 86 yrs., field (MS)
SHAW, Mabry (S1 - 11.1, 36-39) (NC)
SHAW, Mary (10.6, 141-42), 77 yrs. (AR via MS)
SHAW, Tiney (15.2, 266-68), 76 yrs. (NC)
SHAW, Violet (10.6, 143-44), 50 yrs. (AR via MS)
SHEETS, Will (13.3, 236-44), 76 yrs., carried water to field (GA)
SHELBY, Gussie (S2 - 1.10, 349-52), 74 yrs., free (NE via MO)
SHELBY, Will (S2 - 9.8, 3503-05), 86 yrs. (TX)
SHELTON, Frederick (10.6, 145-47) (S2 - 1.3, 121-23), 81 yrs. (AR)
SHELTON, Laura (10.6, 148-53), 58 yrs., free (AR)
SHEPARD, Matilda (S2 - 1.3, 124-29), 107 yrs., field (AR via GA)
SHEPARD, Morris (7.1, 285-94), 85 yrs., field (OK via IL)
SHEPHERD, Callie (5.4, 17-18) (S2 - 9.8, 3506-09), c. 84 yrs. (TX)
SHEPHERD, Cora (S1 - 4.2, 551-60), 82 yrs., house (GA)
SHEPHERD, (SHEPPARD), Maugan (6.1, 340-41) (S1 - 1.1, 361-62), 83 yrs.,
    field (AL)
SHEPHERD, Robert (13.3, 245-63), 91 yrs. (GA)
SHEPPARD, Maugan (AL)
    See Shepherd, Maugan (AL)
SHEPPARD, Perry (11.8, 308), 94 yrs., house (MO)
SHERMAN, William (17.1, 286-99), 94 yrs., field (FL via SC)
SHEROLD, Charlotte (S1 - 11.2, 281-82) (SC)
SHINE, Polly (S2 - 9.8, 3510-27), 90 yrs., chores (TX via LA)
SHIRLEY, Edd (16.2, 23, 86-87), 97 yrs. (KY)
SHORES, Mahalia (10.6, 154-56), 77 yrs., field (AR via GA)
SHOWERS, Marshall (S2 - 9.8, 3528-32), 85-90 yrs., tended livestock
    (TX via GA)
SIDES, Frank (11.8, 309) (MO)
SIDES, Mollie (11.8, 310) (MO)
SIMMONS, Betty (5.4, 19-23) (S2 - 9.8, 3533-43), over 100 yrs., house
    (TX via AL and TN)
SIMMONS, George (5.4, 24-26) (S2 - 9.8, 3544-48), 83 yrs. (TX via AL)
SIMMONS, Hamp (S1 - 10.5, 1933-34), 83 yrs. (MS)
SIMMONS, Mary Jane (S1 - 4.2, 561-70), 90 yrs., house (GA via NC)
SIMMONS, Ransom (3.4, 91), 104 yrs., house (SC via MS)
SIMMONS, Rosa (10.6, 157-58), 85 yrs., field (AR via TN)
SIMMONS, Smith (S1 - 10.5, 1935-43) (MS)
SIMMS, Allen (S1 - 1.1, 365-66), over 85 yrs. (AL via VA)
SIMMS, Andrew (7.1, 295-97), 80 yrs. (OK via TX and FL)
SIMMS, Bill (16.1, 8-13), 97 yrs., field (KS via MO)
SIMMS, Dennis (16.3, 60-62), 96 yrs., field (MD)
SIMMS, Jack (6.2, 175), field (IN via KY)

SIMPKINS, Millie (16.6, 66-69), 109 yrs., house (TN)
SIMPSON, Ben (5.4, 27-29) (S2 - 9.8, 3549-55), 90 yrs. (TX via GA)
SIMPSON, Burke (S2 - 9.8, 3556-66), 86 yrs. (TX via AR)
SIMPSON, Emma (S2 - 9.8, 3567-72), upper 80's, cook and field (TX)
SIMPSON, George (S1 - 2.4, 219-29), 83 yrs., field (MO)
SIMPSON, Ike (S2 - 9.8, 3573-79), c. 90 yrs., carriage boy (TX)
SIMPSON, Jane (11.8, 311-17), 90 yrs., field and house (MO via MS, AR
    and KY)
SIMPSON, Joe (S1 - 10.5, 1944-45), 91 yrs. (MS)
SIMPSON, Marie (S1 - 2.4, 230-34), 80 yrs., house (MO)
SIMS, Allen (6.1, 342-44), upper 70's (AL)
SIMS, Amos (S2 - 9.8, 3580-83), 86 yrs. (TX)
SIMS, Fannie (10.6, 159), 78 yrs., field (AR)
SIMS, Green (S2 - 9.8, 3584-91), 88 yrs. (TX)
SIMS, Jerry (10.6, 160), 72 yrs. (AR via MS)
SIMS, Victoria (10.6, 161-62), 76 yrs., house (AR via AL)
SIMS, Virginia (10.6, 163-65), 93 yrs., house (AR via VA)
SINCLAIR, Ellen (S2 - 9.8, 3592-94), c. 72 yrs., (TX)
SINGFIELD, Senya (10.6, 166), 74 yrs. (AR via VA)
SINGLETON, Ada (S1 - 10.5, 1946-56), 79 yrs. (MS via AL)
SINGLETON, Affie (S1 - 11.2, 283-84), 87 yrs. (SC)
SINGLETON, Cato (S1 - 11.2, 285), 75-80 yrs. (SC)
SINGLETON, James (7.2, 125-27) (S1 - 10.5, 1957-60), 81 yrs., tended
    cows; house (MS)
SINGLETON, Tom (13.3, 264-73), 94 yrs., field (GA)
SKELTON, Lou (S2 - 9.8, 3595-3600), 74 yrs. (TX)
SLATE, Serena Mulberry Anndora (S1 - 11.1, 40-48), 65 yrs., free (NC)
SLAUGHTER, Billy (6.2, 176-80), 79 yrs., field (IN via KY)
SLAUGHTER, Moses (S1 - 5.1, 193-99), 104 yrs., field (IN via TN)
SLAUGHTER, Richard (16.5, 46-49), 89 yrs. (VA)
SLIGH, Alfred (3.4, 92-94), 100 yrs., field (SC)
SLIM, Catherine (16.4, 77-79), 87 yrs., field and house (OH via VA)
SLOAN, Peggy (10.6, 167-69), 80 yrs. (AR)
SMALL, Eliza (S1 - 11.2, 286-89), c. 70 yrs., free (SC)
SMALL, Jennie (16.4, 80-81), 80 yrs., (OH via VA)
SMALL, Liza (S1 - 11.2, 290-94), c. 71 yrs., (SC)
SMALLS, Samuel (on Cato Smith) (17.1, 300-02), 84 yrs. (FL)
SMALLWOOD, Arzella (10.6, 170-71), 60 yrs., free (AR via SC)
SMILEY, Sarah (10.6, 172-73), 76 yrs. (AR via MS)
SMITH, Adam (S1 - 10.5, 1968-75), c. 98 yrs., house (MS via GA)
SMITH, Alex (6.2, 181-84), 83 yrs., field (IN via KY)
    See Smith, Mrs. Alex (Elizabeth) (IN via KY)
SMITH, Mrs. Alex (Elizabeth) (6.2, 181-84), 83 yrs., picked seed from
    cotton; house (IN via KY)
    See Smith, Alex (IN via KY)
SMITH, Alfred (S1 - 12.1, 274-75), 80 yrs. (OK via GA)
SMITH, Andrew (10.6, 174-75), 73 yrs. (AR via MS)
SMITH, Anna (16.4, 82-85) (S1 - 5.2, 444-45), 103 yrs., house (OH via
    KY)
SMITH (MESSERSMITH), August (S1 - 2.4, 240-65), 92 yrs., house (MO)
    See Messersmith, August (MO)
SMITH, Benjamin Whitley (S1 - 10.5, 1976-77), 79 yrs. (MS)
SMITH, Berry (7.2, 128-34) (S1 - 1978-87), 116 yrs., house (MS via AL)
SMITH, Billie (S1 - 10.5, 1989-91), 85 yrs. (MS via AL)
SMITH, Carolina (10.6, 176-81), 83 yrs. (AR via MS)
SMITH, Cassie Blackmond (S1 - 10.5, 1992-93), 95 yrs. (MS)

SMITH, Charles Tye (13.3, 247-77), c. 87 yrs. (GA)
SMITH, Clay (11.8, 318-20) (MO)
SMITH, Dan (3.4, 95-99), 75 yrs. (SC)
SMITH, Edmond (10.6, 182-84) (AR via LA)
SMITH, Eli (S1 - 1.1, 367-68), 95 yrs., house (AL via GA)
SMITH, Emma (10.6, 185-86), 66 yrs., free (AR)
SMITH, Ervin E. (10.6, 187-91), 84 yrs. (AR via SC)
SMITH, Eugene Wesley (13.4, 230-31), 84 yrs. (GA)
SMITH, Frances (10.6, 192), 77 yrs. (AR via MS)
SMITH, Frank (6.1, 345-48), 89 yrs., house (AL via TN)
SMITH, Georgia (13.3, 278-84), 87 yrs., house (GA)
SMITH, Giles (5.4, 30-32) (S2 - 9.8, 3601-09), 79 yrs. (TX via AL)
SMITH, Gus (11.8, 321-32), 92 yrs., field (MO)
SMITH, Hector (3.4, 100-09), 79 yrs., field (SC)
SMITH, Henrietta (10.6, 193-95)(AR via LA)
SMITH, Henry (10.6, 196-97), 79 yrs., field (AR)
SMITH, Henry (S2 - 9.8, 3610-23), team driver (TX via LA)
SMITH, Henry Hence (S2 - 9.8, 3624-29), 85 yrs., field (TX)
SMITH, J.L. (10.6, 198-202), 76 yrs. (AR)
SMITH, James W. (5.4, 33-35) (S2 - 9.8, 3630-36), 77 yrs. (TX)
SMITH, Jane (3.4, 110-11), 80 yrs., house (SC)
SMITH, John (6.1, 349-52), 103 yrs., house and field (AL via NC)
SMITH, John (15.2, 270-75), 108 yrs., field (NC)
SMITH, John (15.2, 277-80), 77 yrs. (NC)
SMITH, John H. (10.6, 203-04), 81 yrs. (AR via MO)
SMITH, John H.B. (S1 - 1.1, 369-74), over 90 yrs. (AL)
SMITH, Jordan (5.4, 36-40) (S2 - 9.8, 3637-45), 86 yrs. (TX via GA)
SMITH, Josephine (15.2, 282-84), 94 yrs. (NC via VA)
SMITH, Liza (7.1, 298-99A), 91 yrs., house (OK via AR and VA)
SMITH, Lou (7.1, 300-05), 83 yrs. (OK via TX and SC)
SMITH, Louis (S2 - 9.8, 3646-47), 81 yrs. (TX)
SMITH, Lucinda (S2 - 9.8, 3648-49), c. 58 yrs., free (TX)
SMITH, Malindy (S1 - 10.5, 1994-97), 77 yrs. (MS)
SMITH, Maria (S1 - 4.2, 571-74), 72 yrs. (GA)
SMITH, Mary (13.3, 285-87), house (GA)
SMITH, Mary (3.4, 112-15), 84 yrs., house (SC)
SMITH, Melvin (13.3, 288-94), 96 yrs., field (GA via SC)
SMITH, Millie Ann (5.4, 41-43) (S2 - 9.8, 3650-55), 87 yrs. (TX)
SMITH, Mose (S1 - 12.1, 276-78), 85 yrs., field (OK via LA)
SMITH, Nancy (13.3, 295-303), c. 80 yrs. (GA)
SMITH, Nellie (13.3, 304-19), 78 yrs. (GA)
SMITH, Nellie (15.2, 286-88), 81 yrs., house (NC)
SMITH, Paul (13.3, 320-38), 74 yrs. (GA)
SMITH, Prince (3.4, 116-18), c. 100 yrs., field (SC)
SMITH, R.C. (S1 - 12.1, 280-92), 96 yrs., field (OK via AR)
SMITH, Richard (S1 - 10.5, 1998-99), c. 121 yrs. (MS)
SMITH, Robert (S1 - 11.2, 294-96) (SC)
SMITH, Robert Franklin (S2 - 9.8, 3656-58), c. 80 yrs. (TX via MD)
SMITH, Sallie (S1 - 1.1, 375-76), over 80 yrs. (AL)
SMITH, Samuel (S2 - 9.8, 3659-62), 97 yrs., chores and stable boy
   (TX via TN)
SMITH, Sarah Ann (15.2, 290-91), 79 yrs. (NC)
SMITH, Silas (3.4, 119-20), 85 yrs., house (SC)
SMITH, Stonewall (S1 - 2.2, 86-88), 65 yrs. (CO via KY)
SMITH, Susan (S1 - 5.1, 206), over 90 yrs. (IN via KY)
SMITH, Susan (5.4, 44-46) (S2 - 9.8, 3663-70), c. 82 yrs., nursemaid

(TX)
SMITH, Sylvester (S1 - 5.1, 207-08), 85 yrs., carried water (IN via NC)
SMITH, Tucker (S2 - 9.8, 3671-88), 87 yrs., cowboy (TX via MO)
SMITH, Wilham (15.2, 293-94), 80 yrs. (NC)
SMITH, William (S2 - 9.8, 3689-96), 92 yrs., carried water (TX via LA)
SNEED, John (5.4, 47-51) (S2 - 9.8, 3697-3706), spinner (TX)
SNOW, Andy (S1 - 10.5, 2000-02), 78 yrs., cared for white children (MS)
SNOW, Charlie (10.6, 207) , 73 yrs. (AR)
    See Snow, Maggie (AR via MS)
SNOW, Centennial (10.6, 88-89), 74 yrs. (AR)
SNOW, Maggie (10.6, 205-06), 69 yrs., free (AR via MS)
    See Snow, Charlie (AR)
SNOW, Susan (7.2, 135-42) (S1 - 10.5, 2003-13), 87 yrs. (MS via AL)
SNYDER, Mariah (5.4, 52-54) (S2 - 9.8, 3707-13), 89 yrs., field (TX
    via MS)
SOLOMON, Robert (10.6, 208-11), 73 yrs. (AR via GA)
SOMMERVILLE, Jim (S2 - 1.11, 359-61), 96 yrs., stableman and groom
    (NY via TN)
SORRELL, Laura (15.2, 296-98), 72 yrs. (NC)
SORRELL, Ria (15.2, 300-05), 97 yrs., house (NC)
SOUTHALL, James (7.1, 306-11), 82 yrs., field (OK via TN)
SOUTHWELL, Patsy (5.4, 55-56) (S2 - 9.8, 3714-17), 83 yrs., spinner
    and weaver (TX)
SOUTHWORTH, Lou (S1 - 2.5, 273-75), 86 yrs. (OR via KY)
SPARKS, Virginia (16.5, 50-54) (VA)
SPARROW, Jessie (3.4, 121-46), 83 yrs., house (SC)
SPEERS, Jackson (S1 - 11.2, 297-300) (SC)
SPELL, Chaney (15.2, 307-08), 101 yrs. (NC)
SPENCER, Elias (S1 - 10.5, 2014-15), field (MS)
SPIGHT, Tuck (S1 - 10.5, 2016-19) (MS)
SPIKE, James (10.6, 212-13), 91 yrs., (AR via TN)
SPIKES, Tanner (15.2, 310-11), 77 yrs. (NC)
SPINKS, Leithean (5.4, 57-60) (S2 - 9.8, 3718-27), 82 yrs. (TX via LA
    and MS)
STANFORD, Kittie (10.6, 214-15), 104 yrs., house (AR)
STANHOUSE, Tom (10.6, 216-17), 74 yrs. (AR via SC)
STANTON, Annie (6.1, 353-55) (S1 - 1.1, 377-79), 84 yrs., house (AL)
STAPLETON, Wright (S1 - 10.5, 2019-24), c. 87 yrs. (MS)
STAR, Joseph Leonidas (16.6, 70-73), 81 yrs., house (TN)
STARKE, Rosa (3.4, 147-50), 83 yrs. (SC)
STARKS, Lydia C. (S1 - 4.2, 575-79), 85 yrs. (GA via SC)
STARNES, Isom (10.6, 218-19), 78 yrs. (AR via AL)
STARR, Milton (S1 - 12.1, 293-95), 80 yrs. (OK via AR)
STEEL, Ky (10.6, 220-21), 83 yrs. (AR via TX and NC)
STEELE, Elmo (S1 - 10.5, 2025-35), 110-115 yrs., free (MS)
STENHOUSE, Maggie (10.6, 222-25), 72 yrs. (AR via NC)
STENTSON, Mattie (S1 - 10.5, 2036-38), 76 yrs. (MS)
STEPHENS, Charlotte (10.6, 226-33), 83 yrs. (AR)
STEPHENS, Fayette (S2 - 9.8, 3728-30), 82 yrs. (TX)
STEPHENSON, Annie (15.2, 313-15), 80 yrs., house (NC)
STEPNEY, Emeline (13.3, 339-42), over 90 yrs. (GA)
STEPNEY, Moses (S2 - 1.10, 353-55), 53 yrs., free (NE via VA)
STEPNEY, Steve (S1 - 10.5, 2039-40) (MS)
STEVENS, Ma (S1 - 4.2, 580-91), 103 yrs. (GA)
STEVENS, Sam (13.4, 264), non-slave (GA)
STEVENS, William (10.6, 234-35), over 70 yrs. (AR)

STEWART, Charley (S1 - 10.5, 2041-46), 85 yrs., field (MS)
STEWART, Guy (5.4, 61-63) (S2 - 9.8, 3731-35), 87 yrs., field (TX via LA)
STEWART, Josephine (3.4, 151-54), 85 yrs., house (SC)
STEWART, Laura (S1 - 4.2, 592-94), 75 yrs., house (GA)
STEWART, Lydia (S1 - 10.5, 2047), 108 yrs. (d. 1925) (MS)
STEWART, Mary (S1 - 5.1, 209), 104 yrs., free (IN)
STEWART, Minnie Johnson (10.6, 236-37), over 50 yrs., free (AR)
STEWART, Nan (16.4, 86-91), 87 yrs., house (OH via WV)
STEWART, Nelson (S1 - 11.1, 49-51), cattle herder (NC)
STEWART, Sam (15.2, 317-23), 84 yrs., field (NC)
STEWART, Theodore (6.1, 356-58) (S1 - 1.1, 380-82), c. 90's, field (AL via GA)
STIER, Isaac (7.2, 143-50) (S1 - 10.5, 2048-59), 99 yrs. (MS)
STIGGERS, Liza (10.6, 238), over 70 yrs. (AR)
STINNETT, J.W. (S1 - 12.1, 296), 75 yrs. (OK via TX)
STINSON, Ella (S1 - 4.2, 595-99), 90 yrs. (GA via SC)
STITH, James Henry (10.6, 239-45), 72 yrs. (AR via GA)
STOKES, Ann (11.8, 333-37), 93 yrs. (MO)
STOKES, Simon (16.5, 45), c. 100 yrs., field (VA)
STONE, Barney (6.2, 185-88), 90 yrs., field (IN via TN and KY)
STONE, Emma (15.2, 325-26), 77 yrs. (NC)
STONE, Miles (S1 - 8.3, 997-1006) (MS)
    See Hewitt, Florida (MS)
STONE, William (5.4, 64-66) (S2 - 9.8, 3736-47), 74 yrs. (TX via AL)
STOVALL, Jim (S1 - 10.5, 2060-61), 84 yrs. (MS via GA)
SPRATLIN, (Dr.) V.B. (S1 - 2.2, 89-91), 79 yrs. (CO via AL and GA)
STRAYHORN, Eva (S1 - 12.1, 297-308), 79 yrs. (OK via AR)
STREET, Felix (10.6, 246-51), 74 yrs. (AR via TN)
STRICKLAND, Ellis (13.4, 261-63, 267), non-slave (GA)
STRICKLAND, George (6.1, 359-62) (S1 - 1.1, 397-99), c. 81 yrs., field (AL via MS)
STRICKLAND, Jane (S1 - 10.5, 2062-63), c. 77 yrs. (MS)
STRICKLAND, Liza (S1 - 10.5, 2064-67), c. 90 yrs., house (MS)
STRINGFELLOW, Yach (5.4, 67-69) (S2 - 9.8, 3748-54), c. 89 yrs., chores (TX)
STRONG, Bert (5.4, 70-72) (S2 - 9.8, 3755-60), 73 yrs. (TX)
STUBBS, Julia (S1 - 10.5, 2068-71), c. 85 yrs., house (MS)
STURDIVANT, George (S1 - 10.5, 2072-73), 86 yrs., field (MS)
STURGIS, Emmaline (S1 - 4.2, 600-02), 80 yrs., house (GA)
SUBER, Bettie (3.4, 155), 96 yrs., house (SC)
SUGG, Hattie (S1 - 10.5, 2074-79), 80 yrs., field (MS)
SUGGS, Adah Isabelle (6.2, 189-92), 85 yrs., house (IN via KY)
SUITS, Isaac (S1 - 11.2, 301-04), 94 yrs., cook (SC via NC)
SULLIVAN, Rachel (13.4, 226-29), c. 85 yrs., nursemaid (GA)
SUTTON, Mrs. (18.1, 30-37)
SUTTON, James R. (S1 - 10.5, 2080-82), 71 yrs. (MS via NC)
SUTTON, Jane (7.2, 151-56) (S1 - 10.5, 2083-93), 84 yrs. (MS)
SUTTON, Katie (6.2, 193-95) (S1 - 5.1, 210-11), over 80 yrs. (IN)
SUTTON, Samuel (16.4, 92-96) (S1 - 5.2, 446-51), c. 82 yrs., house (OH via KY)
STYLES, Amanda (13.3, 343-46), c. 80 yrs. (GA)
SWINDLER, Ellen (3.4, 156), 78 yrs., field (SC)
SYKES, William (15.2, 328-31), 78 yrs. (NC)

TABON, Mary (10.6, 252-53), 67 yrs. (AR)
TABON, Robert (S1 - 2.1, 21), 78 yrs., free (AR via NC)
TANNER, Liza Moore (10.6, 254-56), 79 yrs., hired out (AR via GA)
TASWELL, Salena (17.1, 303-10, 372-73), 93 yrs., house (FL via GA)
TATE, Annie (15.2, 333-34) (S1 - 11.1, 52-53), 73 yrs. (NC)
TATE, Mary Emily Eaton (S1 - 5.1, 212-19), 78 yrs. (IN via TN)
TATE, Preston (S1 - 5.1, 220-21), 81 yrs. (IN via TN)
TATUM, Fannie (10.6, 257-58), 72 yrs. (AR)
TAYLOR, Anthony (10.6, 259-65), 68 or 78 yrs. (AR)
TAYLOR, Cull (6.1, 363-66), 78 yrs. (AL)
TAYLOR, Daniel (6.1, 367-69), 86 yrs., field (AL via SC)
TAYLOR, (Uncle) Dave (17.1, 311-26) (FL via VA)
TAYLOR, Edward (11.8, 338-41), c. 115 yrs., split rails; assisted
    blacksmith (MO via LA)
TAYLOR, Emma (5.4, 73-75) (S2 - 9.8, 3761-67), c. 89 yrs., chores
    (TX via MS)
TAYLOR, George (6.1, 370-73), c. 85 yrs., field (AL)
TAYLOR, George (S1 - 2.5, 276-78), over 85 yrs. (OR via VA)
TAYLOR, Jacob (S1 - 11.2, 305-09), 45 yrs., free (SC)
TAYLOR, Jim (16.3, 63-65), 90 yrs., seaman (MD)
TAYLOR, Lula (10.6, 266-68), 71 yrs. (AR)
TAYLOR, Mack (3.4, 157-59), 97 yrs., field (SC)
TAYLOR, Millie (10.6, 269-70), 78 yrs. (AR via MS)
TAYLOR, Mollie (5.4, 76-77) (S2 - 9.8, 3768-71), 84 yrs., field and
    house (TX)
TAYLOR, R.S. (15.2, 336-41), 80 yrs., field (NC)
TAYLOR, Sarah (10.6, 271-72), 70 yrs. (AR via TN)
TAYLOR, Spencer (S1 - 1.1, 400-01), 103 yrs., field (AL via VA)
TAYLOR, Tishey (11.8, 342-47), 77 yrs. (MO)
TAYLOR, Warren (10.6, 273-79), 74 yrs. (AR via VA)
TAYLOR, William (S1 - 4.2, 603-04), 85 yrs. (GA)
TEAGUE, Sneed (10.6, 280-81), 68 yrs. (AR)
TEEL, Mary (10.6, 282-84), 74 yrs. (AR via MS)
TELFAIR, Georgia (13.4, 1-10), 74 yrs. (GA)
TELLIS, Amanda (6.1, 374-75), 83 yrs., house (AL via SC)
TERRIEL, Jake (5.4, 78-79) (S2 - 9.8, 3772-76), c. 90's, field (TX
    via NC)
TERRILL, J.W. (5.4, 80-82), over 100 yrs., field (TX via LA)
THERMAN, Wade (10.6, 285-86), 67 yrs. (AR via OK)
THOMAS, Acie (17.1, 327-34), 79 yrs., household chores (FL)
THOMAS, Adline (S1 - 10.5, 2094), 110 yrs. (MS)
THOMAS, Allen (5.4, 83-84) (S2 - 9.8, 3777-80), 97 yrs. (TX)
THOMAS, Bill (5.4, 85-88) (S2 - 9.8, 3781-99), 88 yrs., field (TX via
    MO)
    See Thomas, Ellen (TX via MS)
THOMAS, Cordelia (13.4, 11-24), 80 yrs. (GA)
THOMAS, Dan (16.6, 74-75), 90 yrs. (TN)
THOMAS, Dicey (10.6, 287-95), 82 yrs. (AR)
THOMAS, Elias (15.2, 343-47), 84 yrs., field (NC)
THOMAS, Elizabeth (6.1, 380), 100 yrs., house (AL)
THOMAS, Elizabeth (S1 - 1.3, 258-61), 69 yrs., free (DC)
THOMAS, Ellen (6.1, 376-79), 89 yrs., house (AL)
THOMAS, Ellen (5.4, 85-88) (S2 - 9.8, 3781-99), 81 yrs. (TX via MS)
    See Thomas, Bill (TX via MO)
THOMAS, George (S1 - 5.1, 222-28), 86 yrs. (IN via KY)
THOMAS, Ike (13.4, 25-28), c. 85 yrs., carriage boy (GA)

THOMAS, Jacob (15.2, 349-51), 97 yrs., field (NC via GA)
THOMAS, Jim (S1 - 1.1, 471-75), slave interviewer (1884) (AL)
   See Morgan, Uncle Tony (AL)
THOMAS, Kate (S1 - 4.2, 605-10), over 85 yrs. (GA)
THOMAS, Lorena (S1 - 10.5, 2095-97), 73 yrs. (MS)
THOMAS, Louis (11.8, 348-52), 93 yrs., field (MO via MS and AL)
THOMAS, Lucy (5.4, 88-91) (S2 - 9.8, 3800-05), c. 87 yrs., field (TX)
THOMAS, Mandy (10.6, 296), 78 yrs. (AR)
THOMAS, Mike (S1 - 2.2, 92-93), 77 yrs. (CO via MO)
THOMAS, Nancy (S2 - 9.8, 3806-11), 78 yrs. (TX)
THOMAS, Philles (5.4, 92-94) (S2 - 9.8, 3812-18), c. 76 yrs. (TX)
THOMAS, Omelia (10.6, 300-03), 63 yrs., free (AR)
THOMAS, Omelia (10.6, 297-99), c. 70 yrs. (AR via LA)
THOMAS, Rebecca (S2 - 9.8, 3819-23), c. 113 yrs., house and field
   (TX via AR)
THOMAS, Rosa (S1 - 10.5, 2098-2102), 76 yrs. (MS)
THOMAS, Rose (S2 - 9.8, 3824-25) (TX via MS)
THOMAS, Sarah (S1 - 10.5, 2103-09), 80 yrs. (MS via LA)
THOMAS, Shack (17.1, 335-41), 102 yrs., field (FL)
THOMAS, Tanner (10.6, 304-05), 78 yrs. (AR)
THOMAS, Valmo (S2 - 9.8, 3826-34), 77 yrs. (TX via LA)
THOMAS, Webster (10.6, 306), 79 yrs. (AR via MS)
THOMAS, William M. (5.4, 95-99) (S2 - 9.8, 3835-43), 87 yrs., house
   (TX via MS)
THOMPSON, Annie (10.6, 307-08), 55 yrs., free (AR via MS)
THOMPSON, Delia (3.4, 160-62), 88 yrs., house (SC)
THOMPSON, Ellen Briggs (10.6, 309-14), 83 yrs., field (AR)
THOMPSON, George (6.2, 196-97), 83 yrs., field and house (IN via MS,
   AL, and KY)
THOMPSON, Hattie (10.6, 315-17), 72 yrs. (AR via TN)
THOMPSON, Jane (11.8, 353-54), house and field (MO via MS)
THOMPSON, John (S2 - 9.8, 3844-54), 80 yrs. (TX via TN)
THOMPSON, Johnson (S1 - 12.1, 309-12), 84 yrs. (OK via TX)
THOMPSON, Laura (S1 - 2.3, 131-36), 84 yrs., child nurse (MN via KY)
THOMPSON, Mamie (10.6, 318-19), 68 yrs., free (AR)
THOMPSON, Maria Tilden (S2 - 9.8, 3855-59), 101 yrs., house (TX)
THOMPSON, Mary (5.4, 100-02) (S2 - 9.8, 3860-64), 87 yrs., nursemaid
   (TX via AL)
THOMPSON, Mike (10.6, 320-21), 79 yrs. (AR via TX)
THOMPSON, Moslie (S2 - 9.8, 3865-69) (TX)
THOMPSON, Ned (S1 - 12.1, 313-19), over 75 yrs. (OK via AR)
THOMPSON, Penny (5.4, 103-05) (S2 - 9.8, 3870-77), 86 yrs., chores
   (TX via AL)
THOMPSON, Victoria (S1 - 12.1, 320-24), 80 yrs. (OK via AR)
THORNTON, Laura (10.6, 322-29), 105 yrs. (AR via AL)
THORNTON, Margaret (15.2, 353-54), 77 yrs., house (NC)
THORNTON, Tim (S1 - 4.2, 611-15), over 100 yrs., field (GA via VA)
THREAT, Jim (S1 - 12.1, 325-41), 86 yrs. (OK via KS)
THURSTON, Lucy (S1 - 10.5, 2110-20), 101 yrs., field (MS)
"TID, Mother" (S1 - 10.5, 2121) (MS)
TIDWELL, Emma (10.6, 330-33) (AR)
TILLIE(15.2, 356-58) (NC)
TILLMAN, Joe (10.6, 334-35), 79 yrs. (AR)
TILLMAN, Mollie (6.1, 381-82), 87 yrs., house (AL via GA)
TIMS, J.T. (10.6, 336-45), 86 yrs. (AR via KY)
TIPPIN, FAnnie (S2 - 9.8, 3878-81), 73 yrs. (TX via KY)

TOATLEY, Robert (3.4, 163-66), 82 yrs. (SC)
TODD, Albert (5.4, 106-07)(S2-9.8, 3882-85), 86 yrs., chores (TX via KY)
TODD, Mason (S2 - 1.10, 356-58), 68 yrs., free (NE via TX)
TOLBERT, Bettie (S1 - 1.1, 402-04), over 85 yrs. (AL)
TOLER, Richard (16.4, 97-101) (S1 - 5.2, 452-54), c. 101 yrs., field
   (OH via VA)
TOLES, John (S1 - 10.5, 2122-23) (MS via LA and KY)
TOLLIVER, Jerry (S2 - 1.3, 130), 70 yrs., free (AR)
TOMBS, Alonza Fantroy (6.1, 383-84) (S1 - 1.1, 405-06), 86 yrs., field
   (AL via GA)
TOODLE, Pappy (S1 - 10.5, 2124) (MS)
TOOMBS, Jane Mickens (13.4, 29-36), 82 yrs., house (GA)
TORIAN, Cora (16.2, 104-05), 71 yrs. (KY)
TOWNS, Luke (17.1, 342-45), 101 yrs., household chores (FL via GA)
TOWNS, Phil (13.4, 37-47), c. 95 yrs. (GA via VA)
TOWNS, William (6.1, 385-93) (S1 - 1.1, 407-16), 82 yrs., watched
   animals (AL)
TRAVIS, Hannah (10.6, 346-52), 73 yrs. (AR)
TRELL, Ellen (15.2, 360-62), 73 yrs. (NC)
TRENTHAM, Henry James (15.2, 364-66), 92 yrs. (NC)
TRIMBLE, Aleck (5.4, 108-15), 76 yrs. (TX)
TRIP, Annie (17.1, 374) (FL via GA)
TRIPLETT, Allen (S1 - 10.5, 2125) (MS via SC)
TRIPLETT, Billie (S1 - 10.5, 2126) (MS)
   See Triplett, Jane (MS)
TRIPLETT, Jane (S1 - 10.5, 2126) (MS)
   See Triplett, Billie (MS)
TRIPLETT, Oscar (S1 - 2.2, 94-95), 67 yrs. (CO)
TROTT, Emmeline (S1 - 10.5, 2127), 98 yrs., house (MS)
TROTTE, Mark C. (10.6, 353-56), 71 yrs. (AR via MS)
TROTTY, Charlie (S2 - 9.8, 3886-89) (TX)
TRUHART, Buck (S1 - 10.5, 2137), house (MS)
TUCKER, Isham (S1 - 10.5, 2138), field (MS)
TUCKER, Mandy (10.6, 357-59) (S2 - 1.3, 131), 80 yrs. (AR)
TUCKER, Reeves (5.4, 116-17) (S2 - 10.9, 3891-95), 78 yrs. (TX via AL)
TURNBOW, Eliza Hardin (S1 - 10.5, 2139) (MS)
TURNER, Bart (S2 - 1.3, 132-34), slaveowner (white) (AR)
TURNER, Charlie (S1 - 1.1, 417-22), 71 yrs. (AL)
TURNER, Emma (10.6, 360-62), 83 yrs. (AR via MS and GA)
TURNER, (Uncle) Henry (10.6, 363-68) (S2 - 1.3, 135-41), 93 yrs., field
   (AR via MS)
TURNER, Lou (female) (5.4, 118-21) (S2 - 10.9, 3896-3900), 89 yrs.,
   light work around house (TX)
TUTTLE, Seabe (10.6, 369-71), 88 yrs. (AR via TN)

UNDERWOOD, Stepney (6.1, 394-96), 86 yrs., house (AL)
UPPERMAN, Jane Anne Privette (15.2, 368-70), 74 yrs. (NC)
UPSON, Neal (13.4, 48-70), 81 yrs., house (GA)

VADEN, Charlie (11.7, 1-2), 77 yrs. (AR)
VADEN, Ellen (11.7, 3-4), 83 yrs., field (AR)
VAN BUREN, Nettie (11.7, 5-6), 62 yrs., free (AR)

VAN DYKE, Charlie (6.1, 397–400), 107 yrs., field (AL)
VAN HOOK, John F. (13.4, 71–96), 76 yrs. (GA via NC)
VANCE, Molly (S1 – 10.5, 2140–43), c. 80 yrs. (MS)
VANN, Lucinda (S1 – 12.1, 342–53), c. 100 yrs., field (OK via AR)
VARNADO, Harriet (S1 – 10.5, 2144–45) (MS)
VARNER, Stephen (S1 – 1.1, 425–28), over 85 yrs. (AL)
VAUGHAN, Adelaide (11.7, 7–12), 69 yrs. (AR via AL)
VAUGHN, Joe (S1 – 4.2, 623–25), 76 yrs. (GA)
VAUGHN, Nancy (S1 – 1.1, 429–30), over 90 yrs. (AL via SC)
VEALS, Mary (3.4, 167–69), 73 yrs. (SC)
VERNON, David (S1 – 10.5, 2146–47), 80 yrs. (MS)
VINSON, Addie (13.4, 97–114), 86 yrs., field (GA)
VIRGEL, Emma (13.4, 115–22), 73 yrs. (GA)
VIRGIL, Sarah (S1 – 4.2, 626–27), 94 yrs. (GA)

WADDELL, Emiline (AR via GA)
  See Wadille, Emmeline (AR via GA)
WADE, Joe (S1 – 5.1, 229), field (IN via TN)
WADILLE (Waddell), Emmeline (Emiline) (11.7, 13), 106 yrs., nurse
  (AR via GA)
WAGGONER, Sarah (11.8, 357–64), 93 yrs., house (MO via KY)
WAGONER, Sweetie (S1 – 12.1, 354–56), 73 yrs. (OK via AR)
WALDON, Adeline (S2 – 10.9, 3913–20), 80 yrs. (TX via MO)
WALDON, Henry (11.7, 14–18), 84 yrs., field (AR via MS)
WALKER, Agnes (S1 – 12.1, 357–58), 75 yrs. (OK via AR)
WALKER, Bean (S2 – 10.9, 3921–23), c. 85 yrs., field (TX)
WALKER, Clara (11.7, 19–27), 111 yrs., mid-wife and weaver (AR)
WALKER, Dave (S1 – 10.5, 2148–52), 87 yrs., field (MS)
WALKER, Edwin (S1 – 10.5, 2153–56), 88 yrs., field (MS)
WALKER, Fannie Moore (S2 – 10.9, 3924–30), 84 yrs., nursed children
  (TX)
WALKER, Harriet (S1 – 10.5, 2157–61), 85 yrs. (MS)
WALKER, Henry (11.7, 28–35), 80 yrs., field (AR via TN)
WALKER, Irella Battle (5.4, 122–24) (S2 – 10.9, 3931–37), 86 yrs.,
  field (TX)
WALKER, Jake (11.7, 39–41), 68 yrs., free (AR via MS)
WALKER, Jake (11.7, 36–38), 95 yrs., mule driver (AR via MS and AL)
WALKER, Lilah (6.1, 401–03), house (AL)
WALKER, Lula C. (S1 – 1.1, 431–34), 112 yrs., field (AL)
WALKER, Manda (3.4, 170–73), 80 yrs., field (SC)
WALKER, Minksie (11.8, 365–70), 77 yrs. (MO via AR, KY, and TN)
WALKER, Ned (3.4, 174–80), 83 yrs. (SC)
WALKER, Sarah (S1 – 2.5, 279–81) (WA via MO)
WALKER, Simon (6.1, 404–06) (S1 – 1.1, 435–37), 85 yrs., field (AL via
  GA)
WALL, Ben (S1 – 10.5, 2163–64), 85 yrs. (MS)
WALLACE, D.W. (S2 – 10.9, 3938–40), c. 76 yrs. (TX)
WALLACE, Lewis (S1 – 10.5, 2165–66), 87 yrs. (MS)
WALLACE, Willie (11.7, 42–43), 80 yrs., field (AR via AL)
WALLS, Nancy (S1 – 10.5, 2167), 90 yrs. (MS)
WATTERS, William (7.1, 312–13), 85 yrs. (OK via TN)
WALTON, Caroline Walker (S2 – 10.9, 3941–45), 75 yrs. (TX)
WALTON, Henry (S1 – 10.5, 2168–69), 84 yrs. (MS)
WALTON, John (5.4, 125–27) (S2 – 10.9, 3946–51), 87 yrs., field (TX)

WALTON, Liza (S2 - 10.9, 3957), 89 yrs. (TX via NC)
WALTON, Rhodus (13.4, 123-27) (S1 - 4.2, 628-34), c. 85 yrs. (GA)
WALTON, Sol (5.4, 128-30) (S2 - 10.9, 3952-57), c. 89 yrs., carried
    water; field (TX via AL, MS and LA)
WAMBLE, (WOMBLE), Rev. (6.2, 198-205), 78 yrs. (IN via TN and MS)
WARD, Allen (S1 - 10.5, 2170-74), 81 yrs., house and field (MS)
WARD, George (S1 - 10.5, 2175-77), house (MS)
WARD, Robert A. (S1 - 12.1, 359-64), 91 yrs., mill worker (OK via AR)
WARD, William (13.4, 128-33), 103 yrs., field (GA)
WARE, Annie Whitley (S2 - 10.9, 3958-67), c. 80 yrs. (TX)
WARFIELD, Henry (S1 - 10.5, 2178-84), 90 yrs., house and field (MS)
WARFIELD, Lucy Ann (S1 - 5.2, 455-57), 117 yrs., field (OH via KY)
WARING, Daniel (3.4, 181-83), 88 yrs., field (SC)
WARRIOR, Evans (11.7, 44-45), 80 yrs., field (AR)
WASHINGTON, Anna (11.7, 46-48), 77 yrs. (AR)
WASHINGTON, Callie (S1 - 10.5, 2185-95), c. 80 yrs. (MS via AR)
WASHINGTON, Cindy (6.1, 407-10), over 80 yrs., field (AL)
WASHINGTON, Eliza (11.7, 49-56), 77 yrs., washed clothes (AR)
WASHINGTON, Ella (5.4, 131-33) (S2 - 10.9, 3968-76), c. 82 yrs., cared
    for children (TX via LA)
WASHINGTON, George (S1 - 1.1, 438-39), 108 yrs., free (AL via VA and IL)
WASHINGTON,J.W. (S1 - 10.5, 2196), 96 yrs., nursed confederate soldiers
    (MS)
WASHINGTON, (Rev.) James W. (S1 - 10.5, 2197-2205), 81 yrs. (MS)
WASHINGTON, Jennie (11.7, 57-59), 80 yrs. (AR)
WASHINGTON, Lula (13.4, 134-35), 84 yrs. (GA via AL)
WASHINGTON, Nancy (3.4, 184-87), 104 yrs., house (SC)
WASHINGTON, Parrish (11.7, 60-61), 86 yrs. (AR)
WASHINGTON, Rosa (5.4, 134-37) (S2 - 10.9, 3977-83), c. 90 yrs., field
    (TX via LA)
WASHINGTON, Sam Jones (5.4, 138-40) (S2 - 10.9, 3984-91), 88 yrs.,
    cowhand (TX)
WASHINGTON, Susan Grubby (S1 - 10.5, 2206-07), d. 1918 (MS)
WASHINGTON, Virginia (S1 - 5.2, 458-60), c. 90 yrs., house (OH via TN)
WATKINS, Hettie (S2 - 1.7, 282-83) (IN)
    See Watkins, Louis (IN via TN)
WATKINS, Lincoln (S1 - 10.5, 2208-11), 85 yrs., house (MS via SC)
WATKINS, Louis (S1 - 5.1, 230-31) (S2 - 1.7, 280-81), c. 84 yrs.,
    errands (IN via TN)
    See Watkins, Hettie (IN)
WATKINS, Sylvia (16.6, 76-79), 91 yrs. (TN)
WATKINS, William (5.4, 141-43), 87 yrs. (TX via OH and VA)
WATSON, Caroline (11.7, 62-63), 82 yrs. (AR via MS)
WATSON, Charley (3.4, 188-90), 87 yrs. (SC)
WATSON, Dianah (5.4, 144-46) (S2 - 10.9, 3992-97), 102 yrs., house
    (TX via LA)
WATSON, Emma (5.4, 144-47) (S2 - 10.9, 3998-4002), c. 85 yrs., cared
    for children (TX)
WATSON, Mary (11.7, 64-69), 72 yrs. (AR)
WATSON, Mollie (S1 - 12.1, 365-74), 83 yrs., house (OK via TX)
WATSON, Samuel (6.2, 206-08), 75 yrs. (IN via KY)
WATSON, William (S1 - 12.1, 375-79), 85 yrs., field (OK via TN)
WATTS, Emaline (S1 - 10.5, 2212-13), 89 yrs., field (MS)
WATTS, John (S1 - 4.2, 635-36), 83 yrs., field (GA)
WAYNE, Bart (11.7, 70), 72 yrs. (AR)
WEATHERALL, Eugenia (S1 - 10.5, 2214-21), 74 yrs. (MS)

WEATHERBY, Isom (S1 - 10.5, 2236-38), 90 yrs., field (MS)
WEATHERS, Annie Mae (11.7, 71-72) (AR)
WEATHERS, Cora (11.7, 73-75), 79 yrs. (AR)
WEATHERSBY, Dave (S1 - 10.5, 2222-26), 86 yrs., shoe shiner (MS)
WEATHERSBY, Foster (S1 - 10.5, 2227-31), 82 yrs. (MS)
WEATHERSBY, George (S1 - 10.5, 2232-35), 85 yrs., field (MS)
WEATHERSBY, Robert (S1 - 10.5, 2239-44), 90 yrs. (MS)
WEATHERSBY, Steve (S1 - 10.5, 2245-48), 80 yrs., field (MS)
WEBB, Charlie (S2 - 10.9, 4003-05), 84 yrs., chores (TX via AL)
WEBB, Henry (S1 - 5.1, 232), free (IN)
WEBB, Ishe (11.7, 76-81), 78 yrs., field (AR via GA)
WEBB, Jennie (S1 - 10.5, 2249-54), 91 yrs., spinning and weaving (MS)
WEBB, Mary Frances (7.1, 314-15) (OK)
WEBB, Sol (S1 - 1.1, 440-42), over 85 yrs., house (AL)
WEEKS, Emma (S2 - 10.9, 4006-14), c. 80 yrs., house (TX)
WELCH, J.T., (M.D.) (S2 - 10.9, 4015-16), upper 50's, free (TX)
WELLS, Alfred (11.7, 82), 83 yrs., herded cows (AR via MS)
WELLS, Douglas (11.7, 83-84), 83 yrs. (AR via MS)
WELLS, Easter (7.1, 316-21), 83 yrs., house (OK via TX and AR)
WELLS, John (11.7, 85-88), 82 yrs., sheep herder (AR)
WELLS, Julia (S1 - 10.5, 2255), 86 yrs. (MS via MO and TN)
WELLS, Minerva (S1 - 10.5, 2256-61), 84 yrs., nursemaid (MS)
WELLS, Peter (S1 - 4.2, 637-38), 90 yrs. (GA via NC)
WELLS, Sarah (11.7, 89-94), 84 yrs. (AR via MS)
WELLS, Sarah Williams (11.7, 94-95), 71 yrs. (AR)
WESLEY, John (11.7, 96-97), field (AR via TN and KY)
WESLEY, Robert (11.7, 98), 74 yrs. (AR via AL)
WESMOLAND, Maggie (11.7, 99-103), 85 yrs., field (AR)
WEST, Calvin (11.7, 104-05), 68 yrs. (AR via MS)
WEST, James (5.4, 150-52) (S2 - 10.9, 4017-23), 83 yrs., house (TX via MS)
WEST, Mary Mays (11.7, 106), 65 yrs., free (AR via MS)
WESTBROOK, (Dr.) J.H. (S1 - 2.2, 96-97), 60's, free (CO via MS and TN)
WETHINGTON, Sylvester (11.7, 107), 77 yrs. (AR)
WHALLER, Nancy (6.2, 209-10), c. 81 yrs., field (IN via KY)
WHEELER, Martha (S1 - 10.5, 2262-71), 86 yrs. (MS)
WHEELER, William (S1 - 10.5, 2272-75), c. 83 yrs. (MS)
WHITAKER, Joe (11.7, 108), 70 yrs. (AR via TN)
WHITE, Adeline (5.4, 153-54) (S2 - 10.9, 4024-28), c. 80 yrs. (TX)
WHITE, Clara (S2 - 10.9, 4029-32), 78 yrs. (TX via LA)
WHITE, Dave (3.4, 194-95), c. 90 yrs. (SC)
WHITE, Eliza (6.1, 411-12), 80 yrs., house (AL)
WHITE, J.W. (S1 - 11.2, 310-11), 71 yrs., free (SC)
WHITE, Jack (S2 - 10.9, 4033-36), over 80 yrs., light field work (TX)
WHITE, John (7.1, 322-29), 121 yrs., house (OK via TX)
WHITE, Julia A. (11.7, 109-33), 79 yrs., house (AR)
WHITE, Liza (S1 - 1.1, 443-45), c. 90 yrs., house (AL via GA)
WHITE, Lucy (11.7, 134-35), 74 yrs. (AR)
WHITE, Margaret (17.1, 375-76), 84 yrs., house (FL via NC)
WHITE, Maria (S1 - 10.5, 2276-81), 84 yrs. (MS)
WHITE, Mingo (6.1, 413-22), c. 87 yrs., field and house (AL via SC)
WHITE, Nat (3.4, 191-93), 91 yrs. (SC)
WHITE, Sallah (S1 - 5.2, 461-63), over 85 yrs. (OH via TN)
WHITE, Tena (3.4, 196-98), 90 yrs., house (SC)
WHITEMAN, David (11.7, 136), 88 yrs. (AR)
WHITES, Abe (S1 - 1.1, 446-47), over 85 yrs., carried water to field

slaves (AL)
WHITESIDE, Dolly (11.7, 137), 81 yrs. (AR)
WHITESS, Abe (6.1, 423-24), over 90 yrs., field (AL via MS)
WHITFIELD, J.W. (11.7, 138-39), 60 yrs., free (AR)
WHITFIELD, Martha (S1 - 10.5, 2282), house (MS)
WHITLEY, Ophelia (15.2, 372-75), 96 yrs. (NC)
WHITMIRE, Eliza (S1 - 12.1, 380-88), over 85 yrs. (OK via GA and KS)
WHITMORE, Sarah (11.7, 140-41), 100 yrs., field (AR via MS)
WHITTED, Anderson (6.2, 211-13), 88 yrs., field (IN via NC)
WICKLIFFE, Sylvester (5.4, 155-59) (S2 - 10.9, 4037-45), c. 83 yrs.,
    free (TX via LA)
WIDGEON, John (S1 - 11.2, 312-13), 87 yrs. (d. 1938) (SC via VA and MD)
WIGGINS, James (16.3, 66-67), c. 87 yrs., house (MD)
WILBORN, David (S1 - 5.2, 464-67), 81 yrs. (OH via GA)
WILBORN, Dock (11.7, 142-46), 95 yrs. (AR via AL)
WILBURN, Jane McLeod (S1 - 10.5, 2283-96), 82 yrs. (MS)
WILCOX, Tom (15.2, 377-79), 81 yrs. (NC)
WILKINS, Alice (S2 - 10.9, 4046-56), 82 yrs. (TX)
WILKS, Bell (11.7, 147-48), 80 yrs. (AR via TN)
WILLBANKS, Green (13.4, 136-47), 77 yrs. (GA)
WILLIAMS, Allen (S2 - 10.9, 4057-64), 91 yrs., field (TX via AL)
WILLIAMS, Anderson (S1 - 10.5, 2297-2311), 87 yrs., field (MS)
WILLIAMS, Andy (S2 - 10.9, 4065-76), 78 yrs. (TX)
WILLIAMS, Banana (17.1, 365-66), c. 74 yrs. (FL)
WILLIAMS, Bell (11.7, 149), 85 yrs., mid-wife (AR)
WILLIAMS, Belle (16.1, 14-17) (S2 - 1.8, 292-95), c. 87 yrs. (KS via AR)
WILLIAMS, Bessie (S1 - 10.5, 2302-03), 78 yrs., field (MS via AL)
WILLIAMS, Bill (3.4, 199-201), 82 yrs. (SC)
WILLIAMS, Callie (6.1, 425-28) (S1 - 1.1, 448-53), 76 yrs. (AL)
WILLIAMS, Catherine (15.2, 381-84), 86 yrs., house (NC via VA)
WILLIAMS, Chaney M. (S1 - 10.5, 2304-05), 85 yrs. (MS)
WILLIAMS, Charles (S2 - 1.3, 181-249) (AR via MS)
WILLIAMS, (Rev.) Charles (S1 - 5.2, 468-72), 76 yrs. (OH via WV and LA)
WILLIAMS, Charley (11.7, 150-52), 81 yrs. (AR)
WILLIAMS, Charley (7.1, 330-43), 94 yrs., field (OK via LA)
WILLIAMS, Charlie (11.7, 153), 73 yrs. (AR via MS)
WILLIAMS, Columbus (11.7, 154-58), 98 yrs., field (AR)
WILLIAMS, Daphne (5.4, 160-63) (S2 - 10.9, 4077-86), c. 110 yrs.,
    nursemaid (TX via FL)
WILLIAMS, Ed (S1 - 10.5, 2306-12), 79 yrs. (MS)
WILLIAMS, Frank (11.7, 159-60), 100 yrs. (AR via MS)
WILLIAMS, Frank (S1 - 10.5, 2313-21), 85 yrs., cattle driver, house (MS)
WILLIAMS, Gus (11.7, 161-62), 80 yrs. (AR via TN and GA)
WILLIAMS, (Rev.) Handy (15.2, 386-89), 88 yrs. (NC)
WILLIAMS, Henrietta (11.7, 163-65), 82 yrs., field and house (AR via GA)
WILLIAMS, Henry Andrew (11.7, 166-69), 86 yrs., wagoneer (AR via NC)
WILLIAMS, Horatio (5.4, 164-65) (S2 - 10.9, 4087-89), 83 yrs. (TX via
    AR)
WILLIAMS, Hulda (S1 - 12.1, 389-91), 81 yrs. (OK via MS and AR)
WILLIAMS, Jackson Barkley (S2 - 1.3, 250-51), 76 yrs. (AR)
WILLIAMS, James (11.7, 170-71), 72 yrs. (AR via AL)
WILLIAMS, Jane (S1 - 10.5, 2322-25), 95 yrs., house (MS)
WILLIAMS, Jesse (3.4, 202-05), 83 yrs., field (SC)
WILLIAMS, John (11.7, 172-76), 45 yrs., free (AR via TX)
WILLIAMS, John (S1 - 10.5, 2326-33), 75 yrs. (MS)
WILLIAMS, John Thomas (15.2, 391-93), 77 yrs. (NC)

WILLIAMS, Julia (16.4, 102-07) (S1 - 5.2, 473-76), c. 100 yrs., field
  (OH via VA)
WILLIAMS, Julia (S2 - 10.9, 4090-92), c. 77 yrs. (TX)
WILLIAMS, Lewis (S2 - 10.9, 4093-95), 86 yrs., jockey (TX)
WILLIAMS, Lillie (11.7, 177-78), 69 yrs. (AR via MS)
WILLIAMS, Lizzie (S1 - 10.5, 2334-38), 88 yrs., weaving; field (MS)
WILLIAMS, Lizzie (15.2, 394-400), c. 90 yrs., house (NC)
WILLIAMS, Lord Byron (S1 - 10.5, 2339) (MS)
WILLIAMS, Lou (female) (5.4, 166-69) (S2 - 10.9, 4096-4101), c. 108 yrs.
  nursemaid (TX via MD)
WILLIAMS, Louella (S1 - 1.1, 454-60), 85 yrs., house (AL)
WILLIAMS, Maggie (S1 - 4.2, 639-41), over 85 yrs., field (GA)
WILLIAMS, Mary (11.7, 179), 65 yrs., free (AR)
WILLIAMS, Mary (11.7, 180-82), 69 yrs., free (AR)
WILLIAMS, Mary (11.7, 183-88), 82 yrs., weaver (AR via GA)
WILLIAMS, Mary (3.4, 206-07), c. 85 yrs., field (SC)
WILLIAMS, Mattie (S2 - 10.9, 4102-08), 84 yrs., house (TX via TN)
WILLIAMS, Melinda (S1 - 10.5, 2340-42), 76 yrs., house (MS)
WILLIAMS, Melissa (15.2, 411-13), 77 yrs. (NC)
WILLIAMS, Millie (5.4, 170-73) (S2 - 10.9, 4109-16), 86 yrs., house and
  field (TX via TN)
WILLIAMS, Mollie (7.2, 157-64) (S1 - 10.5, 2343-51), 84 yrs., field
  (MS)
WILLIAMS, Olin (S1 - 4.2, 642-48), over 85 yrs., house (GA)
WILLIAMS, Parson Rezin (16.3, 68-78), 115 yrs. (MD)
WILLIAMS, Penny (15.2, 402-05), 76 yrs. (NC)
WILLIAMS, Pete (S1 - 1.1, 461-62), 85 yrs., carried water (AL)
WILLIAMS, Plaz (15.2, 407-09), c. 90 yrs., field (NC via MS)
WILLIAMS, Reverend (16.4, 111-13), 76 yrs. (OH via WV)
WILLIAMS, Robert (S1 - 12.1, 392-96), 87 yrs., house and field (OK via
  MS)
WILLIAMS, Rose (5.4, 174-78) (S2 - 10.9, 4117-30), c. 90 yrs., field
  (TX)
WILLIAMS, Rosena Hunt (11.7, 189-90), 56 yrs., free (AR)
WILLIAMS, Sebia (S1 - 1.1, 463), over 90 yrs., child nurse (AL)
WILLIAMS, Soul (S2 - 10.9, 4131-34), 96 yrs., carriage driver (TX via
  MS)
WILLIAMS, Stephen (S2 - 10.9, 4135-41), 93 yrs. (TX via LA)
WILLIAMS, Steve (5.4, 179-81), 82 yrs. (TX)
WILLIAMS, Wayman (5.4, 182-86) (S2 - 10.9, 4142-53) (TX via MS)
WILLIAMS, William (16.4, 114-16), 80 yrs. (OH via NC)
WILLIAMS, William Ball III (11.7, 191-92), 98 yrs. (AR)
WILLIAMS, Willie (5.4, 187-89) (S2 - 10.9, 4154-60), 78 yrs. (TX via
  LA)
WILLIAMS, Willis (17.1, 347-54), 81 yrs. (FL)
WILLIAMS, Willis (3.4, 208-12), 89 yrs. (SC)
WILLIAMSON, Anna (11.7, 193-95), 75-80 yrs. (AR via TN)
WILLIAMSON, Callie Halsey (11.7, 196-97), 60 yrs., free (AR)
WILLIAMSON, Eliza (13.4, 148-50), c. 80 yrs. (GA via NC)
WILLIAMSON, George (S1 - 10.5, 2352), 96 yrs. (MS)
WILLINGHAM, Frances (13.4, 151-60), 78 yrs. (GA)
WILLIS, Aaron (S1 - 10.5, 2353-56), 79 yrs. (MS)
WILLIS, Adeline (13.4, 161-67), 100 yrs., field (GA)
WILLIS, Charles (S1 - 12.1, 397-99), 112 yrs., field (OK via MS)
WILLIS, Charlotte (11.7, 198-200), 63 yrs., free (AR)
WILLIS, Frances (S1 - 10.5, 2357-59), c. 90 yrs., nurse (MS)

WILLIS, Sampson (S2 - 10.9, 4161-67), 80's, chores (TX via KY)
WILLIS, Uncle (13.4, 168-75), 101 yrs., field (GA)
WILSON, Claude Augusta (17.1, 355-63), 79 yrs., field (FL)
WILSON, Ella (11.7, 201-06), 100 yrs., cook (AR via LA and GA)
WILSON, Emma Countee (S2 - 10.9, 4168-71), 85 yrs., house (TX)
WILSON, Emoline (3.4, 213-15), 90 yrs., field and house (SC)
WILSON, Isaac (S1 - 10.5, 2360-62), 92 yrs. (MS)
WILSON, Jake (S2 - 10.9, 4172-81), 83 yrs., house (TX via GA)
WILSON, James (11.8, 371-72), 87 yrs., handled sailboats (MO via SC)
WILSON, Jane (3.4, 216-17), 77 yrs., house (SC)
WILSON, Jesse (S1 - 5.2, 477-81), free (OH via KY)
WILSON, Julius (S2 - 10.9, 4182-90), 83 yrs., carried water (TX via TN)
WILSON, Luke (S1 - 10.5, 2363-68), 78 yrs. (MS)
WILSON, Lulu (5.4, 190-94) (S2 - 10.9, 4191-98), c. 97 yrs., spinner;
    house (TX via KY)
WILSON, Mary A. (S2 - 10.9, 4199-4204), 80 yrs., errands (TX via SC)
WILSON, Mary Jane (16.5, 55-56), house (VA)
WILSON, President (S2 - 10.9, 4205-06), 80 yrs., farm work (TX)
WILSON, Robert (11.7, 207-09), 101 yrs., field (AR via TN and VA)
WILSON, Robert (S2 - 10.9, 4207-15), 76 yrs. (TX via GA)
WILSON, Sarah (7.1, 344-53), 87 yrs. (OK)
WILSON, Sarah (S2 - 10.9, 4216-25), nursemaid (TX via LA)
WILSON, Smith (S2 - 10.9, 4226-35), 75 yrs., house (TX)
WILSON, Temple (S1 - 10.5, 2369-75), 80 yrs. (MS)
WILSON, Tom (7.2, 165-68) (S1 - 10.5, 2376-80), c. 84 yrs., house (MS)
WILSON, Wash (5.4, 195-200) (S2 - 10.9, 4236-48), c. 95 yrs. (TX via LA)
WINDFIELD, Dicy (S1 - 10.5, 2381-86), 96 yrs., house (MS)
WINDHAM, Tom (11.7, 210-15), 92 yrs., house (AR via GA)
WINFIELD, Cornelia (13.4, 176-78), 83 yrs. (GA)
WINGER, Van Hook (S2 - 10.9, 3901-12), 88 yrs., field (TX via TN)
WINLOCK, George (S1 - 5.1, 233-37), 91 yrs. (IN via KY)
WINN, Willie (5.4, 201-07) (S2 - 10.9, 4249-57), 116 yrs., farmhand
    (TX via LA)
WINSTON, Louis Jr. (S1 - 10.5, 2387), 93 yrs. (MS)
WINSTON, Sarah (S2 - 10.9, 4258-59), c. 83 yrs. (TX via AR)
WISE, Alice (11.7, 216-17) (S1 - 1.3, 252), 79 yrs., house (AR via SC)
WISE, Frank (11.7, 218-21), 80's (AR via GA)
WITHERS, Lucy (11.7, 222-23), 86 yrs., field (AR via SC)
WITHERSPOON, Silvia (6.1, 429-31), c. 90 yrs., house (AL via MS)
WITT, Rube (5.4, 208-10) (S2 - 10.9, 4260-64), 87 yrs., house (TX)
WOFFORD, Acemy (S1 - 12.1, 400-01), c. 100 yrs., field (OK via MS and
    TX)
WOMBLE, George (13.4, 179-93) (S1 - 4.2, 653-57), c. 93 yrs., house
    (GA)
    See Rush, Mrs. (GA)
WOMBLE, Rev. (IN via TN and MS)
    See Wamble, Rev. (IN via TN and MS)
WOOD, Mintie (11.8, 373-77), 90 yrs., field (MO via AR and TN)
WOOD, Ruth (S2 - 10.9, 4265-71), 80 yrs. (TX via MS)
WOOD, Wes (16.2, 24-27), field (KY)
WOODBERRY, Eugenia (3.4, 218-26), 89 yrs., house (SC)
WOODBERRY, Julia (3.4, 227-46) (S1 - 11.2, 214-15), 70's (SC)
WOODS, Alex (15.2, 415-19), 79 yrs. (NC)
WOODS, Anita (S1 - 10.5, 2388-91), 97 yrs., field (MS)
WOODS, Anna (11.7, 224-28) (AR via TX)
WOODS, Cal (11.7, 229-31), c. 85 yrs., field (AR via SC)

WOODS, George (3.4, 247-52), c. 80 yrs., field (SC)
WOODS, Maggie (11.7, 232-34), 70 yrs. (AR)
WOODS, Rebecca (S1 - 10.5, 2392-94), 80 yrs., field (MS)
WOODS, Ruben (5.4, 211-13) (S2 - 10.9, 4272-76), 84 yrs., house (TX via
   AL)
WOODS, Tom W. (7.1, 354-58), 83 yrs., field (OK via VA)
WOODSEN, Willis (TX)
   See Woodson (Woodsen), Willis
WOODSON, Alex (6.2, 214-17), c. low 80's, field (IN)
WOODSON, (Woodsen), Willis (5.4, 214-15) (S2 - 10.9, 4277-80) (TX)
WOODWARD, Aleck (3.4, 253-56), 83 yrs., field (SC)
WOODWARD, Ike (S1 - 10.5, 2395-98), 82 yrs. (MS)
WOODWARD, Mary (3.4, 257-59), 83 yrs., house (SC)
WOOLDRIDGE, Mary (16.2, 106-10), 103 yrs., house and field (KY)
WOORLING, James G. (5.4, 216-18) (S2 - 10.9, 4374-77), 110 yrs., white
   (TX)
WOOTEN, Joe (S1 - 4.2, 658), 104 yrs. (GA)
WORD, Sam (11.7, 235-41), 79 yrs. (AR)
WORD, Sophia (16.2, 66-68), 99 yrs. (KY)
WORTH, Pauline (3.4, 260-65), 79 yrs., house (SC)
WORTHY, Ike (11.7, 242-43), 74 yrs. (AR via LA and AL)
WRIGHT, Alice (11.7, 244-48), 74 yrs. (AR via AL)
WRIGHT, Caroline (5.4, 219-22) (S2 - 10.9, 4281-86), 90 yrs., house
   (TX via LA)
WRIGHT, Daphney (3.4, 266-69), 106 yrs. (SC)
WRIGHT, Ella (S1 - 4.2, 659), 79 yrs. (GA)
WRIGHT, Ellaine (11.8, 378), 97 yrs. (MO)
WRIGHT, Hannah Brooks (11.7, 249-51), 85 yrs., house (AR via MS)
WRIGHT, Henry (13.4, 194-204), 99 yrs., house (GA)
WRIGHT, Maggie (S1 - 11.2, 316-18) (SC)
WRIGHT, Mary (16.2, 61-66) (KY)
WRIGHT, Mary (S1 - 11.2, 319-21), c. 80 yrs. (SC)
WRIGHT, William (S1 - 2.2, 98-100), 68 yrs., free (CO via TN)
WROE, Sallie (5.4, 223-24) (S2 - 10.9, 4287-91), 81, house (TX)
WYMAN, Susannah (S1 - 4.2, 660-65), 103 yrs. (GA via SC)

YARBROUGH, Fannie (5.4, 225-26) (S2 - 10.9, 4292-93), c. 83 yrs.,
   shepherd's helper (TX)
YARBROUGH, Virginia (S2 - 10.9, 4294-99), 78 yrs. (TX via LA)
YATES, Tom (11.7, 252), 66 yrs. (AR via MS)
YELLADY, Dilly (15.2, 426-30), 70 yrs. (NC)
YELLERDAY, Hilliard (15.2, 432-36), 76 yrs. (NC)
YOUNG, Annie (11.7, 253-54), 76 yrs. (AR)
YOUNG, Annie (7.1, 359-62), 86 yrs., house (OK via TN)
YOUNG Anthony (S1 - 5.1, 238-39), 104 yrs. (IN via KY)
YOUNG, Ben (S1 - 10.5, 2399) (MS)
YOUNG, Bill (3.4, 271-72), early 70's (SC)
YOUNG, Bob (3.4, 273-75), 75 yrs. (SC)
YOUNG, Clara (7.2, 169-74) (S1 - 10.5, 2400-06), 95 yrs., field (MS via
   AL)
YOUNG, Dink Walton (Mammy Dink) (13.4, 205-11) (S1 - 4.2, 666-70), c.
   96 yrs., house (GA)
YOUNG, George (6.1, 432-36), 91 yrs., field (AL)
YOUNG, John (11.7, 255-57), 92 yrs., field (AR via VA)

NAME INDEX BY STATE

ALABAMA

AARONS, Charlie
ABERCROMBIE, Anthony
ALLEN, Jeff
AMERSON, Richard
AMMONDS, Molly
AMBERSON, Charity
ASKEW, Gus
BAKER, Father
BAKER, Julia
BAKER, Tom
BALLARD, General Lee
BARNES, Henry
BEAUCHAMP, Nathan
BELL, Bettie M.
BELL, Oliver
BENTON, Sara
BIRDSONG, Nelson
BISHOP, Ank
BOHANNON, Henry
BONNER, Siney
BOOTH, Etta
BOWEN, Jennie
BRADFIELD, Nannie
BRADLEY, Martha
BROWN, Allen
BROWN, Gus
BRYANT, Tommie
BURNES, Mahala
CALLOWAY, Walter
CARVER, George Washington
CASEY, Esther King
CASSIBRY, Georgiana
CHAMBERS, Abraham
CHAPMAN, Amy

CHAPMAN, Emma
CHEATAM, Henry
CLARK, Laura
CLAYTON, Hattie
CLEMONS, Wadley
CLUSSEY, Aunt
COLBERT, William
COLLINS, Tildy
COLQUITT, Sara
COSBY, Mandy McCullough
CRANDLE, Bill
CROCKETT, Emma
CROSS, Cheney
CUMMINGS, Josephine
CUSTIS, Lititia
DANIEL, Matilda Pugh
DAVIS, Annie
DAVIS, Carrie
DAVIS, Clara
DILLARD, George
DILLIARD, Ella
DIRT, Rufus
EARLY, Sarah
EBENEZER, Mr.
EPPES, Katherine
ERWING, Cynthia
FITZPATRICK, Reuben
FLOURNEY, Georgia
FLOURNEY, Lou
FORD, Heywood
FOWLER, M.
FOWLER, M.
FREDERICK, Bert
GARLIC, Delia
GARRETT, Angie
GARRY, Henry
GEORGIA
GIBSON, Fannie
GILL, Frank
GILLARD, Jim
GILLIAM, (Uncle) George
GRAHAM, Martin
GRANDBERRY, Mary Ella
GREEN, Esther
GREEN, Jake
GRIGSBY, Charity
HARRIS, Ella
HAYES, Charles
HILL, Laura
HILL, Lizzie
HINES, Gabe
HODGE (or HODGES), Adeline
HOLLAND, Caroline
HOLLOWAY, Jane
HOLMES, Joseph
HORN, Josh

WITHERSPOON, Silvia
YOUNG, George
ZIEGLER, Frank

ARIZONA

EMBERS, Charley
MERCHANT, Harvey

ARKANSAS

ABBOTT, Silas
ABERNATHY, Lucian
ABROMSON, Laura
ADELINE, Aunt
ADWAY, Rose
AIKEN, Liddie
ALDRIDGE, Mattie
ALEXANDER, Amsy
ALEXANDER, Diana
ALEXANDER, Fannie
ALEXANDER, Lucretia
ALLEN, Ed
ALLISON, Lucindy
AMES, Josephine
ANDERSON, Charles
ANDERSON, Nancy
ANDERSON, R.B.
ANDERSON, Sarah
ANDERSON, Selie
ANDERSON, W.A.
ANONYMOUS
ANONYMOUS
ANTHONY, Henry
ARBERY, Katie
ARMSTRONG, Campbell
ARMSTRONG, Cora
BACCUS, Lillie
BADGETT, Joseph Samuel
BAILEY, Jeff
BAKER, James
BALTIMORE, Uncle William
BANKS, Mose
BANNER, Henry
BARNETT, John W.H.
BARNETT, Josephine Ann
BARNETT, Lizzie
BARNETT, Spencer
BARR, Emma
BARR, Robert
BASS, Matilda
BEAL, Emmett
BEARD, Dina
BECK, Anne

BURRIS, Adeline
BUTLER, Jennie
BYRD, E.L.
BYRD, Emmett Augusta
CANNON, Frank
CAULEY, Zenie
CHAMBERS, Liney
CHARLESTON, Willie Buck Jr.
CHASE, Lewis
CLAY, Katherine
CLAY, Sarah
CLEMMENTS, Maria Sutton
CLEMONS, Fannie
CLINTON, Joe
COLEMAN, Betty
COTTON, Lucy
COTTON, T.W.
COTTONHAM, John
CRAGIN, Ellen
CRANE, Sally
CRAWFORD, Isaac
CROSBY, Mary
CROSS, William
CROWLEY, Ellen
CRUMP, Richard
CULP, Zenia
CUMINS, Albert
CURLETT, Betty
CURRY, J.H.
DANDRIDGE, Lyttleton
DANIELS, Ella
DARROW, Mary Allen
DAVIS, Alice
DAVIS, Charlie
DAVIS, D.
DAVIS, James
DAVIS, Jeff
DAVIS, Jeff
DAVIS, Jordan
DAVIS, Mary Jane Drucilla
DAVIS, Minerva
DAVIS, Rosetta
DAVIS, Virginia
DAVIS, Winnie
DAY, Leroy
DELL, Hammett
DICKEY, James
DIGGS, Benjamin
DILLON, Katie
DIXON, Alice
DIXON, Luke D.
DIXON, Martha Ann
DOCKERY, Railroad
DONALSON, Callie
DORTCH, Charles Green
DORUM, Fannie

DOTHRUM, Silas
DOUGLAS, Hattie
DOUGLAS, Sarah
DOUGLAS, Sebert
DOUGLAS, Tom
DOYL, Henry
DOYLD, Willie
DUDLEY, Wade
DUKE, Isabella
DUKES, Wash
DUNN, Lizzie
DUNNE, Nellie
DUNWOODY, William L.
EDWARDS, Lucius
ELLIOTT, John
EVANS, Millie
EVANS, Mose
FAIRLEY, Rachel
FAKES, Pauline
FANNEN, Mattie
FARMER, Robert
FERGUSSON, Mrs. Lou
FERRELL, Jennie
FIELD, Sally
FIKES, Frank
FILER, J.E.
FINGER, Orleans
FINLEY, Molly
FINNEY, Fanny
FISHER, "Gate-Eye"
FITZGERALD, Ellen
FITZHUGH, Henry
FLAGG, Mary
FLOWERS, Doc
FLUKER, Frances
FLUKER, Ida May
FORD, Wash
FORTENBURY, Judia
FOSTER, Emma
FOSTER, Ira
FRANKLIN, Leonard
FRAZIER, Eliza
FRAZIER, Mary
FRAZIER, Tyler
FREEMAN, (Aunt) Mittie
FRITZ, Mattie
GADSON, Charlie
GAINES, Dr. D.B.
GAINES, Mary
GARDNER, Emma
GENT, William
GIBSON, Jennie Wormly
GILL, James
GILLAM, Cora
GILLESPIE, J.N.
GLASS, Will

PERKINS, Maggie
PERKINS, Rachel
PERRY, Dinah
PETERS, Alfred
PETERS, Mary Estes
PETERSON, John
PETTIS, Louise
PETTUS, Henry C.
PHILLIPS, Dolly
PIGGY, Tony
PITTMAN, Ella
PITTMAN, Sarah
POE, Mary
POLLACKS, W.L.
POPE, (Doc) John
PORTER, William
POTTER, Bob
PRAYER, Louise
QUESNESBERRY, Mrs. Betty
QUINN, Doc
RALLS, Henrietta
RANKINS, Diana
REAVES, Clay
REECE, Jane
REED, Frank
REEVES, James
RHONE, Shepherd
RICHARD, Dora
RICKS, Jim
RIGGER, Charlie
RIGLEY, Ida
RITCHIE, Milton
RIVERS, Alice
ROBERTSON (ROBINSON), George
ROBERTSON, Irene
ROBINSON, Augustus
ROBINSON, George
ROBINSON, Malindy
ROBINSON, Tom
ROGERS, Isom
ROGERS, Oscar James
ROGERS, Will Orr
ROOKS, William Henry
ROSE, Amanda
ROSE, "Cat"
ROSSBERRY, Senia
ROWLAND, Laura
RUCKER, Landy
RUFFIN, Martha
RUFFIN, Thomas
RUMPLE, Casper
RUSSELL, Henry
RYE, Katie
SAMUELS, Bob
SANDERSON, Emma
SCOTT, Mary

BUFFORD, Henry
CHAPMAN, W.
CLARK, Anna
HANNA, Moses
HARRIS, Charles
HARRIS, Susan
HOOD, Willis
JACKSON, James W.
LAMB, Alice
LEWIS, John H.
LITTLE, Kate
LOPER, Frank
MCDONALD, Kate
MANUEL, James J.
RONE, Martin
ROSS, Gertie
SMITH, Stonewall
SPRATLIN, (Dr.) V.B.
THOMAS, Mike
TRIPLETT, Oscar
WESTBROOK, (Dr.) J.H.
WRIGHT, William

DISTRICT OF COLUMBIA

HARRIS, Lancy
THOMAS, Elizabeth

FLORIDA

ANDERSON, Josephine
ANDREWS, Samuel Simeon (Parson)
AUSTIN, Bill
BATES, Frank
BERRY, Frank
BIDDIE, Mary Minus
BOYD, (Rev.) Eli
BOYNTON, Rivana (Riviana)
BROOKS, Matilda
BYNES, Titus
CAMPBELL, Patience
CLAYTON, Florida
COATES, "Father" Charles
COATES, Irene
COKER, Neil
DAVIS, Young Winston
DORSEY, Douglas
DOUGLAS, Ambrose Hilliard
DUCK, Mama
DUKES, Willis
EVERETT, Louisa
EVERETT, Sam

ALLEN, Rev. W.B.
ALLEN, Washington
AMELIA
ANONYMOUS
ATES, Caroline
ATKINSON, Jack
AUSTIN, Hannah
AVERY, Celestia
BAKER, Georgia
BATTLE, Alice
BATTLE, Jasper
BENNEFIELD, Willis
BENTON, Harriet
BETHUNE, Thomas G.
BINNS, Arie
BLAKELY, Sally
BLAND, Henry
BODY, Rias
BOLTON, James
BOSTWICK, Alec
BOUDRY, Nancy
BRADLEY, Alice
BRADSHAW, Tillman
BRISCOE, Della
BROOKS, George
BROWN, Betty
BROWN, Easter
BROWN, Julia ("Aunt Sally")
BROWN, Sally
BROWNING, G.W.
BUNTS, Queen Elizabeth
BURDEN, Augustus
BUTLER, Marshal
BYRD, Mrs.
BYRD, Sarah
CALLOWAY, Mariah
CAMPBELL, Ellen
CARPENTER, Mary
CARRIE
CARTER, George
CASTLE, Susan
CAULTON, George
CAWTHON, Cicely
CHILDS, Mary
CLAIBOURN, Ellen
CLAY, Berry
CODY, Pierce
COFER, Willis
COKER, Emma
COLBERT, Mary
COLE, John
COLE, Julia
COLEMAN, F.C.
COLQUITT, Kizzie
COLQUITT, Martha
DAVIS, Minnie

DAVIS, Mose
DENNIS, Edie
DERRICOTTE, Ike
DILLARD, Benny
DORSEY, Amelia
EASON, George
EASTER, Aunt
ELDER, Callie
EUGENE
EVERETTE, Martha
FAVOR, Lewis
FAVOR, Mr.
FERGUSON, Mary
FLAGG, Randell
FLANNIGAN, Lula
FRYER, Carrie Nancy
FULCHER, Fannie
FURR, Anderson
GAREY, Elisha (Doc)
GARRETT, Leah
GIBON, Fannie
GLADDY, Mary
GLOVER, Julia
GRANT, Anna
GRAY, Sarah
GREEN, Alice
GREEN, Isaiah
GREEN, Margaret
GREEN, Minnie
GRESHAM, Wheeler
GRIFFIN, Abner
GRIFFIN, Heard
GULLINS, David G.
HAMMOND, Milton
HARMON, Jane Smith Hill
HARRIS, Dosia
HARRIS, John
HARRIS, "Uncle Shang"
HARRIS, Squire
HARRISON, Ethel
HAWKINS, Ella
HAWKINS, Tom
HEARD, Bill
HEARD, Emmaline
HEARD, Mildred
HEARD, Robert
HENDERSON, Benjamin
HENDERSON, Harris
HENDERSON, Julia
HENRY, Jefferson Franklin
HENRY, "Uncle Robert"
HILL, John
HOLMES, (Rev.) B.R.
HOLMES, Henry
HOOD, Laura
HUDSON, Carrie

WRIGHT, Henry
WYMAN, Susannah
YOUNG, Dink Walton

INDIANA

ALLEN, Joseph
ARNOLD, George W.
ASH, Thomas
BARBER, Rosa
BARNETT, Lewis
BARTON, Robert
BATTLE, Anthony
BEATTY, George
BLAKELY, Mittie
BLAND, Patsy Jane
BOLDEN, Lizzie
BOONE, Carl
BORLAND, Walter
BOWMAN, Julia
BOYCE, Angie
BOYSAW, Edna
BRACEY, Callie
BRAGG, Tolbert
BUCKNER, Dr. George Washington
BURNS, George Taylor
BUTLER, Belle
CARTER, Joseph William
CAVE, Ellen
CHAVIOUS, Hillery
CHEATAM, Harriet
CHEATHAM, Robert J.
CHILDRESS, James
COLBERT, Sarah
COOPER, Frank
CRANE, Mary
DAUGHERTY, Ethel
DAUGHERTY, Lizzie
DUNCAN, Rachael
EDMUNDS, (Rev.) H.H.
EUBANKS, John
FAIRBANKS, Calvin
FIELDS, John W.
FORTMAN, George
FOWLER, Alex
GIBSON, John Henry
GOHAGEN, Peter
GRAHAM, Sidney
GREEN, L.
GUWN, Betty
HARRIS, Maston
HARVEY, Nealy
HERRINGTON, Harriet
HICKS, (Dr.) S.

HOCKADAY, Mrs.
HOUGH (or HOUSE), Samantha
HOWARD, Robert
HUME, Matthew
HUNTER, Lillian
JACKSON, Henrietta
JOHNSON, Lizzie
JOHNSON, Pete
JONES, Betty
JONES, Ira
JONES, Lark
JONES, Nathan
KATES, Ralph
KELLEY, Alexander
KELLEY, Bell
KNOWLES, Merton
LEE, Elvira
LENNOX, Adeline Rose
LEWIS, Mrs. E.
LEWIS, Ezekiel
LEWIS, Thomas
LOCKE, Sarah H.
LOVE, Maria
MCCLAIN, Hettie
MCKINLEY, Robert
MAGRUDER, Tom
MERRILL, Sarah E.
MILLER, Richard
MILLION, Eliza
MONROE, Roy
MONROE, Woodford
MOORE, Ben
MOORE, John
MOORMAN, (Rev.) Henry Clay
MORGAN, America
MORRISON, George
MOSELY, Joseph
NEAL, Peter
NELSON, (Rev.) Oliver
O'DONNELL, Sarah
O'HARA, Cynthia
PARROTT, Richard
PATTERSON, Amy Elizabeth
PATTERSON, Haywood
PITMAN, Spear
POLK, Nelson
POMPEY, Nettie
PRESTON, Mrs.
QUINN, William M.
RICHARDSON, Candus
ROBERTS, Nancy
ROBINSON, Joe
ROGERS, Rosaline
ROLLINS, Parthena
ROSE, Katie
RUDD, John

RUSSELL, Elizabeth
SAMUELS, Amanda Elizabeth
SCARBER, Mrs. Mary Elizabeth
SCOTT, Lulu
SIMMS, Jack
SLAUGHTER, Billy
SLAUGHTER, Moses
SMITH, Alex
SMITH, Mrs. Alex
SMITH, Susan
SMITH, Sylvester,
STEWART, Mary
STONE, Barney
SUGGS, Adah Isabelle
SUTTON, Katie
TATE, Mary Emily Eaton
TATE, Preston
THOMAS, George
THOMPSON, George
WADE, Joe
WAMBLE, (WOMBLE), Rev.
WATKINS, Hettie
WATKINS, Louis
WATSON, Samuel
WEBB, Henry
WHALLEN, Nancy
WHITTED, Anderson
WINLOCK, George
WOMBLE, Rev.
WOODSON, Alex
YOUNG, Anthony

KANSAS

HOLBERT, Clayton
SIMS, Bill
WILLIAMS, Belle

KENTUCKY

ANDERSON, John
BILLINGSBY, Kate
BOGIE, Dan
BOYD, Annie B.
BRUNNER, Peter
CAMPBELL, Easter Sudie
COX, (Rev.) John R.
DORSEY, George
EAVES, Nannie
FORCE, Tinie
GIBSON, Mandy

GUDGEL, Ann
HENDERSON, George
HUDESPETH, Esther
JONES, Amelia
JONES, Martha
LEWIS, Elvira
MCKEE, Judy
MASON, Harriett
MAYFIELD, Bert
MITCHELL, Scott
MORGAN, Annie
OATS, Will
OWENS, Joana
ROBINSON, Belle
SANDERS, Susan Dale
SCRUGGS, George
SHIRLEY, Edd
TORIAN, Cora
WOODS, Wes
WOOLDRIDGE, Mary
WORD, Sophia
WRIGHT, Mary

MARYLAND

ANONYMOUS
BARNES, Mary
BROOKS, Lucy
COLES, Charles
DEANE, James V.
FAYMAN, Mrs. M.S.
FOOTE, Thomas
GASSAWAY, Menellis
HAMMOND, Caroline
HARRIS, Page
HENSON, Annie Young
JACKSON, (Rev.) Silas
JAMES, James Calhart
JAMES, Mary Moriah Anne Susanna
JOHNSON, Phillip
JONES, George
LEWIS, Alice
LEWIS, Perry
MACKS, Richard
RANDALL, Tom
SIMMS, Dennis
TAYLOR, Jim
WIGGINS, James
WILLIAMS, Parson Rezin

MINNESOTA

ALLEN, Ruth
DORSEY, Nelson
HICKMAN, (Rev.) Robert
JOHNSON, George
NORRIS, Mr.
SELLERS, Mary
THOMPSON, Laura

MISSISSIPPI

ABBEY, Tabby
ADAMS, Lewis
ALBRIGHT, George Washington
ALDREDGE, Jack
ALFORD, Barney
ALLEN, Dinah
ALLEN, Jim
ANDERSON, Cindy
ANN, Aunt
ANONYMOUS
ANONYMOUS
ARCHER, Jim
ASHLEY, Levi
BACKSTROM, Susan
BAKER, Anna
BAMBURG, Red
BANKS, Ephom
BECCA, Aunt
BELCHER, John
BELL, Alex
BELL, Charlie
BELL, Mary
BEST, Nathan
BILLUPS, Ellen
BISHOP, Nancy
BLACK, William Edward
BLACKWELL, Charlie
BLEWETT, Dig
BLEWETT, Harold
BLEWITT, Peter
BOGGAN, Manda
BOHANON, Georganna
BOLDRIDGE, Joe
BOND, Porter
BONES, Tom
BONNER, Elax
BOOTH, Ella
BOVY, Joe
BOWMAN, Amanda
BRADFORD, Elodga
BRADFORD, Sam
BRADLEY, Edmund

COOK, Jerry
CORNELIUS, James
COSTINE, Hannah
COTTEN, Betsey
COX, Albert
COX, Alex
COX, Julia
COX, Tony
COXE, Josephine
CRAFT, Jessie
CRAIG, Letitia
CRAWFORD, Rena
CRUM, Ed
CYRUS, Shadrach
DANIELS, Henry
DANTZLER, Juda
DARBY, _____
DAVENPORT, Charlie
DAVIS, A.K.
DAVIS, Joe
DAVIS, Louis
DAVIS, Ollie
DAWKINS, Frank
DAWKINS, Jake
DICKERSON, Nelson
DILLARD, Lizzie
DILLWORTH, Mattie
DIVINITY, Howard
DIXON, Emily
DIXON, Sally
DODGE, Clara
DOGAN, (Dr.) M.W.
DONALD, George
DONALD, Lucy
DRAKE, Ann
DURDEN, John
DURR, Simon
DURRELL, Betsy
EDMONDS, Mollie
EDMONDSON, Manda
EDWARDS, Malinda
EMANUEL, Gabe
EUBANKS, Jerry
EVANS, Emma
EVANS, Lawrence
EVANS, Minerva
FAIRLEY, J.W.
FARNANDIS, Ben
FELDER, Sarah
FINLEY, Elizabeth
FISHER, George
FLANNAGAN, William
FLOYD, Angie
FLOYD, Sylvia
FLOYD, Tom
FOLTZ, Sally

HOLLIDAY, Wayne
HOLMAN, Charles
HOLMAN, Rose
HOLMES, Augustus
HOLMES, Charlie
HOOVER, Silvia
HOWARD, Perry W.
HOWARD, R.H.
HOWELL, Jerry
HUBBARD, Clark
HUBBARD, James Nelson
HUGHES, Emanuel
HUGHES, Frank
HUNLEY, Tom ("Hambone")
HUNT, Rhoda
HURST, Pattie
IRVIN, Squire
ISOM, Joanna Thompson
"JACK, ARMY"
JACKSON, Dora
JACKSON, Laura Jane
JACOBS, Turner
JAMES, Arena
JAMES, Wash
JARMAGIN, Andrew J.
JEFFERSON, Hattie
JEFFERSON, Lewis
JEMISON, Rube
JENKINS, Nep
JOHNSON, Callie
JOHNSON, Eliza
JOHNSON, Emma
JOHNSON, George
JOHNSON, Jeff
JOHNSON, Prince
JOHNSON, Priscilla
JOHNSON, Tilda
JOHNSTON, Clarence
JOHNSTON, Wiley
JONES, Aaron
JONES, Austin
JONES, Charity
JONES, Edward
JONES, Isam
JONES, Jack
JONES, Julius
JONES, Mandy
JONES, Mary Jane
JONES, Myra
JONES, Oliver
JONES, Susan
JORDAN, Jonce J.
JORDAN, Charlie
KATHERINE, Aunt
KELLEY, Abe
KENNEDY, Hamp

MINGO, Sam
MINTER, Fannie
MITCHELL, Cindy
MITCHELL, Jeff
MONTGOMERY, Adeline
MONTGOMERY, Alex
MONTGOMERY, Isaiah T.
MONTGOMERY, J.P.T.
MONTGOMERY, Laura
MONTGOMERY, Rube
MOODY, Dave
MOORE, Charlotte
MOORE, Crozier ("Crow")
MOORE, Riley
MORGAN, (Aunt) Jane
MORRIS, Tom
MORSE, Peyton
MORSE, Rose
MOSELEY, John Archie
MOSES, Charlie
MOSLEY, Sam
MUNSON, Melissa
MURRAY, Henrietta
MURRAY, Henry
MYERS, Elbert
NECAISE, Henri (Henry)
NEWELL, Tom
NICKERSON, Jim
NICKERSON, Sally
NORFLEET, Lizzie
NORTON, Hester
NORWOOD, Glascow
OLIVER, Mark
PAGE, Sid
PARHAM, Maria
PARKER, Caesar
PATTERSON, Frances
PATTERSON, Sam
PATTERSON, Sarah
PATTON, Grundy
PATTON, Ned
PEALE, Andrew
PEARL, Billy
PETTUS, Joe
PETTY, William
PHILLIPS, Rebecca
PICKETT, Century
PIERNAS, Louis Joseph
PITTS, Dempsey
PLUMMER, Nat
POCHE, Cora
POINDEXTER, Allen
POLK, Lizzie
POSEY, Elsie
POTTER, Isaac
POWELL, Salem

POWERS, Charlie
PRICE, Andrew
PRICE, Dick
PRINCE, John
PRINGLE, "Uncle Ike"
QUINN, James Hamilton
QUINN, S.B.
QUINN, Spart
RABB, Jack
RAMSAY, George Washington
RAMSEY, Filmore
RATLIFF, Bunk
RAYFORD, Jeff
REE, Henry R.
REED, (Uncle) George
REED, Rachel Santee
REVELS, Hiram Rhoades
RICHARDSON, Ben
RILEY, Cicely
RILEY, Ephram
ROBERSON, Uncle
ROBINSON, (Rev.) Ben J.
ROBINSON, Ephriam
ROBINSON, Ibby Barnes
ROBINSON, Manus
ROBINSON, Nancy
ROBY, Edd
ROCKET, Nettie
RODGERS, Caroline
ROGERS, Jane
ROGERS, Noah
ROLAND, Jennie
ROLLEY, Callie
ROLLINS, Joe
ROSE, Mammie
RUSSELL, Rose
SANDERS, Harriet
SANTEE, Hamp
SHAW, Alice
SHAW, Lucindy Hall
SIMMONS, Hamp
SIMMONS, Smith
SIMPSON, Joe
SINGLETON, Adam
SINGLETON, James
SMITH, Adam
SMITH, Benjamin Whitley
SMITH, Berry
SMITH, Billie
SMITH, Cassie Blackmond
SMITH, Malindy
SMITH, Richard
SNOW, Andy
SNOW, Susan
SPENCER, Elias
SPIGHT, Tuck

WEATHERSBY, Steve
WEBB, Jennie
WELLS, Julia
WELLS, Minerva
WHEELER, Martha
WHEELER, William
WHITE, Maria
WHITFIELD, Martha
WILBURN, Jane McLeod
WILLIAMS, Anderson
WILLIAMS, Bessie
WILLIAMS, Chaney M.
WILLIAMS, Ed
WILLIAMS, Frank
WILLIAMS, Jane
WILLIAMS, John
WILLIAMS, Lizzie
WILLIAMS, Lord Byron
WILLIAMS, Melinda
WILLIAMS, Mollie
WILLIAMSON, George
WILLIS, Aaron
WILLIS, Frances
WILSON, Isaac
WILSON, Luke
WILSON, Temple
WILSON, Tom
WINDFIELD, Dicy
WINSTON, Louis Jr.
WOODS, Anita
WOODS, Rebecca
WOODWARD, Ike
YOUNG, Ben O.
YOUNG, Clara
YOUNG, Robert

MISSOURI

ABBOT, James Monroe
ABERNATHY, Betty
ALLEN, Hannah
ALLEN, Parson
ANDERSON, Charles Gabriel
ARNETT, R.C.
BAKER, Jane
BELL, Mary A.
BLACK, William
BOGGS, Daisy L.
BOLDEN, Mary M.
BOLLINGER, George
BRIDGES, Annie
BROOKS, G.W.
BROWN, Betty
BROWN, Steve

BRUNER, Richard
BRYANT, Robert
BUFFORD, Alex
BUTLINGTON, Charles
CASEY, Harriet
CASEY, Joe
CHAMBERS, Lula
COPE, Ermaline
CORN, Peter
CRADDOCK, Ed
DANFORTH, Nelson
DANT, Henry
DAVIS, Lucy
DAVIS, Margaret
DISCUS, Malinda
DISCUS, Mark
DIVINE, Mary
DOUTHIT, Mrs. Charles
ESTELL, John
EULENBERG, Smoly
EVANS, Ann Ulrich
GOINGS, James
GOINGS, Rachal
GRAVES, Sarah Frances Shaw
GREEN. Emily Camster
GRIFFIN, Lou
HAMILTON, Louis
HANCOCK, Filmore T.
HANCOCK, George
HARPER, Dave
HARRELL, Clara McNeely
HEAD
HENDERSON, Isabelle
HIGGERSON, Joe
HILL, Delia
HILL, Louis
HOLSELL, Rhody
HOLT, John A.
ISABELLE
JOHNSON, Charles
JOHNSON, Henry
JONES, Hannah
KNIGHT, Emma
LEE, Harriet
LEE, Mattie
LEE, Wes
MCGEE, Perry
MCGUIRE, John
MADISON, Eliza
MARTIN, Drucilla
MARTIN, Richard
MATTHEWS, Hattie
MEEKS, Letha Taylor
MESSERSMITH, August
MILLER, Wylie
MUNDY, Lewis

MURPHY, Malinda
NASH, Joe
NICKENS, Margaret
OVERTON, Eliza
PATTERSON, Delicia Ann Wiley
PETHY, Marilda
RHODES, Susan Davis
RICHARDSON, Charlie
ROSS, Frederick
SEWELL, Alice
SHEPPARD, Perry
SIDES, Frank
SIDES, Mollie Renfro
SIMPSON, George J.
SIMPSON, Jane
SIMPSON, Marie
SMITH (MESSERSMITH), August
SMITH, Clay
SMITH, Gus
STOKES, Ann
TAYLOR, Edward
TAYLOR, Tishey
THOMAS, Louis
THOMPSON, Jane
WAGGONER, Sarah
WALKER, Minskie
WILSON, James
WOOD, Mintie Gilbert
WRIGHT, Ellaine
YOUNGER, Sim

NEBRASKA

BLACK, Henry
CONWAY, George
CORNEAL, Mrs. Phannie
ELDER, John C.
FORBES, Fred
GRANT, Sarah A.
HARDY, Mrs. Allie O.
HAWES, William
HILL, P.M.E.
MCCOWAN, Samuel
MILES, July
O'DONNEL, (Mrs.) James
ROSIER, Mrs. Sarah K.
ROSS, Nimrod
SELLERS, Fanny
SHELBY, Gussie
STEPNEY, Moses
TODD, Mason

NEW YORK

SOMMERVILLE, Jim

NORTH CAROLINA

ADAMS, Louisa
ADKINS, Ida
ALLEN, Martha
ANDERSON, Joseph
ANDERSON, Mary
ANDREWS, Cornelia
ANNGADY, Mary
ARRINGTON, Jane
AUGUSTUS, Sarah Louise
AUSTIN, Charity
BAKER, Blount
BAKER, Lizzie
BAKER, Viney
BARBOUR, Charlie
BARBOUR, Mary
BARNES, Berle
BARNES, Mariah
BAUGH, Alice
BECKWITH, John
BECTOM, John C.
BELL, Laura
BLALOCK, Emma
BLOUNT, (Uncle) David
BOBBIT, Clay
BOBBITT, Henry
BOGAN, Herndon
BOONE, Andrew
BOST, W.L.
BOWE, Mary Wallace
BROWN, Lucy
BURNETT, Midge
CANNADY, Fanny
COFER, Betty
COGGIN, John
COVERSON, Mandy
COZART, Willie
CRASSON, Hannah
CRENSHAW, Julia
CROWDER, Zeb
CRUMP, Adeline
CRUMP, Bill
CRUMP, Charlie
CURTIS, Mattie
DALTON, Charles Lee
DANIELS, John
DAVES, Harriet Ann
DAVIS, Jerry
DEBNAM, W. Solomon

LONG, Amos
MCALLISTER, Charity
MCCOY, Clara Cotton
MCCULLERS, Henrietta
MCCULLOUGH, Willie
MCLEAN, James Turner
MAGWOOD, Frank
MANSON, Jacob
MANSON, Roberta
MARKHAM, Millie
MATTHEWS, Z.D.
MIALS, Maggie
MITCHELL, Anna
MITCHNER, Patsy
MOORE, Emeline
MOORE, Fannie
MORING, Richard
NELSON, Julius
NICHOLS, Lila
ORGAN, Martha
PARKER, Ann
PENNY, Amy
PENNY, Lily
PERRY, Valley
PITTS, Tempe
PLUMMER, Hannah
POOL, Parker
RAINES, Rena
RANSOME, Anthony
RICHARDSON, Caroline
RIENSHAW, Adora
ROBINSON, Celia
ROGERS, B.E.
ROGERS, George
ROGERS, Hattie
ROUNDTREE, Henry
RUDDICK, Charity
RUDDICK, Samuel
RUFE
SCALES, Anderson
SCALES, Catherine
SCALES, Porter
SCOTT, William
SHAW, Mabry
SHAW, Tiney
SLATE, Serena Mulberry Anndora
SMITH, John
SMITH, John
SMITH, Josephine
SMITH, Nellie
SMITH, Sarah Ann
SMITH, Wilham
SORRELL, Laura
SORRELL, Ria
SPELL, Chaney
SPIKES, Tanner

STEPHENSON, Annie
STEWART, Nelson
STEWART, Sam
STONE, Emma
SYKES, William
TATE, Annie
TAYLOR, R.S.
THOMAS, Elias
THOMAS, Jacob
THORNTON, Margaret
TILLIE
TRELL, Ellen
TRENTHAM, Henry James
UPPERMAN, Jane Anne Privette
WHITLEY, Ophelia
WILCOX, Tom
WILLIAMS, Catherine
WILLIAMS, (Rev.) Handy
WILLIAMS, John Thomas
WILLIAMS, Lizzie
WILLIAMS, Melissa
WILLIAMS, Penny
WILLIAMS, Plaz
WOODS, Alex
YELLADAY, Dilly
YELLERDAY, Hilliard

OHIO

ANDERSON, Charles H.
BARDEN, Mrs. Melissa
BAUMONT, Kate Dudley
BEDFORD, Henry
BLEDSOE, Susan
BOST, Mrs. Phoebe
BROWN, Ben
BURKE, Sarah Woods
CAMPBELL, James
CLARK, Fleming
COFFEE, Anna M.
CRUZE, Rachel
DAVIDSON, Hannah
DEMPSEY, Mary B.
EAST, Nancy
EMMONS, William
FAMBRO, Hanna
GLENN, Wade
GREEN, Charles
GURDNER, Julia
HALL, David A.
HARRIS, Eliza
HAWKINS, Susan
HAWKINS, Tap
HEARD, Clark

HENDERSON, Celia
HOGUE, William P.
JACKSON, Edna
JACKSON, George
JAMES, Julia A.
JAMES, Thomas W.
JAMES, Tippett
JEMISEN, Perry Sid
JONES, Royal Allen
JORDAN, Watt
KING, Julia
LEE, Florence
LESTER, Angeline
LYONS, Phoebe
LYONS, Samuel
MCINTIRE, Thomas
MCKIMM, Kisey
MCMILLAN, Thomas
MANN, Sarah
MARTIN, Dulcinda Baker
MATHEUS, John Williams
NELSON, William
PATE, Charlotte
RAY, Morgan
RINGO, Joseph
RODGERS, Isaac
ROSS, Elsie
SLIM, Catherine
SMALL, Jennie
SMITH, Anna
STEWART, Nan
SUTTON, Samuel
TOLER, Richard
WARFIELD, Lucy Ann
WASHINGTON, Virginia
WHITE, Sallah
WILBORN, David
WILLIAMS, (Rev.) Charles
WILLIAMS, Julia
WILLIAMS, Reverend
WILLIAMS, William
WILSON, Jesse
YOUNG, John I.

OKLAHOMA

ADAMS, Isaac
ALEXANDER, Alice
ANDERSON, Sam
BANKS, Frances
BANKS, Phoebe
BANKS, Sina
BARBER, Mollie
BARNER, L.B.

JENKINS, Lewis
JOHNSON, Nellie
JORDAN, Josie
JORDAN, Sam
KING, (Uncle) George G.
KING, Martha
KYE, George
LAWSON, Ben
LINDSAY, Mary
LOGAN, Mattie
LONIAN, Moses
LOVE, Kiziah
LUCAS, Daniel William
LUSTER, Bert
MCCRAY, Stephen
MCFARLAND, Hannah
MCNAIR, Chaney
MACK, Marshall
MANNING, Allen V.
MAYNARD, Bob
MERCER, Rose
MONTGOMERY, Jane
NAVE, Cornelius Neely
OLIVER, Amanda
OLIVER, Solomon
PERRY, Noah
PERRYMAN, Patsy
PETITE, Phyllis
PINKARD, Maggie
POE, Matilda
PRYOR, Elsie
PUGH, J.L.
PYLES, Henry F.
RICHARDSON, Chaney
RICHARDSON, Red
ROBERTSON, Betty
ROBINSON, Harriet
ROWE, Katie
SAMUEL, C.G.
SCOTT, Annie Groves
SHEPARD, Morris
SIMMS, Andrew
SMITH, Alfred
SMITH, Liza
SMITH, Lou
SMITH, Mose
SMITH, R.C.
SOUTHALL, James
STARR, Milton
STINNETT, J.W.
STRAYHORN, Eva
THOMPSON, Johnson
THOMPSON, Ned
THOMPSON, Victoria T.
THREAT, Jim
VANN, Lucinda

WAGONER, Sweetie I.
WALKER, Agnes
WALTERS, William
WARD, Robert A.
WATSON, Mollie
WATSON, William W.
WEBB, Mary Frances
WELLS, Easter
WHITE, John
WHITMIRE, Eliza
WILLIAMS, Charley
WILLIAMS, Hulda
WILLIAMS, Robert
WILLIS, Charles
WILSON, Sarah
WOFFORD, Acemy
WOODS, Tom W.
YOUNG, Annie

OREGON

SOUTHWORTH, Lou
TAYLOR, George

RHODE ISLAND

JOHNSON, Henry

SOUTH CAROLINA

ABRAMS, George F.
ABRAMS, M.E.
ADAMS, Ezra
ADAMS, Mary
ADAMS, Victoria
ADAMSON, Frank
ANDREWS, Frances
ARTHUR, "Pete"
BACCHUS, Josephine
BALLARD, William
BARBER, Charley
BARBER, Ed
BARBER, Millie
BATES, Anderson
BATES, Millie
BEAS, Welcome
BECKETT, Ransom
BEES, Welcome
BEES, Will
BELL, Anne

GODDARD, Daniel
GODFREY, Ellen
GOODWATER, Thomas
GRANT, Charlie
GRANT, Rebecca Jane
GRAVES, John
GREELEY, Sim
GREEN, Elijah
GREEN, Phyllis
GREEN, W.M.
GREY, Adeline
GRIFFIN, Fannie
GRIFFIN, Madison
GRIGSBY, Peggy
GUNTHARPE, Violet
HAMILTON, John
HAMLIN, Susan
HAMPTON, Wade
HARP, Anson
HARPER, (Rev.) Thomas
HARRIS, Abe
HARRISON, Eli
HARVEY, Charlie Jeff
HASTY, Eliza
HAYGOOD, Burt
HAYNES, Dolly
HENDERSON, Liney
HENRY, Jim
HERNDON, Zack
HEYWARD, Lavinia
HEYWARD, Lucretia
HEYWOOD, Maria
HEYWOOD, Mariah
HILL, Jerry
HOLLINS, Jane
HOLMAN, Gillam
HOLMES, Cornelius
HOLMES, Mundy
HORRY, Ben
HORRY, Stella
HOUSEAL, William P.
HUGHES, Margaret
HUNTER, Forest
HUNTER, Hester
JACKSON, Adeline
JACKSON, Cordelia
JACKSON, George
JAMES, Agnes
JAMES, Fred
JEFFERIES, Isiah
JEFFERSON, Thomas
JEMISON, Ophelia
JENKINS, Henry D.
JENKINS, Maria
JENKINS, Paul
JETER, Emma

AUSTIN, George
AUSTIN, Hattie
AUSTIN, Lou
AUSTIN, Smith
BABINO, Agatha
BAKER, Henry
BALE, Mrs. Betty Elizabeth Brooks
BARBER, James
BARCLAY, Delia
BARCLAY, Jim
BARCLAY, Mrs. John (Sarah Sanders)
BARKER, John
BARNES, Joe (Paul)
BARNES, Lucy
BARNETT, Amelia
BARNETT, Darcus
BARRENS, Jake
BARRETT, Armstead
BARRETT, Harriet
BASARD, Elvira
BATES, John
BEAN, Abe
BECKETT, Harrison
BELL, Frank
BELL, Virginia
BENDY, Edgar
BENDY, Minerva
BENJAMIN, Sarah
BERLINER, Sarah L. Johnson
BESS, Jack
BETTERS, Aunt Kate
BETTS, Ellen
BEVERLY, Charlotte
BIBLES, Della Mun
BIBLES, Johnny
BLACK, Francis
BLACKWELL, Willie
BLANCHARD, Olivier
BLANKS, Julia
BOLDIN, Quentin
BOLES, Elvira
BORMER, Betty
BOUDREAUX, Felice
BOWEN, Charley
BOYD, Harrison
BOYD, Isabella
BOYD, James
BOYKINS, Jerry
BRACKINS, Monroe
BRADSHAW, Gus
BRADY, Wes
BRANCH, Jacob
BRANCH, William
BRATCHER, Minerva
BRICE, Amanda Eilers
BRIM, Clara

BROADDUS, Henry
BROADUS, Ned
BROOKS, Sylvester
BROUSSARD, Donaville
BROWN, Fannie
BROWN, Fred
BROWN, Hattie Jane
BROWN, James
BROWN, Josie
BROWN, Rosella
BROWN, Steve
BROWN, Zek
BRUIN, Madison
BRUNSON, Vinnie
BUNTON, Martha Spence
BURLESON, James
BURRELL, Phoebe Jane
BURRELL, Wesley
BUSH, Sam
BUTLER, Ellen
BUTTLER, Henry H.
BYRD, David L.
BYRD, William
CAIN, Louis
CALHOUN, Jeff
CAMPBELL, Simpson (Simp)
CAPE, James
CARRUTHERS, "Uncle" Richard
CARTER, Cato
CARTHAN, Allen
CAUTHERN, Jack
CHAMBERS, Ben
CHAMBERS, Lucy
CHAMBERS, Sally Banks
CHAPPEL, Clara (Clara Williams)
CHESLEY, Harriet
CHILDERS, Henry
CHOICE, Jeptha (Doc)
CHRISTOPHER, Anthony (Uncle Tony)
CLARK, Amos
CLARK, Mother Anne
COKER, Abraham
COLE, Alice
COLE, Harrison
COLE, Hattie
COLE, Thomas
COLEMAN, Betty (Robertson)
COLEMAN, Eli
COLEMAN, Preely
COLEMAN, William
COLLINS, Bill
COLLINS, Harriet
COLUMBUS, Andrew ("Smoky")
COMPTON, Jake
COMPTON, Josephine Tippit
CONNALLY, Steve

FENNELS, Archie
FIELDS, Alphonse
FINNELY, John
FITTS, Jennie
FORD, Ellen Nora
FORD, Sarah
FORGE, Sam
FORREST, Susan
FORWARD, Millie
FOWLER, Louis
FOWLER, Mat
FRANKLIN, Chris
FRANKLIN, Jim
FRANKLIN, Robert
FRANKS, Orelia Alexie
FRAZIER, Rosanna
FREEMAN, Henry
FULLER, Sarah
GAFFNEY, Mary
GATES, Hattie
GIBSON, Mary Anne
GIBSON, Priscilla
GILBERT, Gabriel
GILMORE, Mattie
GLASKER, George
GLEN, Scot
GLOVER, Mary
GOODMAN, Andrew
GOODMAN, Ellen
GRAND, Austin
GRANT, Austin
GRANT, Dennis
GRANT, Lizzie
GREEN, Catharine
GREEN, James
GREEN, Marie Aurelia
GREEN, O.W.
GREEN, Rosa
GREEN, William
GRICE, Pauline
GRIFFEN, Lucendy
GRUMBERS, James
HADNOT, Josh
HADNOT, Mandy
HADNOT, Maria
HAMILTON, Jeff
HAMILTON, William
HARPER, Pierce
HARRELL, Molly
HARRISON, Jack
HARWELL, Alice
HATLEY, Sarah
HAWTHORNE, Ann
HAYES, James
HAYWOOD, Felix
HENDERSON, Albert

MCCILLERY, Rosie
MCKEEVER, Duncan
MCQUEEN, Nap
MCRAY, Calvin Bell
MADDOX, Jack
MADDOX, Rosa
MAJORS, John
MALONE, Julia
MALONE, Melea
MANUEL, Millie
MAPLES, Ella
MARSH, O.A.
MARSHALL, Adeline
MARTIN, Eva
MARTIN, Isaac
MARTIN, James
MASON, Sam Meredith
MATHEWS, Louise
MATHEWS, Williams
MATTHEWS, Maggie Whitehead
MAUCHISON, Lucy C.F.
MAYES, Hiram
MERRITT, Susan
MICKEY, Ann
MIDDLETON, Cassie
MILES, Josh
MILLER, Anna
MILLER, Mintie Maria
MILLETT, Harriet
MILLS, Tom
MIRE, La San
MITCHELL, Charley
MITCHELL, Peter
MOODY, Andrew
MOODY, Tildy
MOORE, Almont M. ("Mount")
MOORE, Jerry
MOORE, John
MOORE, Laura
MOORE, Van
MOORE, Vina
MOORE, William
MORROW, Mandy
MOSES, Mary
MOSES, Patsy
MOSLEY, John
MOUTON, Leo
MOYE, Calvin
MULLINS, Hannah
NAPIER, Florence
NEEDHAM, W.S., Jr.
NEELY, Sally
NEILL, Louise
NELSON, Andy
NELSON, Bell
NELSON, Ida

NEWMAN, Virginia
NEWTON, George
NICHOLS, Pierce
NICKERSON, Mary
NILLIN, Margrett
NORMAN, Fannie
NORRIS, Isom
NORTON, Annie
NORWOOD, Isaiah
NUNN, Aaron
OCKLBARY, Julia Grimes Jones
ODOM, Charley
OGEE, John
OLIVER, Joe
OSBORNE, Annie
OVERSTREET, Horace
OVERTON, Mary
OWENS, George
OWENS, Henry
PARKER, Jim
PARKER, Will
PATTERSON, Mrs. Mary Anne
PATTON, Martha
PAULS, Jessie
PAXTON, William
PAYNE, Ellen
PAYNE, Jack
PERKINS, Henderson
PERKINS, Lu
PERKINS, Sarah
PERRIER, (Rev.) John
PHILLIPS, Daniel
PHOENIX, Katie
PICKETT, Lee
PIERCE, Lee
PLEASANT, Louvinia Young
POLK, Ellen
POLK, James
POLLARD, Melinda
POLLARD, Rosa L.
PORTER, Ophelia
POWERS, Betty
POWERS, Tillie R.
PRICE, Allen
PRICE, John
PRICE, (Rev.) Lafayette
PROBASCO, Henry
PROCTOR, Jenny
PROUT, Robert
PRUITT, A.C.
PULLEN, Andrew
QUARLS, Harre
RAHLS, Mary
RAINS, Aunt Eda
RAMSEY, Ella Belle
RANDALL, Millie

ZOLLICOFFER, Tobe

VIRGINIA

BERRY, Fannie
CRAWLEY, Charles
FULKES, Minnie
GIWBS, Georgina
GOODWIN, Candis
GRANDY, Charles
HARRIS, Della
HINES, Marriah
HOPSON, Moble
JONES, Albert
KELLY, Susan
SLAUGHTER, Richard
SPARKS, Elizabeth
STOKES, Simon
WILSON, Mary Jane

WASHINGTON

FLOWERS, Mrs. Cornelia J.
FREEMAN, Alice
HILL, Sarah Laws
LAWS, Sarah
LONG, Ellen
MILLER, Mrs. Ellen (Ellen Long)
SELBY, Mrs. Carrie
WALKER, Sarah

SUBJECT INDEX

ABOLITIONISM

   8.1:   p. 183
   8.2:   p. 122
 16.4:   p. 90
 17.1:   pp. 152-53, 208, 265, 337
S1-5.2:   p. 412
S1-7.2:   p. 333
S1-12.1: pp. 128, 129
S2-8.7: pp. 2982-83

AFRICA

  2.1:   pp. 14, 30, 67, 118, 119, 122-23, 198, 252
  2.2:   pp 34, 149, 150, 172-173, 190, 191, 229-30, 235, 297, 306, 310
  3.3:   pp. 64, 65
  3.4:   p. 163
  4.1:   pp. 49, 185, 200, 236, 290, 307
  4.2:   pp. 10, 13, 41, 163, 192, 201, 209, 219, 220, 222, 249, 250,
        290
  5.3:   pp. 2, 17, 40, 148, 204
  5.4:   pp. 27, 78
  6.1:   p. 263
  6.2:   pp. 27, 68, 199, 202
  7.1:   pp. 24, 25, 92, 102, 111, 169, 295, 298, 309
  7.2:   pp. 91, 136
  8.1:   p. 202
  8.2:   pp. 57, 76, 95, 157, 158
  9.3:   pp. 7, 127, 139
  9.4:   pp. 43, 44
 10.5:   pp. 221, 226
 10.6:   p. 76
 11.7:   pp. 19, 20, 212, 213, 232
 11.8:   p. 94
 12.1:   pp. 89, 172, 213, 287
 12.2:   pp. 18, 108, 119

AFRICAN SURVIVALS

S1-3.1: p. 342
S1-4.2: pp. 355, 364
S1-5.1: pp. 23, 45, 48
S1-6.1: p. 219
S1-7.2: pp. 343, 356, 370, 410, 420, 427-28, 429-30, 515, 529, 571, 646, 677, 697, 724, 731
S1-8.3: pp. 808-809, 866, 944, 966, 1087, 1207, 1219-1220, 1270, 1307
S1-10.5: p. 2004
S1-12.1: pp. 65, 268
S2-1.10(NE): p. 328
S2-3.2: p. 893
S2-6.5: pp. 2148, 2206-10, 2253

See Also: BRER RABBIT; FOLKLORE; MYTHS AND SUPERSTITIONS

AGRICULTURAL PRACTICES

2.1: pp. 10, 26, 58-59, 77, 96, 124, 138, 155, 265, 310, 330
2.2: pp. 40, 43, 129, 292
3.3: pp. 56, 65-66, 84, 90, 107, 127, 160, 174, 218, 230, 241, 272 283
3.4: pp. 2, 6, 10, 13-14, 17-18, 36, 56, 58, 60, 65-66, 71, 116-17, 122, 138, 155, 156, 158, 177-78, 186, 200, 209-10, 219, 220-21, 222-23, 234, 249-50, 251, 253-54, 270
4.1: pp. 14, 68, 85, 99-100, 104, 112, 123, 125, 131, 135, 140, 148, 152, 164, 179-80, 182, 185, 186, 190, 191, 203, 221, 222, 226, 227, 236, 250, 261, 267, 270, 277, 283-84, 298
4.2: pp. 1, 7, 15-16, 22, 36, 51, 57, 61, 68, 72, 75, 82, 83, 99, 119, 123-24, 135, 145, 153, 170, 172, 199, 203-04, 210, 229, 231, 247, 255-56, 265, 273-77, 288, 292-93
5.3: pp. 27-28, 41, 49-51, 57-58, 93, 108, 125-26, 167, 170, 171-72, 173, 174, 177-78, 183-84, 185, 193, 199, 205-06, 211, 214, 216-17, 220, 227, 238-40, 242, 259, 265-66
5.4: pp. 13, 24, 37, 42, 47, 48-49, 53, 59, 64, 65, 69, 76, 86, 104, 123, 125-26, 135, 138, 139, 153, 158, 185, 188, 197, 203, 212, 221, 229, 235-36
6.1: pp. 10, 21-22, 47, 87-88, 91, 114-15, 117, 149, 151, 166, 183, 193, 198-99, 213, 279, 295, 338, 365, 371-72, 419, 426
6.2: pp. 107-08, 183, 215
7.1: pp. 1, 2, 9, 39, 40, 46, 49-50, 67, 103-04, 111-12, 125, 136, 157, 176, 188-89, 203-05, 224, 243, 251-52, 285-87, 291, 332, 334-36, 349, 356, 359-60
7.2: pp. 18-19, 87, 120, 129, 158-59, 166
8.1: pp. 81-2, 101, 116, 141-42, 147, 149, 151, 157, 175-76, 203, 230, 260-61, 292, 293, 326
8.2: pp. 52, 101, 103-04, 142, 153-54, 155, 171, 180, 243-45, 280, 326
9.3: pp. 15, 77, 88, 97, 125, 154, 155, 172, 190, 201, 212, 235, 248 347
9.4: pp. 65, 66, 100, 101, 105, 132, 193, 257, 272, 307
10.5: pp. 4, 27, 30, 94, 97, 118, 152, 209, 230, 254, 340
10.6: pp. 1, 8, 43, 68, 104, 183, 241, 246, 259, 285, 320, 364
11.7: pp. 15, 29, 58, 71, 106, 166, 177, 233, 255
11.8: pp. 56, 66, 154, 181, 204, 301, 302, 349, 366, 374
12.1: pp. 22, 23, 64, 71, 80-81, 94, 99, 107, 116-17, 125-26, 161-62,

S1-5.2:   p. 434
S1-6.1:   pp. 60, 119, 127, 167, 217
S1-7.2:   pp. 472, 505, 529-530, 597, 606, 696, 733
S1-8.3:   pp. 821, 921, 1145, 1219, 1232, 1344
S1-9.4:   pp. 1419, 1531, 1585, 1589-91, 1677
S1-10.5: pp. 1918, 1950-51, 1952, 1954, 2010, 2058, 2138, 2165, 2200,
          2274, 2311, 2314-15, 2319, 2366-67
S1-11.1: pp. 11, 34
S1-11.2: pp. 70, 76-77, 135, 180, 234
S1-12.1: pp. 76, 92, 103, 104, 287
S2-1.1(AL): p. 9
S2-1.3(AR): pp. 54, 209, 236
S2-1.5(FL): p. 264
S2-1.10(NE): pp. 309, 335
S2-2.1:   pp. 83, 183, 210, 271, 395, 416
S2-3.2:   pp. 481-82, 513, 525, 861
S2-4.3:   pp. 1008, 1035, 1049, 1196, 1405
S2-5.4:   pp. 1544, 1799, 1838-39, 1886, 1918
S2-6.5:   pp. 1931, 1991, 2104, 2203, 2216, 2229, 2245, 2247-48,
          2303, 2324, 2341, 2353
S2-7.6:   pp. 2469, 2538, 2605, 2640, 2641, 2742, 2757, 2759, 2785,
          2787, 2825, 2841, 2852, 2878, 2914
S2-8.7:   pp. 2949, 2965, 3020, 3021, 3030, 3048, 3110, 3175, 3189,
          3259
S2-9.8:   pp. 3500, 3534, 3596-97, 3638, 3655, 3692, 3802, 3817, 3841,
          3862, 3871-72
S2-10.9: pp. 3943, 3950, 4184, 4254

BASS, SAM

   5.3:   pp. 146-47
   S2-7.6:   pp. 2893-95

BENEFICIARY (IN A WILL)

   2.2:   p. 30
   3.4:   p. 83
   4.1:   p. 31
   4.2:   pp. 48, 116
   5.3:   p. 62
   5.4:   p. 50
   6.2:   pp. 77, 96
   7.1:   pp. 79, 277
   8.2:   p. 319
   9.3:   pp. 87, 91, 191, 265, 308
   9.4:   pp. 40, 52
   11.8: pp. 11, 90, 102, 103, 363
   12.2: p. 293
   13.4: p. 131
   14.1: pp. 54, 55, 145, 262
   15.2: 153, 225
   16.1(KN): pp. 2, 8
   16.2(KY): p. 82
   16.6(TN): pp. 31, 50

S1-1.1: p. 60
S1-6.1: p. 191
S1-7.2: pp. 535, 687
S1-8.3: p. 1162
S1-12.1: pp. 20, 83
S2-7.6: pp. 2516, 2589, 2590, 2625
S2-8.7: p. 3141
S2-10.9: pp. 4068-69, 4353

BENEVOLENT ORGANIZATIONS (BLACK)

18.1: p. 230
S1-2.2(CO): pp. 96-97
S1-4.2: p. 671
S1-8.3: p. 1326
S1-9.4: pp. 1377, 1703-1704
S2-1.10(NE): pp. 304, 307
S2-4.3: p. 1413
S2-6.5: pp. 1951, 1993, 2317
S2-7.6: pp. 2487-88, 2634, 2638
S2-9.8: p. 3831

BIBLE (REFERENCES TO)

2.1: p. 120, 193, 229
2.2: pp. 78, 142, 174, 261
4.1: p. 148
5.3: p. 119, 213
6.1: p. 155, 299-305, 435
7.1: pp. 303-04
9.3: p. 149
10.5: p. 259
12.1: pp. 13, 89, 180, 219, 254, 257, 294-95, 323, 349
12.2: pp. 19, 42, 69, 85, 109, 186, 203, 215, 231, 247, 287, 340
13.3: pp. 61, 125
13.4: p. 78
14.1: pp. 35, 303
15.2: p. 249
16.2(KY): p. 15
16.4(OH): p. 89
16.6(TN): p. 42
18.1: pp. 10, 111, 113
19.1: p. 44
S1-1.1: p. 188
S1-2.2(CO): pp. 51, 81-82
S1-2.3(MN): p. 107
S1-2.4(MO): p. 193
S1-3.1: pp. 20, 182, 257, 334
S1-5.1: pp. 48, 56, 66
S1-6.1: pp. 4, 95, 100, 156, 216, 306
S1-7.2: pp. 408, 528, 598, 693-694, 700
S1-8.3: pp. 828, 831, 908, 1063, 1072, 1100, 1117, 1241, 1334, 1341, 1342
S1-9.4: pp. 1391, 1613, 1634, 1650, 1776
S1-11.2: pp. 66-67, 213, 216, 221
S1-12.1: pp. 292, 324

S2-10.1(AL): pp. 4,6
S2-10.10(NE): p. 350
S2-10.15(SC): p. 388
S2-2.1: pp. 56, 64, 214, 388
S2-3.2: pp. 584, 636, 801
S2-4.3: pp. 1008, 1015, 1053, 1074, 1115, 1286, 1357, 1384
S2-5.4: pp. 1493, 1628-29, 1631, 1765, 1828, 1911-12
S2-6.5: pp. 2021, 2112, 2139, 2147, 2169, 2236, 2271, 2279, 2281,
         2326, 2329, 2346, 2363, 2398, 2408
S2-7.6: pp. 2466, 2580, 2599, 2625, 2629, 2652, 2718, 2732, 2735,
         2748, 2782, 2801, 2837-39, 2843, 2852, 2884
S2-8.7: pp. 2921, 2952, 2972, 2998, 3003, 3039, 3041, 3042, 3077,
         3121, 3189, 3216, 3217, 3266, 3301, 3337, 3360, 3366, 3380,
         3381
S2-9.8: pp. 3446, 3479, 3489, 3503, 3518, 3593, 3645, 3660, 3666,
         3718, 3754, 3760, 3880
S2-10.9: pp. 3945, 3955, 4004, 4035, 4036, 4048, 4082, 4150, 4196,
          4206, 4285

BRER RABBIT

S1-1.1: pp. 310-12
S1-11.1: pp. 36, 38

See Also: FOLKLORE

BUCHANAN, JAMES

S1-8.3: p. 974

CHILD AND INFANT CARE

2.1: pp. 39, 82, 98, 99, 119, 120, 176, 181, 230, 261 308, 337
2.2: pp. 12, 13, 23, 35, 59, 67, 68, 138, 146, 179, 183, 228, 242,
      289, 327
3.3: pp. 5, 17, 24, 56, 60, 62, 63, 83, 118, 130, 152, 213, 232,
      243
3.4: pp. 10, 32, 36, 65, 76, 96, 126, 143, 156, 161, 171, 189, 242,
      253, 260
4.1: pp. 19, 25, 40, 109, 121, 174, 175, 205, 217, 240, 243, 249
4.2: pp. 5, 15, 33, 56, 63, 120, 126, 135, 169, 177, 208, 209, 255
5.3: pp. 4, 15, 24, 56, 89, 110, 139, 188, 220, 225, 243
5.4: pp. 10, 17, 67, 73, 103, 113, 118, 166, 170, 211
6.1: pp. 28. 33, 42, 67, 90, 133, 155, 195, 201, 261, 294, 331,
      353, 398, 426, 429
6.2: pp. 13, 27, 52, 77, 107, 169
7.1: pp. 8, 45, 76, 120, 138, 172, 178, 188, 227, 257, 258, 296,
      310, 345, 356
7.2: pp. 11, 12, 27, 34, 50, 72, 91, 101, 119, 126, 152, 165, 170
8.1: pp. 1, 25, 34, 49, 97, 112, 143, 151, 181, 197, 234, 243, 301,
      317, 338
8.2: pp. 13, 42, 57, 91, 92, 119, 132, 189, 206, 214, 215, 248, 260,
      292, 312, 344
9.3: pp. 15, 28, 87, 142, 154, 181, 231, 287, 310, 326, 339, 374,

```
              3143, 3144, 3184, 3203, 3204-3205, 3208, 3221-23, 3229-30,
              3239, 3263, 3280, 3284-85, 3294, 3300, 3311, 3332-33, 3395
  S2-9.8:   pp. 3485, 3602, 3722
  S2-10.9:  pp. 4155, 4158, 4318
```

CHURCH (BLACK)

```
    2.1:    pp. 28, 170, 197, 231, 348
    2.2:    pp. 40, 73, 128, 168, 236, 241
    3.3:    pp. 21, 41, 60, 89, 148, 168, 186, 202, 248, 249
    3.4:    pp. 2, 38
    4.1:    pp. 10, 33
    4.2:    pp. 6, 9, 11, 13, 14, 51, 57, 62, 75, 76, 178, 208, 221, 294
    5.3:    pp. 96, 186, 255
    6.1:    pp. 7, 80, 93, 134, 144, 163-164, 167, 184, 191, 249, 309-310,
              316, 372, 373, 400
    6.2:    pp. 16, 22, 77, 80, 119, 140, 185, 209
    7.1:    pp. 49, 208, 353
    7.2:    pp. 41, 42, 168, 171, 172
    8.1:    pp. 35, 133, 267, 295
    8.2:    pp. 3, 16, 128, 197, 220, 290, 314
    9.3:    pp. 40, 41, 75, 200, 201, 256, 262, 280, 323, 325, 363, 388,
              392
    9.4:    pp. 32, 37, 52, 62, 80, 118, 271, 293, 294
   10.5:    pp. 161, 259, 294
   10.6:    pp. 28, 44, 243, 313, 355
   11.7:    pp. 132, 133, 160, 175, 227, 246
   11.8:    pp. 9, 23, 83, 119, 132, 133, 136, 157, 212, 288, 289, 299
   12.1:    pp. 52, 68, 97, 98, 114, 182, 190, 197-198, 219, 224, 228,
              234, 263, 269, 295-296, 314
   13.3:    pp. 29, 42, 61, 124, 125, 158, 221, 282, 328
   13.4:    pp. 4, 5, 8, 9, 33, 91, 92, 100, 129, 201, 214, 227, 234, 237
              364
   14.1:    pp. 37, 226
   15.2:    pp. 160, 182, 187, 221, 240, 395
   16.2(KY):  pp. 6, 26, 36, 98
   16.3(MD):  p. 35
   16.4(OH):  pp. 33, 40, 44, 59, 61, 107, 111, 112
   16.5(VA):  pp. 8, 9
   16.6(TN):  pp. 23, 25, 27, 32, 35, 40, 46, 80
   17.1:    pp. 98, 244-45, 255, 261, 290-91, 309, 343-44, 353
   18.1:    pp. 4, 12, 25, 48, 49, 54, 57, 83, 179
   19.1:    pp. 11, 40, 58, 67, 72, 145
   S1-1.1:  pp. 71, 87, 103-104, 113, 115-116, 148, 174, 234, 355, 358,
              366, 370, 381, 383, 438
   S1-2.3(MN):  pp. 112-13
   S1-2.4(MO):  p. 158
   S1-3.1:  pp. 122, 213, 306
   S1-4.2:  pp. 351, 371, 380-81, 406, 564-65, 673
   S1-5.1:  pp. 18, 171-72
   S1-5.2:  pp. 406, 420, 446, 472, 478
   S1-6.1:  pp. 30, 31, 46, 102, 123, 145, 285, 318
   S1-7.2:  pp. 362, 364, 372, 391-92, 395, 419, 490, 507-508, 542-543,
              589, 608-609, 615, 630, 645-46, 651, 671, 680, 721, 744,
              749, 752, 759, 774, 797
   S1-8.3:  pp. 827, 845, 867-868, 903-904, 914-915, 934, 940-941,
```

S1-2.4(MO): pp. 148, 169, 180-83, 192, 196, 212, 220-21, 226-27
S1-3.1: pp. 1, 26, 31, 65, 83, 92, 122, 132, 198, 213, 219-20, 225,
         233, 251, 331
S1-4.2: pp. 350, 412, 448, 455, 471, 490, 505, 537, 539, 554, 564,
         596, 614, 626, 635, 646, 669
S1-5.1: pp. 2, 7, 11, 14, 99, 189, 206-07, 240
S1-5.2: pp. 278-79, 282, 286, 328, 350-51, 366, 399, 411-12, 423,
         434, 446, 487
S1-6.1: pp. 4, 30, 45, 58, 64, 82, 104, 149, 157, 160, 161, 218,
         261, 271, 282, 283, 291, 299, 310, 315, 323
S1-7.2: pp. 372-373, 390, 400, 405, 418, 425, 439, 443, 492, 537,
         562, 580, 594-595, 598, 623, 628, 640, 656, 692, 744, 757,
         759, 764, 777
S1-8.3: pp. 818, 892-893, 914, 934, 953, 958, 965, 978, 1035, 1083,
         1128-1129, 1171, 1197, 1205-1206, 1212, 1221, 1230, 1244-
         1245, 1253, 1275-1276, 1321
S1-9.4: pp. 1390, 1411, 1488-89, 1511, 1567, 1644, 1676, 1679, 1761
S1-10.5: pp. 1921, 1973, 1995, 2001, 2006, 2008, 2038, 2049, 2075,
         2087, 2097, 2107, 2113, 2159, 2188-89, 2202, 2233, 2237,
         2241, 2247, 2251, 2279, 2315, 2337, 2364, 2370, 2396, 2410
S1-11.1: pp. 31, 49
S1-11.2: pp. 113-14, 135, 181, 252, 272, 281-82, 291
S1-12.1: pp. 2-3, 9, 13, 21, 37, 44, 80, 97, 100, 112-13, 115, 118,
         130, 172, 174, 183, 195-96, 264, 273, 350, 378-79, 399
S2-1.3(AR): pp. 54, 125, 137-38, 251
S2-1.7(IN): p. 280
S2-1.9(MD): p. 299
S2-1.10(NE): pp. 320-21, 326
S2-2.1: pp. 3, 12-13, 29, 30, 89, 97, 142, 150, 151, 160, 176, 189,
         195, 197, 200, 229-230, 254, 256, 257, 282, 285, 326, 353-
         354, 357-358, 363, 401, 410, 430, 443
S2-3.2: pp. 509, 532, 667, 692, 880, 909
S2-4.3: pp. 955-56, 1008, 1033-34, 1053, 1090, 1175, 1202, 1302
S2-5.4: pp. 1446, 1474, 1478, 1479-80, 1493, 1516-17, 1524, 1539-41,
         1542-43, 1549, 1559-60, 1588, 1625, 1628, 1727, 1739, 1765,
         1772, 1804, 1817, 1828, 1850, 1885, 1897
S2-6.5: pp. 1929, 1931, 1948-49, 1969, 1988, 1998, 2018, 2038, 2042,
         2107, 2123, 2129, 2139, 2147, 2160, 2194, 2235-36, 2251,
         2274, 2279, 2358, 2405
S2-7.6: pp. 2465, 2483, 2494, 2501, 2507, 2517, 2528-29, 2567, 2570,
         2579, 2606-2607, 2613-14, 2638, 2642, 2647, 2652, 2654,
         2707, 2727, 2732, 2734, 2746, 2757, 2765, 2801, 2812, 2838-
         39, 2865, 2881, 2886
S2-8.7: pp. 2918, 2921, 3003, 3027, 3041, 3045, 3051, 3052, 3062-63,
         3085, 3101-3102, 3109, 3114, 3120-21, 3139, 3170, 3197,
         3209, 3220, 3230, 3235, 3239, 3251, 3258, 3260, 3263, 3266,
         3273, 3289, 3301, 3304, 3306, 3335, 3345, 3358, 3364, 3366,
         3371, 3380-81, 3398
S2-9.8: pp. 3404, 3431, 3446, 3479, 3481, 3495, 3499-3500, 3503,
         3504, 3517-18, 3580-81, 3605, 3639, 3653, 3660, 3666, 3677,
         3715-16, 3729, 3733, 3738, 3756, 3770, 3774, 3775, 3779,
         3838, 3873
S2-10.9: pp. 3893, 3917, 3945, 3955, 3971, 3980, 3995, 4018, 4026,
         4035, 4070, 4078, 4098, 4114, 4118, 4127-28, 4166, 4169,
         4206, 4218, 4284

CIVIL WAR (BATTLES)

573, 596, 618, 629, 657, 732, 781, 798
S1-8.3: pp. 849, 861, 890, 908, 917-18, 945, 971, 972-73, 1012, 1057,
1065, 1107, 1177, 1198, 1210, 1222-1223, 1242, 1258, 1284,
1328, 1333, 1340-1341, 1347
S1-9.4: pp. 1376-77, 1406, 1448, 1462-63, 1510, 1532, 1541-44, 1659,
1719, 1759, 1798, 1849, 1877
S1-10.5: pp. 1968, 1974, 2016, 2028, 2049, 2164, 2178, 2196, 2395
S1-11.1: pp. 44-45
S1-11.2: p. 318
S1-12.1: pp. 177, 229
S2-1.3(AR): pp. 20-21, 62, 70-71, 101, 102, 116
S2-1.8(KS): p. 285
S2-1.10(NE): pp. 317, 336-37
S2-1.13(OK): pp. 371-72
S2-1.15(SC): pp. 389-90, 393
S2-1.16(WA): p. 401
S2-2.1: pp. 119, 134, 201-202, 363, 402-03, 429-30, 434-35, 459
S2-3.2: pp. 557-59, 684, 783, 807, 810-19
S2-4.3: pp. 1004-1005, 1078, 1204-1205
S2-5.4: pp. 1670, 1883, 1886, 1892, 1903-1904
S2-6.5: pp. 1992, 2028, 2037, 2043-44, 2093, 2162, 2181, 2186-88,
2389, 2399
S2-7.6: pp. 2618, 2780-81, 2909
S2-8.7: pp. 2972-77, 2996, 3017, 3021, 3155, 3158-3159, 3167, 3233,
3305-3316
S2-9.8: pp. 3482, 3803, 3806, 3811, 3812, 3824

CIVIL WAR (GENERAL)

2.1: pp. 5, 8, 12, 17, 19, 22, 26, 31, 40, 46, 51, 53, 56, 69, 71,
72, 73, 76, 77, 83, 86, 87, 89, 98, 105, 118, 119, 122, 125,
129, 137, 142, 145, 151, 153, 154, 163, 167, 177, 216, 219,
235, 238, 247, 248, 258, 261, 264, 300, 302, 315, 319, 329,
334
2.2: pp. 45, 54, 85-86, 93-94, 115, 116, 131-132, 141, 147, 195-196,
203-205, 210-211, 216-217, 229, 247, 248, 249-250, 276-277,
335
3.3: pp. 14, 20, 26, 28, 34, 38, 40, 43, 45, 49, 62, 66, 72, 90, 91,
102, 106, 115, 128, 131-132, 134-135, 136, 146, 165, 170, 192-
193, 195, 198, 202, 203, 216, 226, 229, 234-235, 252, 258-259,
261, 265, 268, 269, 275, 280
3.4: pp. 5, 7-8, 12-13, 14, 33, 46, 48, 49, 60, 61, 79, 85, 88, 92,
96, 100, 110-111, 116, 119, 121, 131-132, 149, 150, 152-153,
158-159, 161, 171, 182, 183, 186, 191, 196, 203, 207, 208,
209, 210, 214, 215, 239, 250, 251, 254, 255, 258, 262, 266,
268, 271, 274
4.1: pp. 10, 11, 15, 19, 22, 31, 38, 47, 50, 56, 60, 64, 66, 69, 81,
82, 85, 98-99, 108, 110, 113, 115, 131, 135, 141, 144, 155,
170, 171, 181, 183-184, 190, 192, 194, 207-209, 223, 229-234,
238, 244, 252, 276, 280, 287, 291, 299-300
4.2: pp. 6, 8, 19, 28-29, 33, 39, 48, 53, 56, 61, 64, 66, 69, 72
77-78, 85, 88, 91, 100, 123, 128, 131, 136, 139, 146, 156,
170, 179, 181, 210, 224, 227, 230, 236, 241, 247-248, 286,
288, 289
5.3: pp. 5, 12, 16, 17, 20, 26, 30, 36, 52-53, 61, 70, 79-80, 107,
111-112, 122-123, 126, 130, 150, 158, 161, 164, 168, 173,

12.2:   pp. 17, 26, 30, 35, 45, 53-55, 63, 70, 76, 89, 92, 95, 100,
        108, 112, 121-122, 129, 140, 152, 177, 196, 209, 218, 230,
        236, 239, 277-278, 282-283, 293, 298, 301-302, 306-307, 325-
        326, 330, 354
13.3:   pp. 19-20, 77, 82, 86, 102, 106, 109-110, 116, 137, 144, 146,
        152, 162, 196, 243, 255-256, 291-292, 300-301, 309-310, 332
13.4:   pp. 25-26, 34, 45-46, 59-60, 89-90, 94, 106-107, 126, 130-131,
        135, 192, 203, 224, 234, 238, 343-346
14.1:   pp. 1, 6, 10-12, 24, 35, 55, 67, 68, 72, 76, 80-81, 88-89, 96-
        97, 104, 115-116, 124, 127, 136, 149-150, 157, 161, 171, 174,
        178, 180-181, 192-193, 197, 214-215, 238, 242, 244-245, 249-
        251, 256-257, 268, 271, 279, 288-289, 297, 304-305, 309, 321,
        334, 343-345, 348, 357-358, 364, 367-369, 373, 376, 380-381,
        383-384, 387, 391, 398, 400, 402-403, 407, 415, 419-420, 423,
        425, 430, 435, 439, 442-443, 451-452, 455, 459-460
15.2:   pp. 4-5, 10, 21, 28, 32, 35-36, 52, 55, 67, 69-70, 75, 87-88,
        92, 98-99, 110-111, 118-119, 136, 140, 149-150, 152-153, 164,
        172, 175, 189-190, 200-201, 205-206, 214, 217-218, 223-224,
        227-228, 231, 261-262, 266-268, 271, 273, 278-279, 287-288,
        329, 340-341, 346-347, 353, 374, 382-383, 388, 397-399, 403-
        404, 408, 412, 428-429
16.1(KS): p. 1
16.2(KY): pp. 29, 40, 47, 53, 68, 107, 116
16.3(MD): pp. 2, 39, 40, 42, 43
16.4(OH): pp. 3, 12, 20, 21, 30, 36, 39, 43, 46, 62, 65, 67, 72, 74,
           75, 81, 85, 92, 93, 97, 102, 108-109
16.5(VA): pp. 1, 3, 8, 14, 19, 34, 46, 52, 53, 55
16.6(TN): pp. 1, 2, 9, 14, 15, 25, 28, 33, 43, 49, 50, 51, 52, 57,
           61, 68
17.1:   pp. 15-16, 44-46, 53, 63, 69, 82, 110, 140, 156, 160-162, 169,
        176-177, 179-180, 181, 200, 204-205, 212, 214-215, 231-232,
        250-251, 254, 281, 292-297, 307-308, 312-313, 331, 351-352,
        359-361, 364, 367-369
18.1:   pp. 3, 7, 14, 49, 58, 77, 114-115, 124-125
S1-1.1: pp. 1-2, 18, 37, 41-42, 49, 66, 74, 84, 87-88, 90, 95, 105,
         114-115, 120, 140, 144, 162, 168, 177, 182, 187-188, 205,
         223-224, 227, 230-232, 242, 263, 281, 289-290, 302-303, 353,
         366, 414, 435, 444
S1-2.1(AR): pp. 1, 5
S1-2.2(CO): p. 73
S1-2.3(MN): p. 116
S1-2.4(MO): pp. 144, 148, 161, 175-176, 196, 212, 220, 226-227, 230
S1-3.1: pp. 19, 29, 43, 46, 51, 66, 74, 93, 116, 132, 143, 147, 161-
         163, 173, 178, 227-228, 234, 241, 247, 261, 263-264, 306,
         315-316, 317-318, 333
S1-4.2: pp. 345, 358-359, 362, 370, 387, 401-402, 403, 416, 451, 469,
         473, 476, 498, 508, 539, 542, 556-557, 568-569, 608-609,
         614, 633, 636-637, 642-643
S1-5.1: pp. 2, 7, 11, 15, 29, 48, 51, 58, 70, 73, 78, 84-85, 95, 99,
         110-111, 112-113, 119, 132, 135, 176, 180-181, 185, 194-196,
         207, 213, 215, 233-237
S1-5.2: pp. 309-316, 342, 352, 357, 361-362, 366, 386, 411-412, 415,
         424-425, 448-450
S1-6.1: pp. 11, 13, 21, 28, 41, 42, 50, 61, 62, 66, 73, 79, 80, 84,
         85, 86, 87, 91, 93, 102, 106, 107, 114, 115, 116, 125, 130,
         131, 132, 140, 157-158, 160, 180, 181, 187, 198, 202, 209,

2661-64, 2683-84, 2692, 2702, 2703, 2706, 2710 11, 2712, 2714
15, 2722, 2727, 2729, 2732-33, 2738, 2739, 2745-46, 2749, 2750
2751, 2754, 2761, 2769-70, 2774-75, 2787, 2795, 2805, 2816,
2841, 2856-58, 2890, 2906

S2-8.7:   pp. 2922, 2929, 2932, 2933-34, 2944, 2945, 2954, 2970, 2987,
2998, 3004, 3027-28, 3042, 3045-46, 3050, 3054, 3060-62,
3082, 3083-84, 3089-90, 3094, 3113, 3123-24, 3139-40, 3145-
46, 3150, 3163-64, 3167-71, 3201, 3202, 3207, 3218, 3227-
28, 3230, 3307-3308, 3362, 3366, 3372-73, 3379, 3386-88,
3397, 3400

S2-9.8:   pp. 3403, 3407-3408, 3409-10, 3414, 3449, 3484, 2508, 3523-
24, 3542, 3545, 3552, 3561, 3570, 3610-23, 3655, 3661-62,
3681-82, 3712, 3729, 3731, 3737, 3758, 3766, 3770, 3776,
3779, 3813, 3825, 3861, 3876, 3882, 3888

S2-10.9: pp. 3946, 3956, 4004, 4054-55, 4060-61, 4115, 4145, 4173,
4195-96, 4330

CIVIL WAR (PRO-NORTHERN VIEWS)

2.1:   pp. 46, 105, 151, 214
2.2:   pp. 84, 157, 182, 341
4.1:   pp. 11, 144
4.2:   pp. 10, 38, 39, 92, 108, 111, 116, 188, 212, 222
5.3:   pp. 11, 70, 130, 154-155
5.4:   pp. 14, 154
6.1:   pp. 78-9, 346-47
6.2:   pp. 1, 8, 10, 21, 30, 47-48, 68, 74, 79-80, 92, 123, 124-25,
146, 177, 178, 188, 212, 213, 215
7.1:   pp. 3, 10, 11, 29, 31, 39, 59, 117, 189, 202, 211, 315
7.2:   pp. 39, 97, 168
8.1:   pp. 55, 135, 203, 226, 247
9.3:   pp. 8, 9, 28, 29, 71, 74, 78, 122, 123
9.4:   pp. 42, 52, 67, 77, 169, 215, 216, 217, 224, 242
10.5:   pp. 7, 8, 44, 100, 188, 240, 287
10.6:   pp. 10, 212, 213, 338
11.7:   pp. 113, 132, 140, 147, 159, 191, 192, 194, 207, 210, 211, 216
223, 255, 257
11.8:   pp. 4, 20, 21, 144, 216, 217, 250, 284, 285, 300, 325, 349,
381
12.1:   pp. 21, 133, 171, 192, 316-17
12.2:   p. 236
13.3:   p. 77
13.4:   p. 126
14.1:   pp. 24, 81, 97, 161, 171, 238, 335, 403, 419, 425
15.2:   pp. 56, 79, 80, 118, 149, 224, 228, 426, 427
16.1(KS): pp. 1, 9
16.2(KY): pp. 46, 68, 84, 107
16.3(MD): pp. 18, 43
16.4(OH): pp. 31, 76, 90
16.5(VA): p. 34
16.6(TN): p. 51
17.1:   pp. 49, 60, 103, 140, 152, 204-05, 214, 293-97, 313, 359
18.1:   pp. 16, 33
S1-1.1: pp. 74-75, 139
S1-2.1(AR): pp. 13, 22-23
S1-2.4(MO): p. 154

S1-3.1:   p. 66
S1-4.2:   p. 436
S1-5.1:   pp. 48, 51, 58, 119, 156-57, 180
S1-5.2:   p. 233
S1-7.2:   p. 785
S1-8.3:   pp. 1245-1246, 1254, 1310
S1-11.1: p. 55
S1-12.1: pp. 23, 40, 225, 285, 303-04, 330
S1-2.1:   p. 327

CIVIL WAR (PRO-SOUTHERN VIEWS)

2.1:   pp. 17, 98, 238
2.2:   p. 45
3.3:   pp. 2, 26, 27, 46, 144
3.4:   pp. 3, 26, 91, 258
4.1:   pp. 81, 119, 223, 300, 306
4.2:   pp. 28, 29, 53, 73, 78, 99, 209, 235, 257, 258
5.3:   p. 63
6.1:   pp. 23, 50, 67, 77, 78, 216-17, 219, 225-26, 270-71, 274, 280,
        331, 341
6.2:   pp. 50, 124-25, 132
7.1:   pp. 44, 46, 51, 79, 95, 174, 205, 271
7.2:   pp. 10, 28, 47, 64, 122, 147, 174
8.1:   pp. 29, 41, 110, 236
8.2:   pp. 27, 225
9.3:   pp. 1, 3, 17, 21, 143, 169, 185, 233, 284, 307, 310, 359, 360
9.4:   pp. 140, 151, 239, 245
10.5:   pp. 52, 120, 206, 367
10.6:   pp. 5, 45
11.7:   pp. 13B, 28, 91, 107, 196, 197, 218, 219, 235, 239, 240, 241,
        246, 249, 250
11.8:   pp. 41, 150, 151, 152, 153, 154, 165, 166, 178, 181, 195, 232,
        296, 346, 375
12.1:   pp. 8, 12-13, 56, 58, 130-31, 192, 248, 262, 275
12.2:   pp. 8, 35, 61, 71, 116, 133, 218, 241, 262-63, 283, 306
13.3:   pp. 152, 196
13.4:   pp. 45, 59, 60, 90, 107
14.1:   pp. 64, 86, 245, 250, 268, 367, 368
15.2:   pp. 4, 28, 150, 426
16.1(KS): p. 14
16.2(KY): pp. 41, 53
16.3(MD): pp. 47, 92, 93, 105, 106
16.5(VA): p. 19
16.6(TN): p. 51
17.1:   pp. 49-50, 59, 192, 205
S1-3.1:   pp. 19-20, 332-33
S1-5.1:   p. 2
S1-6.1:   pp. 6, 80, 86, 180, 323
S1-7.2:   pp. 333, 334, 363, 432, 538-539, 551, 564, 603-604, 685-686,
          708
S1-8.3:   pp. 812, 844-845, 875, 931, 956, 1010-1011, 1096, 1181-82,
          1278-79, 1299-1300
S1-10.5: pp. 2128, 2286-87
S1-11.2: p. 318
S1-12.1: pp. 88, 177

S2-2.1: pp. 141, 247, 276-8, 315, 338
S2-9.8: p. 3732

CLAY, HENRY

16.6(TN): p. 69

CLOTHING

2.1: pp. 10, 27, 30, 53, 57-58, 71-72, 104, 138, 189-190, 206, 210, 221, 230, 240, 304, 331

2.2: pp. 2, 23, 27-28, 36, 46, 47, 62, 67, 69, 75, 88, 101, 127-128 139, 172, 183, 201, 210, 212, 255, 266, 310, 334

3.3: pp. 15, 18, 56, 89, 113, 118, 143, 147, 172, 173, 177, 180, 200, 210, 244, 245, 252, 272

3.4: pp. 17, 36, 51, 52, 57, 65, 71, 82, 96, 128, 156, 186, 211, 219, 235, 240

4.2: pp. 1, 6, 9, 16, 18, 22, 45, 56, 59, 61, 67, 75, 82, 86, 121, 132, 135, 144, 152, 160, 169, 179, 203, 220, 221, 225, 232, 235, 238, 244, 247, 249, 252, 254, 264, 288

5.3: pp. 2, 3, 6, 10, 15, 30, 41, 90, 114, 125, 157, 160, 163, 173, 188, 211, 218-219, 241, 263, 275

5.4: pp. 11, 12, 33, 48, 52, 55, 68, 71, 84, 86, 88, 89, 106, 109, 123, 136, 148, 150, 161, 167, 180, 187, 202, 215, 217, 221, 235

6.1: pp. 10, 22, 36, 42, 45, 67, 106, 155, 158, 166, 183-84, 213, 231, 236, 248, 273, 278, 284, 295, 297, 332, 338, 343, 359, 364, 365, 388-89, 411, 429-30

6.2: pp. 26, 73, 116-17, 125, 129, 142, 145, 148, 165

7.1: pp. 13, 18, 25, 27, 30, 36, 49, 50, 73, 77, 94, 112, 128, 132, 134, 146, 172, 176, 200, 204, 207, 214, 225, 227, 242, 263, 267, 270, 286, 287, 301, 314, 335, 349, 356, 360

7.2: pp. 3, 24, 37, 44, 87, 91, 115, 137, 138, 144, 152, 158, 166

8.1: pp. 47, 116, 129, 238, 313

8.2: pp. 11, 25, 73, 172, 194

9.3: pp. 11, 15, 128, 139, 142, 155, 196, 216, 219, 236, 275, 390, 392

9.4: pp. 117, 151, 155, 199, 237, 308

10.5: pp. 69, 77, 125, 277, 302, 318

10.6: pp. 39, 44, 164, 182, 190, 234, 253, 269, 331, 348, 350

11.7: pp. 22, 30, 72, 85, 100, 101, 102, 122, 139, 177, 185, 188, 194, 199, 214, 225, 229

11.8: pp. 6, 9, 12, 40, 44, 52, 56, 74, 87, 105, 115, 120, 122, 130, 131, 136, 146, 158, 159, 180, 181, 184, 207, 213, 218, 219, 222, 241, 245, 249, 252, 258, 261, 268, 293, 296, 299, 302, 308, 321, 349, 353, 359, 360, 368

12.1: pp. 3, 4, 23, 41-42, 54, 65, 75, 80, 81-82, 87, 94-95, 108, 115, 128-129, 137, 142, 144, 156-157, 169, 173-174, 179, 186-187, 191, 203, 205, 217-218, 234, 240, 241, 255-256, 267, 279, 291, 300, 301-302, 308-309, 316, 320-321, 347

12.2: pp. 4, 33, 40, 51, 59, 62, 70, 75, 83, 93, 107, 129, 140-141, 149-150, 174, 183-184, 213-214, 224, 235, 240, 247, 257-259, 271, 275, 285-286, 290-291, 297, 317-318, 324-325, 339, 348, 356

13.3: pp. 23, 26, 27, 36, 41, 48, 60, 72, 73, 81, 82, 137, 150, 151, 153, 173, 174, 179, 211, 230, 239, 253, 267, 298, 308, 323

COURTING

13.4: pp. 35, 51, 120, 169
14.1: pp. 95, 96, 101, 118, 167, 185, 209, 282
15.2: pp. 65, 66, 170, 171, 172, 188, 195, 298, 350, 434
16.4(OH): p. 105
16.5(VA): p. 26
17.1: pp. 107-08, 147, 156-57, 324-25, 330-31
18.1: p. 132
19.1: p. 204
S1-3.1: pp. 26, 41, 115, 123, 225
S1-4.2: pp. 396, 413, 426, 448-49, 456, 565, 630
S1-5.2: p. 298
S1-7.2: pp. 384, 623-624, 640-641, 706, 745, 748
S1-8.3: pp. 967, 1008-1009, 1190-1191
S1-10.5: pp. 2012, 2151, 2173, 2235, 2369, 2385
S1-12.1: p. 378
S2-1.1(AL): p. 14
S2-1.3(AR): pp. 142-77
S2-3.2: p. 843
S2-6.5: pp. 1940, 2124, 2161
S2-7.6: pp. 2467, 2539, 2541, 2572-73, 2861-62
S2-8.7: pp. 2948, 3040, 3114, 3354
S2-10.9: p. 3950

See Also: MARRIAGE (GENERAL)

COWBOYS (BLACK)

  S2-1.2(AZ): p. 18
  S2-5.4: pp. 1594-95, 1889-90
  S2-6.5: pp. 2004, 2014, 2017, 2071, 2316, 2340, 2346
  S2-9.8: pp. 3656, 3657-58, 3671-75, 3679, 3700, 3704, 3787
  S2-10.9: pp. 3938, 3984, 3987-88

DAVIS, JEFFERSON

  2.1: pp. 28, 171
  2.2: pp. 2, 38, 151, 281
  3.3: pp. 57, 129, 204
  3.4: pp. 6, 73, 250
  4.1: p. 292
  5.4: p. 117
  6.1: p. 4
  7.1: pp. 75, 137, 226, 229, 327
  7.2: pp. 10, 52, 93, 116, 138, 149
  8.1: p. 106
  8.2: p. 27
  9.3: p. 295
 11.7: p. 235
 11.8: pp. 144, 255, 347
 12.1: pp. 8, 56, 58, 85, 102, 140, 182, 224, 263, 314, 317, 352
 12.2: pp. 8, 105, 114, 134, 192, 218, 231, 241, 250
 13.3: pp. 102, 273
 13.4: p. 113
 14.1: pp. 193, 294, 310, 317, 378, 434

DISEASE

See: MEDICAL CARE

EDUCATION (AFTER SLAVERY)

7.1: pp. 21, 25, 41, 46, 68, 80, 94, 123, 143, 205, 229, 315
7.2: pp. 9, 15, 43, 60, 74, 127, 167
8.1: pp. 18, 21, 25, 65, 79, 121, 132, 133, 144, 182, 216, 223,
      252, 265, 293, 309, 321
8.2: pp. 2, 4, 19, 20, 37, 73, 74, 84, 89, 99, 122, 125, 130, 137,
      152, 153, 159, 165, 167, 173, 174, 181, 190, 194, 199, 204,
      231, 279, 301, 312, 320, 329, 338, 341, 344
9.3: pp. 2, 12, 25, 28, 41, 51, 66, 68, 71, 80, 85, 103, 130, 131,
      151, 152, 177, 199, 209, 213, 228-229, 244, 255, 280, 296,
      313, 363
9.4: pp. 4, 10, 11, 32, 45, 46, 67, 73, 81, 98, 131, 142, 150,
      161, 163, 214, 223, 243, 295, 305
10.5: pp. 6, 22, 26, 31, 47, 49, 51, 75, 80, 115, 121, 126, 179,
      190, 191, 204, 211, 222, 245, 246, 271, 272, 278, 319, 333,
      336, 343, 359, 363
10.6: pp. 15, 19, 22, 36, 43, 51, 92, 100, 137, 138, 142, 151, 165,
      172, 175, 183, 190, 191, 192, 204, 209, 226, 227, 228, 255,
      301, 304, 332, 342, 343, 349, 358, 361
11.7: pp. 5, 6, 29, 37, 40, 42, 44, 61, 62, 67, 73, 74, 75, 81,
      83, 100, 102, 109, 113, 115, 116, 132, 133, 158, 175, 208,
      211, 213, 216, 219, 240, 241, 242, 250, 254, 256
11.8: pp. 7, 11, 19, 22, 23, 26, 27, 74, 82, 133, 136, 171, 185,
      189, 212, 213, 218, 220, 225, 233, 234, 239, 275, 276, 284,
      300, 301, 309, 343, 351, 353, 380
12.1: pp. 21, 68-69, 78, 102, 162, 210, 219, 223, 262-63. 280, 335,
      336, 352
12.2: pp. 8, 30, 45-46, 88, 101, 113, 133, 144, 181, 191, 202, 231,
      242-43, 341
13.3: pp. 83, 86, 97, 102, 117, 134, 144, 301 302, 312
13.4: pp. 3, 21, 63, 64, 93, 146, 231
14.1: pp. 4, 17, 35, 36, 77, 146, 170, 224, 235, 244, 268, 320, 321
      326, 376, 439
15.2: pp. 40, 86, 87, 125, 160, 211, 240, 247, 248, 249, 291, 314,
      369, 382, 383, 392, 416, 429
16.1(KS): pp. 4, 5, 13
16.2(KY): pp. 3, 50, 58, 89
16.3(MD): pp. 13, 21, 35, 64
16.4(OH): pp. 1, 4, 9, 13, 20, 26, 43, 47, 60, 73, 95, 106, 111-13
16.5(VA): pp. 10, 14A, 24, 55, 56
16.6(TN): pp. 22, 32, 40, 44, 64, 72
17.1: pp. 16-17, 39, 46, 50, 136-37, 201, 210, 215-16, 260-61,
      308-09, 331, 352
18.1: pp. 48, 51, 67, 88, 89, 90, 103, 116
19.1: pp. 44, 166-68
S1-1.1: pp. 4, 45, 59, 64, 75, 115, 328, 355, 385, 414
S1-2.2(CO): pp. 25, 28, 35, 49-50, 53-54, 59, 62, 74, 83, 89, 94,
             96, 99
S1-2.3(MN): pp. 101, 107, 134
S1-2.4(MO): pp. 150, 214, 222-23
S1-3.1: pp. 119, 283-84, 312-13
S1-4.2: pp. 352-54, 423, 528-29, 558
S1-5.1: pp. 2, 10-12, 22, 70, 111, 240
S1-5.2: pp. 278, 288, 294, 317-20, 330, 378, 399, 424, 446-47, 465
S1-6.1: pp. 16, 17, 30, 45, 63, 64, 74, 95, 117, 145, 147, 148,
         260, 272, 294, 295, 303
S1-7.2: pp. 354, 367, 426, 443, 483-485, 516, 539, 586, 590,

EDUCATION (DURING SLAVERY)

        279, 299, 301, 302, 311, 332, 348, 376, 377, 390, 410, 417,
        433
6.2:   pp. 11, 12, 38, 56, 78, 103, 109, 113, 131, 159, 189, 196,
        211
7.1:   pp. 9, 14, 31, 51, 74, 78, 97, 129, 135, 145, 168, 291, 296,
        318, 351
7.2:   pp. 5, 24, 38, 79, 87, 101, 145, 160, 167, 170
8.1:   pp. 102, 117, 197, 231, 234
8.2:   pp. 1, 17, 74, 137, 167, 199, 242, 267, 292
9.3:   pp. 12, 28, 70, 73, 220, 253, 276, 311
9.4:   pp. 28, 73, 80, 199, 229
10.5:   pp. 10, 40, 105, 108, 130, 173, 210
10.6:   pp. 56, 187, 204, 257, 273, 324
11.7:   pp. 21, 34, 71, 143, 155, 185
11.8:   pp. 6, 23, 27, 28, 32, 40, 47, 48, 53, 59, 77, 110, 111, 157,
        189, 213, 235, 252, 299, 333, 363, 375
12.1:   pp. 5, 10, 44-45, 68, 83, 109, 114, 180, 202, 219, 234, 257,
        270, 310, 323, 349
12.2:   pp. 5, 33-34, 42, 62, 109, 120, 130-131, 185, 210, 215, 226,
        247, 274, 283, 354
13.3:   pp. 4, 61, 105, 182, 240
13.4:   pp. 40, 54, 143, 214, 231, 297, 317, 318
14.1:   pp. 23, 33, 34, 48, 62, 69, 95, 107, 122, 133, 141, 193, 199
        204, 256, 260, 303, 316, 332, 333, 355, 372, 413, 429, 439
15.2:   pp. 3, 17, 57, 58, 62, 64, 74, 97, 102, 120, 132, 138, 187,
        206. 214, 218, 221, 224, 277, 287, 294, 304, 320, 338, 346,
        366, 373, 386, 396
16.1(KS): pp. 1, 5, 16
16.2(KY): pp. 6, 10, 15, 18, 30, 34, 69
16.3(MO): pp. 4, 9, 10, 18, 28, 32, 35, 39, 46, 54
16.4(OH): pp. 13, 17, 22, 23, 28, 29, 31, 39, 52, 59, 66, 75, 78,
           81, 84, 89, 98, 104, 109, 114
16.5(VA): pp. 18, 30, 42, 53, 55
16.6(TN): pp. 3, 5, 29, 67, 77
17.1:   pp. 16, 54, 95-96, 134, 142, 146-48, 162, 165, 175-176, 178,
        238, 245, 253, 279, 290, 365
18.1:   pp. 41, 45, 129
19.1:   p. 147
S1-1.1:   pp. 87, 92, 138, 242, 245, 255, 293, 299, 352, 403, 405,
           443, 466
S1-2.1(AR): p. 2
S1-2.3(MN): pp. 119, 123-24
S1-2.4(MO): p. 150
S1-2.6(WA): pp. 282, 287
S1-3.1:   pp. 34-35
S1-4.2:   pp. 349-50, 418, 548, 663
S1-5.1:   pp. 3, 12, 45, 57, 166, 171-72, 206
S1-5.2:   pp. 424, 461
S1-6.1:   pp. 10, 21, 58, 108, 123, 124, 160, 218, 285
S1-7.2:   pp. 344, 364, 365, 372, 391, 394, 405, 408, 414, 418, 443,
           449, 483, 493, 497, 512, 537, 546-547, 571, 580, 656, 677,
           682, 691, 745, 756-757, 764, 776, 799
S1-8.3:   pp. 811, 820, 821, 940, 965, 1015, 1045, 1052, 1061, 1083,
           1112, 1153, 1159-1160, 1161, 1170-1171, 1196, 1221, 1232,
           1237-1238, 1253, 1275, 1292, 1321, 1329
S1-9.4:   pp. 1477, 1488, 1533, 1548, 1664, 1731, 1792-93, 1846

FAMILY (GENERAL)

See Also: FAMILY (SEPARATIONS); MARRIAGE (AFTER SLAVERY); MARRIAGE (DURING SLAVERY)

FAMILY (SEPARATIONS)

See Also: AFRICAN SURVIVALS; BRER RABBIT; MYTHS AND SUPERSTITIONS;
            SPIRITUALS

GAMBLING

GAMES AND RECREATION

          3162-63, 3201-3202, 3219-20, 3223, 3239, 3263, 3301-3302,
          3338, 3398-99
S2-9.8: pp. 3408-3409, 3448, 3480, 3508, 3521-22, 3574, 3638, 3655,
          3661, 3680, 3703, 3802
S2-10.9: pp. 3950, 3998, 4000, 4078, 4080, 4134, 4254

  See Also: ENTERTAINMENT; GAMBLING; HOLIDAYS

GERONIMO

  S2-6.5: pp. 2379-80, 2384-85

GHOSTS

  See Also: AFRICAN SURVIVALS; MYTHS AND SUPERSTITIONS

HEALTH

  See: MEDICAL CARE

HISTORY (GENERAL)

  S1-2.6(WA): pp. 279-92
  S1-5.1: pp. 249-51, 254-56

HOLIDAYS

  2.1: pp. 63, 124, 167, 171, 190-191, 207, 301-302, 305, 333, 334,
       343
  2.2: pp. 2, 32, 40, 51, 58, 69, 105, 143-144, 210, 212, 238
  3.3: pp. 1, 90, 115, 169, 201, 219, 273, 277, 285, 286
  3.4: pp. 54, 72, 85, 89, 90, 178, 213, 214, 248
  4.1: pp. 2, 37, 71, 73, 74, 107, 118, 122, 131, 135, 149, 150, 178,
       183, 186, 190, 199, 200, 206, 237, 238, 243, 247, 258, 286
  4.2: pp. 7, 23, 47, 52, 56, 61, 76, 82, 92, 99, 102, 103, 122, 124,
       128, 152, 153, 154, 161, 173, 234, 235
  5.3: pp. 2, 3, 8, 60, 98, 109, 115, 117, 160, 186, 198, 214, 222,
       226, 234, 243
  5.4: pp. 36, 44, 49, 69, 71, 79, 82, 100, 117, 129, 136, 148, 161,
       169, 181, 204, 220, 237
  6.1: pp. 11, 43, 46, 68, 85, 88-89, 107, 114, 131, 134, 150-51,
       155, 162, 194, 200, 216, 229, 237, 239, 256, 295, 298, 322,
       324, 329, 354, 380, 387, 391, 398, 412, 418
  6.2: pp. 53, 107, 130, 148, 165
  7.1: pp. 26, 30, 31, 40, 76, 99, 111, 136, 147, 205, 207, 224,
       227, 304, 311, 320, 351
  7.2: pp. 6, 19, 80, 86, 92, 126, 145, 154, 167
  8.1: pp. 30, 115, 147, 325
  8.2: pp. 28, 104
  9.3: pp. 12, 51, 68, 227, 291
  9.4: pp. 116, 258
  10.5: pp. 119, 357
  10.6: p. 43
  11.7: pp. 100, 101, 126, 131, 168, 187, 233

                2281-82, 2297, 2305, 2328, 2337, 2345, 2354, 2368, 2405,
                2413
S2-7.6:   pp. 2451-2452, 2467-2468, 2483, 2495, 2502, 2510, 2597,
                2606, 2615, 2647-48, 2652-53, 2665-66, 2708, 2712, 2719,
                2723, 2728, 2741-42, 2758-59, 2793, 2802-03, 2814, 2841,
                2842-43
S2-8.7:   pp. 2918, 2979, 2998-99, 3020, 3021, 3027, 3041, 3045, 3060,
                3085, 3093, 3101, 3114, 3163, 3167, 3176, 3203, 3213, 3223,
                3225, 3264, 3273-74, 3289, 3294-95, 3301, 3307, 3325, 3332,
                3337-38, 3346, 3377, 3390
S2-9.8:   pp. 3447-48, 3485, 3496, 3499, 3520-22, 3552, 3569-70, 3604,
                3638, 3652, 3658, 3661, 3666, 3679, 3701-3702, 3716, 3723,
                3724, 3729, 3753, 3758, 3775, 3824, 3863
S2-10.9: pp. 3954, 3981, 4028, 4080, 4090, 4094, 4284, 4319-20

ILLNESS

   See: MEDICAL CARE

INDIAN RELATIVES

   2.1:   pp. 131, 132, 148, 300, 301, 302
   2.2:   p. 190
   3.3:   p. 127
   3.4:   pp. 19, 229
   4.1:   pp. 9, 93, 117, 164
   4.2:   pp. 42, 44, 66, 87, 201, 219, 228, 229
   5.3:   p. 148
   5.4:   pp. 17, 79, 82, 155, 167, 190, 192
   6.1:   pp. 26, 234, 316
   6.2:   pp. 3, 43-44, 47, 48, 84, 85, 86-87, 134, 169
   7.1:   pp. 187, 266, 349
   7.2:   p. 36
   8.1:   pp. 34, 50, 53, 78, 120, 137, 202, 326, 342
   8.2:   pp. 2, 43, 57, 95, 169, 170, 215, 262, 293, 313
   9.3:   pp. 28, 31, 105, 157, 209, 264, 273, 282m 347, 369
   9.4:   pp. 43, 132, 304
   10.5: pp. 33, 51
   10.6: pp. 134, 140, 160, 187, 194, 208, 234, 271, 307, 318
   11.7: pp. 108, 173, 214, 247
   11.8: pp. 59, 121, 147, 175, 200, 216, 243, 246, 290, 296, 299
   12.1: pp. 113, 189, 335
   12.2: p. 49
   13.3: pp. 80, 118, 127
   14.1: pp. 15, 233, 234, 361
   15.2: p. 3
   16.3(MD): pp. 34, 70
   16.4(OH): p. 42
   16.5(VA): pp. 24, 31-33
   16.6(TN): pp. 43, 47, 52, 57
   17.1: pp. 27, 172, 179, 201, 279, 288, 367, 370
   18.1: p. 225
   19.1: p. 187
   S1-1.1: pp. 295, 360

S1-2.1(AR): p. 2
S1-2.2(CO): p. 41
S1-2.4(MO): pp. 154, 178, 219
S1-3.1: pp. 45, 198, 203, 311, 322
S1-4.2: p. 603
S1-5.1: p. 63
S1-5.2: pp. 422, 438, 464
S1-6.1: pp. 92, 99, 190, 206, 287, 288, 290, 295
S1-7.2: pp. 389, 559-560, 760
S1-8.3: pp. 910, 1094, 1236, 1290
S1-9.4: pp. 1415, 1419-20, 1424-25, 1426, 1838, 1854
S1-10.5: pp. 2025, 2041, 2175, 2215
S1-11.2: pp. 63, 291, 314-15
S1-12.1: pp. 11, 73-74, 82, 108, 132, 197, 250, 267, 281, 351, 354-
          56, 360
S2-1.3(AR): pp. 68-69, 70, 75, 102
S2-1.4(FL): p. 263
S2-1.10(NE): pp. 303, 314-14, 322, 323, 339, 344
S2-2.1: pp. 181, 289, 294, 296, 362, 373
S2-3.2: pp. 481, 483, 653
S2-4.3: pp. 1070, 1231, 1309, 1354
S2-5.4: pp. 1546, 1548, 1571, 1572, 1577-78, 1706-1707, 1876
S2-6.5: pp. 1960, 2022, 2051-52, 2064, 2068, 2069, 2294, 2314, 2373,
          2403
S2-7.6: pp. 2485, 2490, 2623, 2695, 2902, 2903
S2-8.7: pp. 2958, 2960-62, 3006, 3007, 3012-13, 3017, 3031, 3032,
          3037-38, 3072, 3087, 3143, 3144, 3365
S2-9.8: pp. 3503, 3507, 3627, 3714, 3776
S2-10.9: pp. 4038, 4191, 4226

INDIANS (GENERAL)

2.1: pp. 198, 299, 302-03, 315
2.2: pp. 213, 230, 235, 248
3.3: pp. 152, 226
3.4: p. 19
4.1: pp. 1, 117, 133, 145, 146
4.2: pp. 2, 44, 45, 195, 259, 265
5.3: pp. 64, 82, 94, 97-98, 148, 172
5.4: pp. 4, 41, 82, 90, 142-143, 155, 158, 167, 190, 196, 200
6.1: pp. 26, 234, 287
6.2: pp. 43-44, 49, 84-85, 176
7.1: pp. 8, 9, 10, 11, 33, 42, 43, 53, 54, 55, 56, 57, 58, 59, 87,
       115, 116, 117, 118, 119, 120, 121, 122, 123, 155, 156, 157,
       158, 159, 178, 179, 180, 181, 192, 217, 237, 240, 241, 257,
       259, 266, 267, 268, 269, 285, 287, 288, 326, 344, 350
7.2: pp. 36, 128
8.1: pp. 107, 190
8.2: p. 147
9.3: pp. 7, 192, 264
9.4: pp. 149, 220
10.5: pp. 35, 103, 115
10.6: pp. 115, 189, 217, 350
11.7: pp. 96, 213, 214
11.8: pp. 68, 175, 353, 359
12.2: pp. 8, 21

LABOR PRACTICES (HIRING OUT)

LAND OWNERSHIP, BLACK

See: PRIVATE PROPERTY (CONTROLLED BY BLACKS)

LAND PEONAGE (AFTER SLAVERY)

9.4:   pp. 2, 3, 6, 26, 31, 40, 41, 66, 88, 98, 101, 105, 132, 134,
        147, 153, 183, 224, 233, 237, 262, 269, 272, 294, 300, 301,
        302, 307, 310
10.5:   pp. 45, 49, 80, 102, 162, 170, 195, 266, 294
10.6:   pp. 28, 34, 67, 68, 87, 95, 151, 165, 196, 197, 224, 250,
        251, 263, 267, 269
11.7:   pp. 31, 44, 56, 78, 79, 86, 101, 134, 135, 157, 174, 175, 205,
        219, 242
11.8:   pp. 117, 192, 211, 296, 305, 308, 328, 350, 351, 374, 375
12.1:   pp. 68, 115, 176, 210, 297, 335
12.2:   pp. 87, 176-177, 190-191
13.4:   pp. 21, 35, 81, 90, 91, 113, 172, 203, 204, 239, 240, 241
14.1:   pp. 61, 172, 178, 205, 294, 326, 327, 334, 420, 430
15.2:   pp. 25, 33, 41, 70, 85, 103, 104, 136, 224, 230, 255, 318,
        319, 334, 345, 361, 362, 435, 436
16.1(KS): pp. 4, 9-10
16.2(KY): pp. 19, 46
16.4(OH): pp. 53, 108, 114
16.5(VA): p. 14
16.6(TN): pp. 16, 48, 62
17.1:   pp. 53, 55, 60, 98, 130, 232, 239, 331-332
18.1:   p. 83
S1-1.1: pp. 147, 220, 359
S1-2.4(MO): pp. 140, 247
S1-2.6(WA): p. 281
S1-3.1: p. 202
S1-4.2: pp. 392, 422, 433, 540, 625
S1-5.1: pp. 4, 47, 83, 165, 167
S1-5.2: pp. 342, 358, 421, 474
S1-6.1: pp. 251-2
S1-7.2: pp. 337, 377, 401, 420, 444-45, 504, 539, 546, 551-552,
        566, 568, 597-598, 604-605, 611, 624, 640, 648-649, 667,
        672, 719, 720, 750, 774, 778, 786
S1-8.3: pp. 813, 836, 847, 850, 868, 893, 902, 911, 931-932, 957,
        960, 966, 976, 1066, 1124, 1135, 1143, 1178-1179, 1241,
        1301, 1325, 1347-48
S1-9.4: p. 1391
S1-10.5: pp. 2054, 2118-19, 2155, 2261, 2296, 2324, 2338, 2385
S1-12.1: pp. 338-39, 373-74, 396
S2-1.1(AL): p. 4
S2-1.3(AR): p. 71
S2-1.7(IN): p. 279
S2-3.2: pp. 692, 729, 779-80
S2-4.3: pp. 997, 1000, 1027, 1039-40, 1146, 1432
S2-5.4: pp. 1453-54, 1471, 1720, 1844, 1922
S2-6.5: pp. 1930, 1950, 1977, 2065, 2106, 2134, 2263, 2329, 2372
S2-7.6: pp. 2454, 2486, 2540, 2579, 2595, 2620, 2626, 2664, 2684,
        2739, 2806-07, 2858, 2860-61, 2862, 2863-64, 2871
S2-8.7: pp. 2934-35, 2951, 2955, 2956, 2970-71, 2998, 3020-21,
        3022, 3024, 3038, 3051, 3090, 3117, 3125, 3140, 3141, 3147,
        3198, 3252, 3276-77, 3302, 3318, 3331, 3339, 3343, 3364,
        3374, 3386, 3390, 3401
S2-9.8: pp. 3479, 3502, 3570-71, 3768, 3771, 3840
S21-10.9: pp. 3952, 3956, 3964, 4047, 4089, 4101, 4374

S2-1.9(MD): pp. 298, 299-300
S2-3.2: p. 736
S2-4.3: pp. 1049, 1176, 1271
S2-5.4: pp. 1646, 1691, 1693, 1874
S2-7.6: pp. 2553, 2609, 2656, 2657-58, 2907
S2-8.7: pp. 2929, 3062, 3114, 3155, 3161, 3373
S2-9.8: pp. 3407-3408, 3643, 3800, 3803, 3844, 3845
S2-10.9: pp. 3973, 3893, 4060

LYNCHING

12.1: p. 281
16.4(OH): p. 53
16.6(TN): p. 44
18.1: pp. 32, 39, 41, 52, 70-1, 84-5, 101-102
S1-1.1: p. 107
S1-2.4(MO): p. 243
S1-4.2: p. 578
S1-5.1: p. 134
S1-6.1: p. 182
S1-7.2: p. 471
S1-11.2: pp. 299, 303
S2-1.3(AR): p. 70
S2-1.10(NE): pp. 307-08
S2-6.5: pp. 2217, 2245, 2289, 2316-17
S2-7.6: p. 2645
S2-8.7: p. 2982
S2-9.8: pp. 3551, 3669, 3685
S2-10.9: p. 4140

MANUMISSION

12.1: pp. 7, 12, 20-21, 49-50, 68, 102, 111, 139-140, 209, 247-248,
        262, 270-271, 325
12.2: pp. 45, 55, 59, 76-77, 95, 190, 209-10, 230, 236, 330
16.1(KS): p. 2
16.2(KY): pp. 79, 81, 83
16.3(MD): p. 22
16.4(OH): p. 111
16.6(TN): pp. 31, 70
18.1: p. 150
S1-2.4(MO): p. 240
S1-5.1: p. 115
S1-5.2: pp. 418-19
S1-6.1: p. 77
S1-7.2: pp. 384, 425-426, 440, 490, 493, 497, 511, 550-551, 585,
        597, 604, 611, 615, 648, 664, 699, 719, 729-730, 738, 758,
        765, 773, 786,
S1-8.3: pp. 828, 846-847, 849-850, 858, 880, 902, 918-919, 926,
        945, 969, 972, 990, 1027, 1039, 1044, 1052, 1075, 1087,
        1119, 1135, 1142-1143, 1148, 1151, 1174-1175, 1192, 1198,
        1213, 1226, 1245-1246, 1249, 1261, 1285, 1347
S1-10.5: pp. 2042-43, 2053, 2060, 2063, 2067, 2070-71, 2077, 2086,
        2100, 2142, 2151, 2155, 2169, 2173, 2201-02, 2210, 2212

MARRIAGE (AFTER SLAVERY)

MARRIAGE (DURING SLAVERY)

11.8:   pp. 1, 2, 3, 6, 26, 28, 33, 73, 87, 114, 115, 121, 129, 131, 137, 147, 184, 264, 266, 271, 312, 341, 350, 353, 371
12.1:   pp. 24, 108, 113, 137, 142, 168, 301, 319
12.2:   pp. 12, 74, 99, 174-75, 185, 233
13.3:   p. 87
13.4:   pp. 77, 124, 180, 290, 291, 292-308
14.1:   pp. 2, 28, 118, 160, 213, 215, 217, 386, 387, 454
15.2:   pp. 24, 31, 44, 96, 128, 148, 150, 193
16.1(KS): p. 5
16.2(KY): pp. 19, 30, 38, 46, 57, 67
16.4(OH): pp. 6, 10, 26, 28, 38, 52, 64, 65, 75, 79, 80, 85, 109
16.5(VA): pp. 12, 50-51
16.6(TN): pp. 1, 4, 16, 19, 21, 58, 60
17.1:   pp. 13, 66-70, 90, 94, 102, 127-30, 139, 166, 168, 173, 184-86, 297
18.1:   pp. 30, 84-85
S1-3.1: pp. 94, 98
S1-4.2: pp. 541, 623, 630, 664
S1-5.1: pp. 206, 229
S1-6.1: pp. 20, 76, 81, 82, 83, 130, 179, 200, 203, 235, 239, 308, 310
S1-7.2: pp. 365, 595, 599
S1-8.3: pp. 897, 1024, 1131, 1134, 1256-1257, 1331, 1338
S1-9.4: pp. 1597-99, 1602, 1727, 1891-93
S1-10.5: pp. 1978, 2042, 2064
S1-11.1: p. 30
S1-12.1: pp. 4, 80-81, 187, 215, 328
S2-1.3(AR): p. 128
S2-1.7(IN): p. 278
S2-1.10(NE): p. 331
S2-2.1: pp. 23, 24, 66, 75, 139, 175, 237
S2-4.3: pp. 1007, 1029, 1053, 1355
S2-5.4: p. 1578
S2-6.5: pp. 1928, 1945, 1960, 2025, 2136, 2145, 2150, 2152, 2253, 2254, 2403, 2404
S2-7.6: pp. 2521, 2530, 2576, 2581-82, 2599, 2610, 2643-45, 2648, 2651, 2689, 2706, 2717, 2718, 2766, 2798
S2-8.7: pp. 2969, 2990-91, 2996-97, 3082-83, 3137-38, 3218, 3239, 3240, 3269, 3282, 3359, 3370
S2-9.8: pp. 3549-53
S2-10.9: pp. 4025, 4118, 4194

See Also: WHITES, NEGATIVE ATTITUDE TOWARD

MASTER, POSITIVE ATTITUDE TOWARD

2.1:   pp. 6, 9, 26, 60, 67, 74, 131, 140, 166, 208, 216, 244, 256, 295, 300, 304-05
2.2:   pp. 2, 9, 11-12, 31, 35, 42, 57, 74, 80, 84, 91, 97, 106, 113, 126, 134, 136, 138, 171, 178, 209, 216, 226-227, 228, 238, 240, 259, 289, 317, 327, 331, 336, 338, 342
3.3:   pp. 1, 2, 33, 36, 37, 38, 39, 43, 45, 56, 87, 92, 102, 113, 140, 142, 206, 207, 208, 221, 236, 237, 266, 277, 282
3.4:   pp. 10, 25, 45, 51, 57, 51, 80, 82, 88, 91, 117, 119, 120, 125, 126, 127, 128, 147, 148, 149, 150, 152, 155, 161, 181, 199, 204, 213, 221, 254, 269

12.1:   pp. 27, 58, 115, 159, 171, 176, 182, 200, 249, 262, 271, 351
12.2:   pp. 45, 55, 76-77, 143, 152, 176, 205, 236, 242, 287, 326,
        333, 353
13.3:   p. 87
13.4:   pp. 45, 90, 126, 348, 350
14.1:   pp. 6, 25, 31, 61, 65, 76, 95, 96, 107, 124, 144, 185, 316,
        445
15.2:   pp. 41, 86, 119, 182, 195, 205, 235, 387, 391
16.1(KS):   p. 15
16.2(KY):   p. 108
16.3(MD):   pp. 28, 76
16.4(OH):   pp. 63, 65, 73, 79, 106, 108
16.5(VA):   pp. 3, 7, 15, 21, 25
16.6(TN):   pp. 68, 77
17.1:   pp. 24-25, 36, 98, 103, 130, 160-61, 166, 169, 177, 187, 232,
        246, 251, 254-55, 282, 293, 313, 331, 351, 360
S1-1.1:   p. 435
S1-3.1:   p. 222
S1-4.2:   pp. 416, 641, 664
S1-5.1:   pp. 95, 165, 197
S1-5.2:   pp. 473-74
S1-6.1:   pp. 43, 67, 81, 107, 197, 202, 211, 237, 252, 278, 311
S1-7.2:   pp. 384, 440, 490, 515, 521, 615, 635, 648, 786
S1-8.3:   pp. 926, 1119, 1143
S1-9.4:   pp. 1391, 1449, 1556
S1-10.5:   pp. 2295, 2373, 2382-83
S1-12.1:   pp. 239, 373
S2-1.3(AR):   pp. 53-54, 71, 90, 184
S2-3.2:   p. 841
S2-5.4:   pp. 1469, 1497, 1917
S2-6.5:   pp. 1937, 2345, 2405
S2-7.6:   pp. 2579, 2607-08, 2619, 2664, 2684, 2699, 2724, 2772, 2882,
        2892
S2-8.7:   pp. 2923, 2955, 2992, 3011-12, 3037, 3073-74, 3090, 3110,
        3197, 3309, 3317-18, 3320, 3329, 3336-37, 3374
S2-9.8:   pp. 3496, 3637, 3661, 3683, 3771, 3857-58

MASTER, SLAVE'S DECISION TO REMAIN WITH

2.1:   pp. 5, 12, 26, 63, 190, 242, 248, 305, 321, 327, 328
2.2:   pp. 135, 137, 211, 263, 330, 336, 340
3.3:   pp. 3, 205, 266
3.4:   pp. 9, 11, 24, 27, 56, 58, 71, 79, 89, 93, 119, 120, 150,
       176, 182, 226, 251
4.1:   pp. 3, 11, 12, 43, 46, 50, 57, 65, 71, 74, 82, 110, 115, 148,
       149, 187, 208, 209, 215, 222, 238, 247, 253, 272, 277, 292
4.2:   pp. 230, 239, 244, 248, 250, 254, 289
5.3:   pp. 2, 5, 21, 27, 36, 42, 83, 107, 119, 121, 130, 155, 161,
       164, 170, 182, 192, 194, 206, 216, 226, 235, 267, 272
5.4:   pp. 8, 30, 35, 50, 54, 60, 70, 72, 75, 88, 105, 124, 130, 139,
       152, 169, 172, 178, 189, 209, 213, 224
6.1:   pp. 102, 138, 176-77, 190, 195-96, 231, 314-14, 392
6.2:   pp. 2, 40, 65, 89, 102, 112, 140, 156, 165, 183, 196, 204, 207,
7.1:   pp. 7, 18, 26, 37, 51, 71, 90, 130, 169, 191, 202, 222, 234,
       255, 291, 308
7.2:   pp. 20, 30, 41, 70, 81, 148, 155, 173

S2-3.2: pp. 619, 675, 703, 877-78, 897, 914
S2-4.3: pp. 1041, 1084, 1144, 1167, 1216, 1304, 1352, 1429
S2-5.4: pp. 1452-53, 1519, 1528, 1566, 1581, 1605, 1695-86, 1720,
         1844
S2-6.5: pp. 1930, 1933, 1937, 1938, 1946, 1964, 2000, 2014, 2016,
         2041, 2045, 2106, 2113, 2121, 2129, 2130, 2138, 2142, 2150,
         2163, 2170, 2216, 2222, 2241, 2260-61, 2286, 2287-88, 2328,
         2332, 2388
S2-7.6: pp. 2475, 2484, 2496, 2503, 2508, 2519, 2538, 2555, 2579,
         2648, 2684, 2699, 2706, 2707, 2724, 2733, 2746, 2752-53,
         2754, 2762, 2806, 2810, 2814, 2816, 2858, 2876, 2882, 2897
S2-8.7: pp. 2923, 2928, 2934, 2948, 2955, 2998, 3004, 3028, 3042,
         3046, 3051, 3103, 3110, 3125, 3126, 3140, 3146, 3164, 3188,
         3198, 3219, 3226, 3252, 3256, 3264, 3276-77, 3282, 3303,
         3353, 3364, 3386, 3390
S2-9.8: pp. 3444, 3450, 3482, 3524, 3546, 3570, 3606, 3623, 3627,
         3633, 3647, 3657, 3668, 3703, 3726, 3735, 3755, 3791, 3811,
         3889
S2-10.9: pp. 4062, 4095, 4146, 4311

MASTERS, BLACK

  5.4: p. 156
 15.2: pp. 237, 319, 329
 16.1(KY): pp. 106, 110
 S1-5.1: p. 94
 S1-8.3: p. 807
 S2-2.1: pp. 296-98

MEDICAL CARE

  2.1: pp. 12, 24, 27, 39, 63, 125, 150-151, 167, 171, 193-194, 221-
        222, 242, 305, 307, 328, 334
  2.2: pp. 2, 31, 38, 55-56, 89, 135, 146-147, 167, 175-176, 191, 210,
        329,
  3.3: pp. 3, 9, 15, 63, 101, 106, 128, 160, 175, 252, 273
  3.4: pp. 11, 58, 73, 85, 90, 103, 156, 168, 214, 228, 229, 263
  4.1: pp. 50, 64, 69, 71, 74, 80, 81, 97, 141, 142, 170, 178, 207,
        212, 214, 262, 271, 298
  4.2: pp. 3, 16, 18, 24, 32, 42, 60, 91, 92, 104, 111, 123, 131, 142,
        154, 158, 161, 193, 209, 222, 247, 252, 254, 285, 291, 292,
        293, 294
  5.3: pp. 13, 65, 77, 109, 126, 143, 175, 178, 198, 215-16, 226,
        242, 279
  5.4: pp. 13, 43, 79, 100, 112-113, 130, 148, 169, 226, 237
  6.1: pp. 7, 19, 21, 28, 44-45, 47, 68-69, 82, 85-86, 115, 122, 134,
        151-152, 174-175, 184, 216, 235, 236, 239, 256, 258, 283, 298,
        308, 312, 327, 332, 333, 343, 355, 361, 372, 384, 391, 402,
        410, 412, 433
  6.2: pp. 28, 37, 47, 132, 152, 179, 193, 196, 201
  7.1: pp. 24, 28, 35, 36, 41, 69, 106, 107, 112, 113, 114, 126, 147,
        173, 184, 189, 190, 194, 204, 252, 273, 287, 299, 305, 321,
        332, 351, 358, 361
  7.2: pp. 7, 52, 69, 137, 144, 160, 166
  8.1: pp. 66, 67, 79, 113, 312
  8.2: pp. 69, 283

10.5:   pp. 245, 259
10.6:   pp. 227, 332
11.7:   pp. 61, 67, 115, 132, 133, 149, 175, 208, 209, 253
11.8:   pp. 19, 22, 212, 267, 362
12.1:   pp. 12, 77, 97, 114, 186, 234, 249, 269–270, 295–296, 323
12.2:   pp. 5, 16, 85, 179, 192–193, 205, 209, 239, 292, 340
13.3:   pp. 61, 181, 280, 335
13.4:   pp. 4, 9, 33, 92, 129, 169, 178, 201, 214, 234, 237, 319, 363, 364
14.1:   pp. 261, 263–69, 287, 391
15.2:   pp. 119, 339
16.2(KY): pp. 3, 16, 28, 98, 109
16.3(MD): pp. 29, 32, 41, 43, 55, 69, 77
16.4(OH): pp. 44, 48, 54, 55, 89, 111, 112
16.6(TN): p. 40
17.1:   pp. 18–19, 40, 50, 165–66, 180, 214–15, 236, 244–45, 261
S1–1.1:   pp. 87, 286–87, 298, 323, 326, 330, 339, 344, 369, 438
S1–2.3(MN): pp. 109, 113
S1–2.4(MO): p. 164
S1–3.1:   pp. 4, 12, 182, 213, 278, 280–81, 293, 331–32
S1–4.2:   pp. 555, 565, 624, 671–73
S1–5.1:   pp. 165, 168
S1–5.2:   pp. 352, 393, 435, 468
S1–6.1:   pp. 31, 58, 143, 148, 265, 266, 306, 323
S1–7.2:   pp. 344, 390, 486, 567, 646, 651, 692, 744, 797
S1–8.3:   pp. 866, 907, 914, 934, 940, 978, 1062, 1072, 1127, 1129–30, 1260, 1294–1295, 1322
S1–10.5: pp. 1955, 2147, 2175, 2202–03, 2217–18, 2220–21, 2352
S1–12.1: pp. 13, 24, 29, 85, 113
S2–2.1:   pp. 65, 97, 343, 450

MISCEGENATION

12.1:   p. 253
12.2:   pp. 50, 118, 173
16.2(KY): pp. 23, 61, 72, 112
16.3(MD): pp. 34, 54
16.4(OH): pp. 61, 77, 92
16.5(VA): pp. 11, 19
16.6(TN): pp. 2, 4, 8, 27, 30, 32, 40, 45, 50, 61, 78, 81
18.1:   pp. 1, 2, 3, 8, 11, 123, 251–52, 298
S1–5.1:   p. 62
S1–6.1:   pp. 124, 190, 191
S1–7.2:   p. 488
S1–8.3:   pp. 801, 832, 855, 860, 1240, 1244, 1264, 1281
S1–9.4:   pp. 1371, 1514, 1560, 1622–23, 1702
S1–11.1: p. 25
S2–1.2(AZ): p. 17
S2–1.3(AR): pp. 36–37, 68, 117
S2–1.10(NE): pp. 303, 311, 314–15, 322, 338, 340–341, 344
S2–1.15(SC): p. 395
S2–1.16(WA): pp. 397, 401
S2–2.1:   pp. 26, 103, 141
S2–3.2:   pp. 719, 853
S2–4.3:   pp. 1218, 1238–39, 1311
S2–5.4:   pp. 1580, 1581–82

16.6(TN): pp. 18, 22, 23, 27, 30, 32, 34, 35, 38, 41, 48, 60, 64,
            68
17.1: pp. 4-9, 14-15, 136, 162, 191, 192, 213, 310, 353, 370
18.1: pp. 26, 38-39, 70, 100, 139, 167-68, 224, 316-17, 319
19.1: pp. 159, 207-208
S1-1.1: pp. 20, 42, 59, 72, 80, 92-93, 150, 171, 216, 223, 229-30,
          245, 275, 280, 294, 330, 363, 404, 468
S1-2.1(AR): pp. 10, 12, 19
S1-2.2(CO): pp. 56, 98
S1-2.4(MO): pp. 149, 164-65, 194-95, 250-51
S1-3.1: pp. 1, 28, 31, 52, 75, 79, 107-08, 127-28, 135-40, 144, 188,
          204-10, 221, 227, 235, 240, 265-69, 273, 321, 332, 335, 337,
          342
S1-4.2: pp. 355-56, 392, 399, 415, 421-22, 426, 429, 432, 437, 451,
          495-96, 499, 501, 558-59, 581-91, 597, 618-19, 624, 632,
          649-58, 674-75
S1-5.1: pp. 49, 73-74, 88-91, 93, 103, 175-78, 186, 189, 210
S1-5.2: pp. 287, 340, 406, 423, 471
S1-6.1: pp. 31, 32, 47, 48, 61, 71, 158, 159, 172, 176, 177, 219,
          220, 229, 238, 254, 260, 271, 310, 314, 316, 327, 328
S1-7.2: pp. 369-370, 376, 383, 409-410, 420, 426, 428-429, 443,
          480, 508-509, 515, 529-530, 571, 584, 598-599, 607-608,
          622-623, 628, 639, 665-666, 677, 680, 697, 698-699, 722,
          724, 750, 773, 790
S1-8.3: pp. 804, 813-814, 830-831, 893, 904-905, 927, 933-934, 943-
          944, 959, 966, 990, 1046-1047, 1056, 1086-1087, 1099, 1103-
          1104, 1111, 1171, 1200-1201, 1206-1207, 1209, 1212-1214,
          1219-1221, 1233, 1255, 1258-1259, 1273-1274, 1276, 1285,
          1292
S1-9.4: pp. 1459, 1492, 1584-85, 1590-91, 1717-18, 1899
S1-10.5: pp. 1911, 1917, 1939, 1974, 1982, 2012-13, 2078, 2160,
          2171-72, 2191-92, 2203-04, 2210, 2234, 2260-61, 2279,
          2283, 2292-93, 2305, 2350, 2360, 2361
S1-11.1: pp. 10, 19-20, 36-39, 41
S1-11.2: pp. 60, 93-94, 118-19, 135-36, 140, 146, 173-74, 191, 210-
          12, 223, 226, 229-32, 233, 254-56, 257, 281, 297
S1-12.1: pp. 25, 81, 161-62, 171, 200, 220-21, 332-33, 374
S2-1.1(AL): p. 4
S2-1.3(AR): pp. 98-99, 105-06, 114, 117-18, 122-23, 127, 129, 130,
              133-34, 196-98, 252
S2-1.7(IN): pp. 275-77
S2-1.9(MD): p. 301
S2-2.1: pp. 16-22, 31-32, 36, 171-72, 201, 223, 233-5, 258, 287,
          328, 360, 369, 389, 402, 438, 445-45, 453
S2-3.2: pp. 484, 578, 609, 633, 674, 691, 693, 708, 755, 848-49,
          891-92, 896, 926
S2-4.3: pp. 1004, 1010, 1037-38, 1050, 1102, 1134-40, 1255-58,
          1263-64, 1301-1302, 1315-16, 1329, 1378-79, 1430-31
S2-5.4: pp. 1449-50, 1481-82, 1496, 1544-45, 1563-64, 1610, 1611,
          1624, 1680, 1817, 1889
S2-6.5: pp. 1931, 1946, 1966-68, 1980-82, 2002-2003, 2035-2038,
          2042, 2044, 2094, 2097, 2103, 2122, 2148-49, 2150, 2161-62,
          2167, 2170, 2174, 2175, 2180, 2205-2206, 2234, 2236-37,
          2265-68, 2271, 2283-84, 2334, 2341-42, 2366-67. 2391-93,
          2404
S2-7.6: pp. 2450, 2452, 2468, 2470-2471, 2513-14, 2579-80, 2587,

OTHER SLAVES, SIGNIFICANT AND/OR RELATED (IDENTIFIED)

OVERSEERS, DRIVERS, AND FOREMEN (WHITE)

POLITICAL PARTICIPATION, BLACK

S1-9.4: pp. 1414, 1458, 1546-47, 1564, 1595, 1700, 1706-1708, 1731,
         1760, 1767, 1768, 1820-21, 1823, 1826-35, 1873
S1-10.5: pp. 1941, 1985, 2023, 2119, 2137, 2225, 2311-12, 2321
S1-11.2: pp. 101-02, 137-38, 241-42, 264-67, 308
S1-12.1: p. 95
S2-1.3(AR): pp. 72-74, 94, 103, 110-11, 129
S2-1.5(FL): pp. 265-66
S2-1.10(NE): pp. 310, 329, 330, 339, 343, 345
S2-1.15(SC): pp. 392-96
S2-1.16(WA): pp. 397-98
S2-2.1: pp. 14, 59, 102, 117, 141-42, 203, 242, 349-50, 354, 368,
         395, 403, 436, 466
S2-3.2: pp. 495-96, 543-44, 597, 616-17, 781-82, 835, 906
S2-4.3: pp. 1042, 1068, 1086, 1106-1107, 1114, 1117, 1267-68, 1272-
         76, 1314, 1326-27, 1398-99, 1435
S2-5.4: pp. 1456, 1499, 1568-69, 1640, 1650, 1656, 1701, 1824, 1844-
         45, 1881, 1918, 1925
S2-6.5: pp. 1938, 2165, 2192, 2217, 2223, 2247-48, 2252, 2289
S2-7.6: pp. 2444, 2456-2457, 2475-2476, 2487, 2497-98, 2504, 2591-
         92, 2609, 2666, 2715, 2735, 2762, 2808, 2872, 2878, 2883
S2-8.7: pp. 2979-80, 2981, 2982, 3043, 3097, 3127, 3165, 3198, 3205-
         3206, 3255, 3279, 3344, 3355, 3392
S2-9.8: pp. 3415, 3456, 3526-27, 3554-55, 3571, 3599-3600, 3636,
         3644, 3686-87, 3695, 3730, 3759-60, 3817, 3830, 3841-42
S2-10.9: pp. 3910, 4044, 4063-64, 4235, 4243

POOR WHITES, BLACK ATTITUDES TOWARD

12.1: pp. 14, 95, 109, 187, 241
12.2: pp. 45, 222, 236
16.3(MD): pp. 9, 49
16.4(OH): pp. 8, 25, 27, 39, 40, 88, 103
16.5(VA): pp. 9, 55
18.1: pp. 8, 264
S1-1.1: pp. 10, 118, 181, 279, 283
S1-2.4(MO): pp. 135-36
S1-3.1: pp. 20, 102, 283
S1-5.1: pp. 54, 239
S1-6.1: pp. 19, 218, 235
S2-7.2: pp. 420-421, 559, 627, 630, 690, 772
S1-8.3: pp. 804, 1221-1222
S1-10.5: p. 1986
S1-11.2: p. 168
S1-12.1: pp. 174, 201
S2-8.7: p. 2940

PRIVATE PROPERTY (CONTROLLED BY BLACKS)

2.1: pp. 191, 246
4.1: pp. 2, 71, 131, 132, 248
4.2: pp. 9, 11, 12, 14, 26, 31, 40, 49, 51, 54, 103, 108, 114, 133,
      139, 143, 144, 150, 156, 157, 158, 168, 200, 214, 225, 245,
      251, 252, 258, 259, 264, 285
5.3: pp. 3, 36, 122, 125, 161, 173, 178, 275
5.4: pp. 22, 24, 43, 48, 55, 141
6.1: pp. 10, 149, 154, 212, 267, 283, 337-38

S2-10.9: pp. 3939, 4164

RECONSTRUCTION (GENERAL)

2.1:   pp. 46–47
2.2:   p. 151
3.3:   pp. 29, 30, 31, 32
3.4:   pp. 7, 20, 34, 74, 93, 242, 266, 267
4.1:   pp. 3, 11, 19, 38, 43, 47, 50, 52, 54, 57, 60, 64, 65, 69, 71,
       74, 82, 86, 98, 102, 108, 110, 113, 115, 149, 152, 162, 164,
       194, 195, 209, 210, 233, 234, 247, 253, 256, 292
4.2:   pp. 7, 8, 19, 20, 23, 33, 46, 48, 54, 58, 79, 95, 101, 106,
       108, 111, 139, 147, 148, 158, 162, 199, 236
5.3:   pp. 2, 3, 17, 29, 33, 47, 53, 70, 81, 112, 119, 137, 199,
       234, 267, 277
5.4:   pp. 23, 31, 56, 62, 63, 90, 97, 111, 163, 165, 183, 230, 231
6.1:   pp. 29–30, 43, 54, 112, 132, 140–41, 163, 175, 178–79, 180,
       218–19, 231, 252, 314–15, 420–21, 435
6.2:   pp. 2, 23, 39, 52, 65, 70, 102, 123, 124, 129, 134, 135, 146,
       153, 171, 183, 207, 212, 215
7.1:   pp. 4, 16, 21, 22, 26, 29, 31, 51, 63, 71, 74, 79, 85, 102,
       103, 106, 126, 143, 163, 167, 168, 191, 205, 208, 209, 224,
       253, 254, 255, 261, 268, 273, 282, 283, 291, 292, 301, 311,
       340, 341, 349, 352, 353
7.2:   pp. 9, 15, 16, 20, 23, 29, 41, 42, 54, 59, 60, 63, 65, 66, 67
       70, 74, 82, 96, 104, 105, 106, 107, 108, 109, 110, 111, 116,
       132, 140, 141, 148, 149, 155, 164
8.1:   pp. 9, 12, 14, 33, 38, 41, 56, 92, 105, 112, 114, 127, 135,
       143, 147, 162, 182, 197, 208, 216, 227, 294, 296, 300, 304,
       315, 320, 333, 340, 349
8.2:   pp. 3, 5, 12, 14, 19, 39, 40, 59, 63, 64, 76, 77, 79, 89, 120,
       171, 181, 202, 213, 231, 237, 238, 247, 258, 259, 280, 290,
       301, 308, 349
9.3:   pp. 78, 124, 180, 198, 199, 204, 230, 232, 245, 267, 268, 280
9.4:   pp. 13, 20, 42, 43, 45, 48, 78, 79, 88, 89, 144, 147, 183, 184
       233, 234, 237, 247, 269, 270, 278, 279, 282, 286, 287, 288,
       294, 300, 301, 302, 307, 310
10.5: pp. 22, 23, 27, 28, 34, 45, 47, 61, 66, 80, 81, 124, 132, 133,
       134, 154, 163, 170, 171, 190, 191, 195, 224, 246, 247, 255,
       280, 281, 298, 299, 307, 308, 316, 317, 319, 336, 341, 345,
       352, 353
10.6: pp. 2, 3, 4, 29, 46, 49, 54, 57, 83, 98, 99, 106, 109, 170,
       198, 220, 230, 235, 247, 249, 250, 261, 267, 273, 293, 302,
       333, 342, 348, 349, 370
11.7: pp. 31, 44, 56, 78, 79, 86, 101, 134, 135, 157, 174, 175, 205,
       219, 242
11.8: pp. 7, 19, 26, 29, 34, 63, 99, 105, 117, 123, 185, 187, 192,
       211, 232, 254, 296, 305, 306, 308, 328, 350, 351, 374, 375
12.1: pp. 21, 193, 329
12.2: pp. 231, 242
13.3: pp. 10, 29, 64, 107, 111, 147, 148, 163, 183, 210, 223, 242,
       302, 303, 310, 315, 334
13.4: pp. 72, 73, 172, 239, 348–350
14.1: pp. 6, 7, 17, 56, 61, 72, 128, 150, 172, 178, 220, 252, 253,

RELIGION (GENERAL)

S1-2.4(MO): pp. 139, 175, 217
S1-2.5(OR): p. 273
S1-3.1: pp. 7, 15, 19, 26, 64, 83, 89, 125, 145, 148, 170, 213,
         251, 258, 260, 278, 293, 295, 306, 331, 335, 341
S1-4.2: pp. 359, 377, 380-381, 391, 432, 440-41, 443, 461, 488, 537,
         539, 548-549, 571, 577, 596, 635, 674
S1-5.1: pp. 45, 56, 68, 127, 129-30, 166, 187
S1-5.2: pp. 283, 288, 294, 349, 388, 400, 411, 432, 456-57
S1-6.1: pp. 41, 73, 76, 77, 95, 100, 202, 261, 271, 282, 311
S1-7.2: pp. 335, 344-45, 348, 349, 408, 421-422, 437, 598, 628, 663,
         677, 680, 682, 693, 696, 701, 754, 769, 784, 787
S1-8.3: pp. 827-828, 884, 886, 889, 892-893, 991, 1072-1073, 1076,
         1083-1084, 1136, 1146, 1221, 1223-1224, 1225, 1231, 1245,
         1250, 1264-1265, 1298, 1321
S1-9.4: pp. 1417, 1420, 1472, 1767, 1768, 1769, 1815, 1822-26, 1846-
         48
S1-10.5: pp. 1912, 1913, 1915, 1921-22, 1938, 1960, 1997, 2009-10,
          2011, 2023-24, 2061, 2079, 2096, 2097, 2107, 2167, 2181,
          2188-89, 2218, 2220-21, 2227, 2290, 2300, 2311, 2365
S1-11.1: pp. 64, 65, 66, 71, 72, 82, 84, 85, 95, 113, 117-18, 141,
          171, 180-81, 188, 213, 215, 218, 219, 220, 224-25, 226,
          227-28, 238, 252, 268, 281-82, 310-11, 318
S1-12.1: pp. 13, 57, 60, 70, 97, 106, 111, 118, 167, 267, 297, 324,
          350, 378-79
S2-1.1(AL): p. 9
S2-1.3(AR): pp. 35, 126, 232, 236, 243-48
S2-1.4(DC): p. 257
S2-1.10(NE): pp. 322, 325-326, 328, 330, 338, 346, 348, 349, 353
S2-1.13(OK): pp. 372-74
S2-1.15(SC): pp. 381-82, 394
S2-2.1: pp. 46, 74, 97, 214-15, 229-30, 326, 349, 410-11, 430, 431,
         455
S2-3.2: pp. 555-56, 584, 630, 693, 708, 733, 751-52, 928-29
S2-4.3: pp. 966, 1014-15, 1022, 1052, 1068, 1087, 1088, 1163, 1240,
         1259, 1261-62, 1271-72, 1307, 1364, 1410, 1422, 1424
S2-5.4: pp. 1466, 1487, 1510, 1516, 1530, 1559-60, 1576, 1585,
         1594, 1598, 1653-54, 1660-61, 1731, 1770-72, 1823-24, 1833-
         36, 1862, 1883, 1911-12
S2-6.5: pp. 1945, 1950-51, 2006, 2015, 2033-34, 2038, 2086, 2147,
         2178, 2201-2202, 2211, 2218, 2219-20, 2228, 2247, 2251,
         2253, 2271, 2281, 2296, 2303, 2369, 2388
S2-7.6: pp. 2446-2447, 2465-2466, 2485, 2492, 2493, 2494, 2499,
         2518, 2519-20, 2529, 2577, 2583, 2585, 2587, 2595-96, 2602,
         2627-32, 2636, 2642, 2658, 2684, 2702, 2722, 2728, 2732,
         2735, 2743, 2757, 2766, 2780-85, 2789, 2814, 2838-39, 2873,
         2907
S2-8.7: pp. 2918, 2919, 2943, 2945, 2951-52, 2973, 2979, 2997-98,
         3004, 3015, 3018, 3034, 3041, 3043, 3056, 3062-63, 3078,
         3079-81, 3098-99, 3112, 3160, 3266-67, 3270, 3281, 3289,
         3290-91, 3324-25, 3361-62, 3398
S2-9.8: pp. 3475, 3482, 3489-90, 3501, 3502, 3507, 3569, 3582,
         3630, 3636, 3666-67, 3695, 3711, 3738-39, 3760, 3809, 3827,
         3861
S2-10.9: pp. 3943, 4094, 4138, 4150-53, 4263-64

See Also: BIBLE; CHURCH, BLACK; CHURCH (GENERAL); MINISTERS (BLACK);

RELIGIOUS CONVERSION: SPIRITUALS

RELIGIOUS CONVERSION

   19.1: pp. v-218

RESISTANCE TO SLAVERY (DAY TO DAY)

   12.1: pp. 23, 110, 188, 292, 350
   12.2: pp. 14-15, 26-27, 87, 236, 240, 323
   16.2(KY): pp. 32, 67
   16.4(OH): pp. 27, 98, 108
   16.6(TN): pp. 9, 31, 34, 38, 45, 47, 67
   18.1: pp. 9, 11, 12, 34, 54, 55, 134
   S1-2.3(MN): p. 110
   S1-5.1: pp. 180-81
   S1-7.2: pp. 435-436, 502, 558, 683-684, 742
   S1-8.3: pp. 899-900, 929, 952, 1038, 1083, 1132, 1216, 1221, 1299,
            1303
   S1-9.4: pp. 1488, 1806
   S1-12.1: pp. 36, 38, 97, 143, 389-90
   S2-1.1(AL): p. 20
   S2-2.1: pp. 26, 32, 54
   S2-6.5: pp. 1971, 2043, 2045-2253
   S2-7.6: pp. 2472, 2530, 2562, 2590, 2642, 2766, 2834-35, 3853-54
   S2-8.7: pp. 3080, 3288, 3360, 3369
   S2-9.8: p. 3810

RESISTANCE TO SLAVERY (GENERAL)

   2.1: pp. 18, 45, 166, 247, 320
   2.2: pp. 9, 10, 24, 25, 36, 110, 111, 130, 145, 149, 150, 197, 212,
         221, 233, 337
   3.3: pp. 2, 15, 16, 25, 57, 92, 101, 130, 161, 227, 277
   3.4: pp. 52, 63, 72, 112, 113, 117, 206
   4.1: pp. 16, 22, 26, 27, 33, 37, 42, 49, 56, 60, 61, 70, 98, 156,
         157, 190, 198, 199, 206, 229, 237, 266, 299
   4.2: pp. 56, 202, 213, 214, 250
   5.3: pp. 1, 2, 20, 38, 39, 63, 69, 83, 85, 135, 186, 210, 226, 243,
         246, 248, 249, 258, 263, 264, 275, 279
   5.4: pp. 1, 37, 38, 41, 43, 75, 78, 101, 107, 117, 129, 132, 145,
         154, 164, 171, 191, 220, 236
   6.1: pp. 7, 30, 35-36, 42, 46, 60, 68, 78, 118, 123-24, 150, 168,
         173, 184, 185-86, 220, 232, 239, 263, 283, 293, 311, 346,
         389-90, 416-17, 418
   6.2: pp. 8, 10, 17, 46, 48, 51, 53, 57-58, 62-63, 66, 107, 108-09,
         118, 126, 128-29, 135, 136, 142, 143, 157, 158, 162, 170,
         171, 188, 190, 196, 200, 201, 212, 213
   7.1: pp. 9, 13, 17, 21, 65, 78, 89, 94, 101, 112, 118, 124, 132,
         134, 136, 140, 145, 160, 177, 218, 234, 272, 302, 346, 362
   7.2: pp. 13, 37, 129, 138
   8.1: pp. 10, 20, 40, 42, 43, 45, 46, 63, 110, 126, 154, 264, 323,
         336, 337
   8.2: pp. 36, 37, 42, 50, 78, 90, 168, 169, 255, 256, 258, 282, 288,
         311, 329
   9.3: pp. 12, 38, 63, 64, 67, 88, 120, 121, 128, 134, 150, 151, 166,

See Also: SEXUAL PRACTICES, SLAVE; SLAVE MORALITY

SLAVE COMMUNICATION (SECRET)

SLAVE DANCING

SLAVE HUMOR

SLAVE PUNISHMENT

S2-1.1(AL): pp. 6, 7
S2-1.3(AR): pp. 19-20, 126
S2-1.11(NY): p. 359
S2-1.15(SC): p. 386
S2-1.16(WA): p. 402
S2-2.1: pp. 3, 24, 25, 33, 52, 90, 146, 165, 198, 200, 204, 205, 238
303, 364, 372, 399-400, 436
S2-3.2: pp. 554, 564, 575, 605, 628-29, 643, 687, 708, 718-19, 736,
778, 867-70
S2-4.3: pp. 963, 967-68, 971-72, 1002, 1008, 1009, 1031-32, 1075,
1090, 1120-22, 1283, 1287, 1289, 1363, 1365-66, 1390
S2-5.4: pp. 1444-45, 1485-86, 1490-91, 1492, 1537-39, 1557, 1571,
1595, 1608, 1622, 1644, 1653, 1726-27, 1755, 1877
S2-6.5: pp. 1928, 1935, 1936, 1941, 1942, 1945, 1949, 1952, 1961,
1963, 1964, 1973, 1988, 1991-92, 1996-98, 2005-2006, 2015,
2025, 2040, 2046, 2047, 2079, 2110, 2125, 2127, 2128, 2137,
2138, 2140, 2145, 2146-48, 2158, 2161, 2168-69, 2178, 2179,
2183, 2194, 2201, 2214, 2220, 2250-51, 2253, 2254, 2259,
2274, 2276-77, 2280, 2295, 2299-2300, 2322, 2327, 2331, 2335
2337, 2338, 2365, 2377, 2405, 2408
S2-7.6: pp. 2446-2447, 2463-2464, 2466, 2472, 2479, 2482, 2493-95,
2500, 2509, 2518, 2527, 2530, 2534, 2536, 2560, 2562, 2567,
2585, 2605, 2617, 2624, 2634-35, 2641, 2642, 2648, 2652,
2682-83, 2690, 2706, 2711, 2731, 2737-38, 2744, 2751, 2760,
2764, 2775, 2799-2800, 2802, 2834-35, 2837, 2881-82, 2898,
2906
S2-8.7: pp. 2921-22, 2939, 2940, 2944, 2947, 2961, 2969, 2990-91,
2997, 3002, 3008, 3019, 3026, 3033, 3040, 3048-49, 3053,
3059, 3083, 3093, 3099, 3106, 3108, 3114, 3119, 3121-22,
3134, 3136-37, 3138-39, 3145, 3207, 3213, 3222, 3224, 3230,
3232, 3239, 3266, 3287, 3290, 3295-96, 3304, 3306, 3312-13,
3326, 3348, 3360, 3365-66, 3369-71, 3379, 3388, 3397
S2-9.8: pp. 3405, 3437, 3445, 3479, 3489, 3495-96, 3499, 3504, 3505,
3507, 3513, 3514, 3515-16, 3575, 3603, 3623, 3625, 3632,
3639, 3642, 3647, 3652, 3657m 3674-75, 3678, 3698, 3708,
3725, 3728, 3753, 3761, 3764, 3769-70, 3774, 3783-84, 3792,
3802, 3821, 3838, 3856-57, 3861-62, 3872, 3883, 3886
S2-10.9: pp. 3899, 3911, 3947, 3953, 3970, 3978, 3985, 4025, 4088,
4158-59, 4165, 4205, 4343-44

See Also: SLAVE TREATMENT (GENERAL, NEGATIVE)

SLAVE QUARTERS

2.1: pp. 14, 39, 82, 104, 150, 173, 189, 205, 330
2.2: pp. 31, 35, 46, 74, 83, 113, 139, 143, 172, 216, 254, 266, 272
338
3.3: pp. 2, 14, 63, 64, 101, 112, 119, 158, 167, 200, 210, 227, 232
281
3.4: pp. 32, 33, 46, 81, 96, 101, 102, 128, 152, 161, 164, 170, 177
188, 199, 219, 247, 253, 260
4.1: pp. 9, 15, 18, 32, 35, 37, 43, 45, 49, 54, 73, 85, 109, 110,
124, 131, 133, 138, 143, 147, 157, 177, 179, 180, 182, 185,
188, 191, 197, 203, 212, 236, 252, 266, 285
4.2: pp. 1, 6, 7, 8, 22, 35, 50, 55, 56, 60, 68, 71, 82, 98, 119,
121, 136, 137, 148, 153, 160, 169, 178, 180, 182, 183, 185,

SLAVE TRADE

SLAVE TREATMENT (GENERAL, NEGATIVE)

SLAVERY, POSITIVE ATTITUDE TOWARD

SPIRITUALS

S2-1.3(AR): pp. 119, 126
S2-1.10(NE): pp. 313, 326, 348, 351-52
S2-3.2: pp. 510-11, 704, 770-71, 860, 890
S2-4.3: pp. 1015, 1022, 1033, 1282, 1302, 1319-21, 1357, 1419
S2-5.4: pp. 1464-65, 1588-89, 1631, 1824, 1828-29, 1834, 1912
S2-6.5: pp. 1969, 2026, 2075, 2111, 2119-20, 2131-32, 2198, 2259, 2271, 2279, 2296, 2339, 2388, 2390-91
S2-7.6: pp. 2466, 2642, 2652, 2719, 2722, 2781, 2783, 2801, 2812-13, 2838
S2-8.7: pp. 2918, 3018, 3041, 3057-58, 3079-80, 3085, 3109, 3121, 3174-76, 3203-3204, 3258, 3290, 3301-3302, 3327-28, 3361-62 3366
S2-9.8: pp. 3653-54, 3660, 3700=3701, 3711, 3716, 3724, 3754, 3757, 3818, 3852
S2-10.9: pp. 4150-51, 4152-53, 4253, 4263

SPYING (UPON FELLOW SLAVES)

12.1: pp. 128, 198
12.2: pp. 17, 235
16.2(KY): p. 16
18.1: pp. 9-10, 76, 116-17
S1-5.1: p. 5
S1-7.2: pp. 377, 474, 750
S1-8.3: p. 899
S2-7.6: p. 2737
S2-8.7: p. 3138

STEAMBOATS

See: RIVERBOATS

STONO (S.C.) REBELLION

S1-11.2: pp. 98-100

SUICIDE

16.2(KY): p. 67
S2-6.5: p. 2140
S2-7.6: pp. 2578, 2684
S2-8.7: pp. 3312-13, 3374

TEXAS RANGERS

S2-3.2: pp. 698-99
S2-6.5: pp. 2055-57
S2-8.7: pp. 2983-84

TUBMAN, HARRIET

S2-3.2: p. 809

TUL3A (OK) RACE RIOT (1921)

  7.1: p. 235

TURNER, NAT

  S1-6.1: p. 226

UNCLE TOM'S CABIN

  See HARRIS, ELIZA (S1-5.1, pp. 245-48) (OH via KY)

UNDERGROUND RAILROAD

  16.2(KY): pp. 69, 79, 85-86, 121
  16.3(MD): pp. 20, 21, 63-64, 67
  16.4(OH): pp. 57-58, 72
  16.6(TN): p. 47
  17.1: pp. 146, 148-54, 265, 337
  18.1: p. 13
  S1-2.3(MN): p. 112
  S1-2.4(MO): p. 269
  S1-5.1: pp. 7, 246, 252, 262
  S1-5.2: pp. 370, 478
  S1-10.5: p. 2189
  S1-11.2: pp. 206-07
  S1-12.1: p. 287

WHITES, NEGATIVE ATTITUDE TOWARD

  2.1: pp. 44-45
  2.2: pp. 98, 109
  3.3: pp. 94, 194, 211, 260, 261
  3.4: p. 273
  4.1: pp. 134, 192
  4.2: pp. 7, 11, 12, 37, 43, 59, 63, 202, 206, 207, 217, 228, 230
  5.3: pp. 18-19, 227
  6.1: pp. 12, 43, 55-56, 212, 340
  6.2: pp. 62, 165, 188
  7.1: pp. 66-67, 77, 87, 112, 131, 136, 210, 296, 345
  8.1: pp. 123, 248
  8.2: p. 53
  9.3: pp. 103, 265
  9.4: p. 7
  10.5: pp. 4, 12, 112
  10.6: pp. 210, 351
  11.7: pp. 8, 15, 16, 26, 27, 118, 140, 154, 157, 178, 201, 241
  11.8: pp. 3, 44, 81, 82, 83, 94, 95, 107, 115, 117, 143, 162, 163,
         176, 194, 195, 215, 240, 281, 316, 346, 372
  12.1: pp. 14, 51, 144, 347
  14.1: pp. 64, 137, 326, 338, 361
  15.2: pp. 263, 273, 274, 300, 301, 319

```
16.1(KS):  pp. 5, 10
16.2(KY):  pp. 23, 59, 65
16.4(OH):  p. 76
16.5(VA):  p. 11
17.1:  pp. 13, 19
18.1:  pp. 22, 27, 71, 151-53, 276
S1-3.1:  pp. 9, 16, 21, 335
S1-4.2:  pp. 355, 452
S1-5.1:  pp. 99, 130
S1-5.2:  p. 403
S1-6.1:  pp. 1, 253
S1-8.3:  pp. 1101, 1207
S1-9.4:  p. 1402
S1-10.5:  p. 2399
S1-11.2:  p. 204
S1-12.1:  pp. 7, 9, 79, 340-341
S2-5.4:  pp. 1810, 1907
S2-6.5:  pp. 2165, 2217, 2277, 2345
S2-7.6:  pp. 2475, 2521, 2522-23, 2530, 2568, 2571, 2578, 2689,
         2716, 2734, 2807, 2858-59, 2860, 2872
S2-8.7:  pp. 3074, 3126-27
```

See Also: MASTER, NEGATIVE ATTITUDE TOWARD

WHITES, POSITIVE ATTITUDE TOWARD

```
2.1:  pp. 36, 60, 67, 167, 201
2.2:  pp. 11, 31, 32, 113, 240, 263
3.3:  pp. 1, 2, 3, 5, 6, 8, 9, 10, 18, 19, 30, 31, 32, 41, 42, 43,
      44, 45, 48, 49, 50, 53, 54, 56, 64, 74, 75, 76, 77, 78, 79,
      105, 119, 126, 127, 132, 140, 142, 157, 166, 168, 169, 172,
      204, 206, 207, 208, 211, 221, 231, 236, 237, 246, 247, 266,
      285
3.4:  pp. 10, 45, 51, 71, 72, 73, 74, 80, 88, 93, 117, 134, 135,
      152, 161, 182, 198, 199, 204, 218, 226, 243, 244, 254, 269
4.1:  pp. 61, 132
4.2:  pp. 13, 20, 23, 29, 40, 43, 45, 64, 67, 68, 75, 137, 159, 164,
      166, 171, 177, 191, 208, 226, 232, 234. 235, 242, 247, 272,
      278, 279
5.3:  pp. 6, 34, 120, 124, 232
6.1:  pp. 14, 55-56, 95, 106, 136, 165, 191, 271, 364-65, 373
6.2:  pp. 24, 94
7.1:  pp. 84, 129, 222a, 284, 319, 327
7.2:  pp. 55, 124, 130, 149
8.1:  pp. 12, 40, 49, 65, 86, 129, 148, 155, 167, 195, 234, 242,
      284, 309, 338
8.2:  pp. 113, 119, 149, 197, 267, 313
9.4:  pp. 29, 260
10.5:  pp. 3, 6, 8, 123, 126, 207, 216, 295
10.6:  pp. 5, 15, 35, 188, 203, 226, 261, 320, 371
11.7:  pp. 13B, 102, 185, 229
11.8:  pp. 10, 34, 67, 110, 141, 213, 339, 359, 364
12.1:  pp. 13, 249-250, 277
12.2:  pp. 36-37, 46, 64, 101-102, 283, 302
13.3:  pp. 55, 228, 261
13.4:  p. 24
```

```
14.1:  pp. 56, 57, 126, 173, 199, 408
15.2:  pp. 28, 245, 345, 377, 388
16.1(KS):  p. 5
16.2(KY):  pp. 23, 91
16.3(MD):  pp. 17, 45, 80, 82
16.6(TN):  pp. 39, 75
17.1:  pp. 150-51, 317-18
18.1:  pp. 9, 26, 40
S1-1.1:  pp. 33, 39, 61, 158, 172, 175-76, 227, 261
S1-3.1:  p. 45
S1-4.2:  pp. 487, 551, 648, 666
S1-5.2:  pp. 326, 380
S1-6.1:  pp. 7, 83, 168, 288
S1-7.2:  p. 609
S1-8.3:  pp. 1064, 1120-1121, 1164
S1-9.4:  pp. 1458, 1531, 1875
S1-10.5:  pp. 2165, 2190, 2215, 2283, 2366, 2367
S1-11.1:  p. 22
S2-1.1(AL):  p. 7
S2-1.3(AR):  p. 73
S2-1.9(MD):  p. 287
S2-2.1:  pp. 243, 395-96
S2-3.2:  p. 900
S2-5.4:  p. 1891
S2-6.5:  pp. 1935, 1947, 1965-66, 2084, 2123, 2145, 2147, 2237, 2248-
         49, 2282, 2305, 2333, 2358-60, 2361, 2408
S2-7.6:  pp. 2469, 2483-84, 2502, 2513, 2688, 2689, 2697, 2734, 2735,
         2803, 2912
S2-8.7:  pp. 2916, 2917, 2919, 2935, 2941, 2960, 2963, 2965-66, 2993,
         3016, 3040, 3073, 3075, 3076, 3096, 3198, 3222, 3265, 3278,
         3318, 3322, 3355, 3357
S2-9.8:  p. 3544

See Also:  MASTER, POSITIVE ATTITUDE TOWARD

WORK SKILLS, BLACK (SPECIFIC)

2.1:  pp. 27, 49, 52, 53, 58, 85, 100, 146, 169, 173, 201, 227, 239,
      311
2.2:  pp. 1, 6-7, 38, 129, 159, 184, 206-207, 266, 279, 293, 294,
      327, 333
3.3:  pp. 17, 18, 27, 36, 53, 56, 65, 94, 143, 167, 168, 183, 226,
      249, 250, 271
3.4:  pp. 9, 55, 76, 97, 125, 222, 223
4.1:  pp. 14, 96, 110, 193, 302
4.2:  pp. 1, 6, 7, 8, 10, 15, 16, 17, 18, 20, 22, 26, 33, 35, 36,
      39, 40, 41, 42, 43, 44, 45, 47, 49, 50, 51, 54, 55, 56, 64,
      67, 69, 71, 72, 74, 75, 76, 82, 83, 85, 88, 90, 94, 95, 99,
      103, 110, 113, 116, 119, 121, 124, 126, 129, 132, 133, 135,
      138, 139, 142, 143, 144, 148, 151, 153, 154, 155, 156, 158,
      160, 170, 171, 172, 173, 178, 179, 180, 181, 183, 184, 188,
      196, 198, 199, 200, 203, 204, 206, 209, 221, 222, 225, 226,
      227, 229, 232, 238, 239, 241, 242, 244, 246, 247, 251, 252,
      253, 256, 259, 261, 262, 264, 265, 266, 267, 270, 273, 274,
      275, 276, 278, 280, 285, 288, 289, 292, 293
5.3:  pp. 63, 88, 139, 205, 259
```

YOUNGER GENERATION, BLACK ATTITUDES TOWARD (1930's)